MARION MILN
THE LIFE

Artist, poet, educationalist and autobiographer, Marion Milner is considered one of the most original psychoanalytic thinkers, whose life (1900–1998) spans a century of radical change. *Marion Milner: The Life* is the first biography of this extraordinary woman. It introduces Milner and her works to the reader through her family, colleagues and, above all, through her books, charting their evolution and development as well as their critical reception and contribution to current twenty-first century debates and discourses.

In this book Emma Letley draws on primary sources, including the newly opened Marion Milner Collection at the archives of the British Psychoanalytical Society in London, as well as interviews and the re-contextualised series of Milner texts. She traces the process of Milner's writing of her books, her discovery of psychoanalysis, her training and her place in that world from the 1940s onwards. The book also includes discussion of Milner's connection with D.W. Winnicott and her emergence as a most individual member of the Independent Group.

Marion Milner: The Life shows how Milner's Personal Notebooks offer fascinating insights into her relationships, both personal and professional, and into many of her important ideas on creativity, the body–mind relationship, her revolutionary ideas on education and her particular personality as a clinician working with both children and adults. Further, Letley explores Milner's literary character from her very early diaries and narratives to her last book written in her nineties, published in 2012.

Marion Milner: The Life places Marion Milner firmly in her Edwardian family setting and contains new material from primary sources, including a new view of her collegial connections. It provides a wealth of material on her life and works that will be invaluable to psychoanalysts, psychotherapists, art psychotherapists, students, those involved with life writing and autobiography and the general reader.

Emma Letley is a writer and psychoanalytic psychotherapist. She trained with the Arbours Association and is currently in practice at King's College London and in private practice in Notting Hill Gate. She is Series Editor of the Marion Milner works (Routledge, 2010–2012).

MARION MILNER
THE LIFE

Emma Letley

LONDON AND NEW YORK

First published 2014
by Routledge
27 Church Road, Hove, East Sussex BN3 2FA

Simultaneously published in the USA and Canada
by Routledge
711 Third Avenue, New York, NY 10017

Routledge is an imprint of the Taylor & Francis Group, an informa business

© 2014 Emma Letley

British Library Cataloguing in Publication Data
A catalogue record for this book is available from the British Library

Library of Congress Cataloging-in-Publication Data
Letley, Emma.
  Marion Milner: the life/Emma Letley.
  pages cm
  Includes bibliographical references and index.
  1. Milner, Marion, 1900–1998. 2. Psychoanalysts—
  Great Britain—Biography. I. Title.
  BF109.M55L48 2013
  150.19'5092–dc23
  [B]
  2012050424

ISBN: 978–0–415–56737–4 (hbk)
ISBN: 978–0–415–56738–1 (pbk)
ISBN: 978–0–203–76712–2 (ebk)

Typeset in Garamond Three
by Florence Production Ltd, Stoodleigh, Devon, UK

MIX
Paper from
responsible sources
FSC® C013604
www.fsc.org

Printed and bound by CPI Group (UK) Ltd, Croydon, CR0 4YY

In affectionate memory of John Milner who very
sadly died when this book was in production

CONTENTS

ILLUSTRATIONS

ACKNOWLEDGEMENTS
AND INTRODUCTION

'I don't wish it to be legible,' the young Milner wrote in her notebook early in her training analysis, and her handwriting bears this out. Beautiful, wonderfully dressed and disarmingly private, Milner was proudly English. She loved the streams of visitors, many of them Americans, who came flocking to her door, drawn by her books – small pyramids of fan letters attest to her enduring charm. So many people knew her through her books, and this is one way the biographer must also meet her. I, too, knew her through the books, through a reading – in my twenties – of her great book on creativity, *On Not Being Able to Paint*; to find her through people – not through books – was more difficult. In her autobiographical book of her (and the twentieth century's) eighties, *Eternity's Sunrise*, she wonders why there are so few 'beads' about people – there are images, places, objects of culture and inner joys with people, but somehow this is not the point. Ironically, this biography is about showing how and why this might be.

Milner is surrounded by a ring fence of set pieces – which conceal – and by colleagues who are respectfully silent about a certain biographical reticence. Her patients, of course, have benefitted from this legacy of discretion. I do not know (and have not sought vigorously to find out) who 'Susan' is or where she might be. Milner loved and valued silence, the great emptiness, and to some extent this is what remains. And yet the silence can be broken – and I am, first of all, enormously grateful to those who have felt able to talk about Marion Milner.

First of all, my thanks must go to Milner's literary executors, her son, John Milner and Margaret Walters, her close friend of many years, who have allowed me to have access to papers and letters, art work and photographs; and then to her family. The company of Milner's son John has been one of the great pleasures of this book. An invitation to his seventy-fifth birthday in Harting, a place significant to Milner from the 1940s onwards, was the start of many congenial meetings; it was also a boost to the project of writing the biography and the preparation of Milner's six books for re-issue in a new edition, completed in 2012 with the publication of her posthumous, long-awaited autobiography *Bothered by Alligators*.

The kindness of Milner's niece, Giovanna Bloor, helped me more than I can say; on a visit to her home in North Wales, she provided me with much detail on the wider family background and history, including invaluable family trees. MM's grandsons, Giles and Quentin, have also been very kind, and an early visit to Quentin in Devon allowed me glimpses of MM's art, her couch (one of them) and some vignettes of her life as a grandmother.

In the early stages of the work, Moris and the late Nina Farhi welcomed me with the greatest warmth and encouragement, Nina's own work being inspirational in continuing Milner's legacy. I would like to single out the kindness of Pearl King in seeing me at the beginning of this project despite declining health. Mary Reid (Pears) I have known for over forty years; fortunately for me and for the book, it turned out that she was a close friend of Milner's for much of the middle part of her life, and her recollections over the years have been invaluable. Her daughter Nicola Pears has always been the best of literary friends.

As Milner was someone who valued silence, it has been a great help and privilege to *hear* Milner's voice – The Squiggle Foundation, Ken Robinson, Christopher Reeves and Bernard Barnett all provided me with recordings, letting me hear the Edwardian nuances of a great psychoanalytic thinker. (Her pronunciation of 'Winnicott' says much.)

The Archives of the British Psychoanalytical Society at the Institute of Psychoanalysis in London have been an excellent resource. I am very grateful to Ken Robinson, Honorary Archivist, for all his help, and extend a very large thank you to Joanne Halford, who has been unfailingly kind while I have been working in the Archives. The establishing and launching of the Marion Milner Collection is a most timely and exciting initiative without which this book would not have been possible. Thanks, too, to Helene Martin – and to Joanne Halford's predecessors, Allie Dillon and Polly Rossdale.

Many others have helped in different ways, and I thank: Tessa Adams, Lisa Appignanesi, Sheila Beskine, Christopher Bollas, Michael Brearley, Lesley Caldwell, Donald Campbell, Sarah Dewsbery, Simon Edwards, Margaret Gardiner, Andreas Giannacoulas, Brenda James, Jennifer Johns, Angela Joyce, Harry Karnac, Roger Kennedy, Zachary Leader, Elizabeth Meakins, Pippa Michaels, Mary Oley, Michael Parsons, Michael Pye, Janet Sayers, Lore Schacht, Dominika Schoenborn-Joseph, Michael Shayer, Jonathan Sklar, Karin Wach, James Ware, Jean White and Roger Willoughby.

My colleagues at King's College London have shown interest and support, and I am especially grateful to Ann Conlon for granting me periods of study leave to write the biography.

I am grateful for permission to quote from letters held in Archives of the British Psychoanalytical Society and for permission from the Winnicott Trust and the Marsh Agency to quote from letters from D.W. Winnicott. The Wellcome Foundation has also kindly allowed me to quote from letters held in their archives. For letting me see and quote from correspondence between

MM and Adrian Stokes, I thank Janet Sayers, Ian Angus and Ann Stokes and Phillip Stokes. 'The Tree' is included by permission of the Marsh Agency on behalf of the Winnicott Trust; Martina Thomson's 'Marion' is included with her permission. In a biography that looks at finding its subject through her books I am aware that I have needed to quote quite extensively from Milner's works; the bulk of quotations from these are taken from the new series, and I am very glad to thank Routledge for this.

Mathew Hale has been consistently generous with his time and thoughts and also in providing me with the photograph of MM's room just after her death. I am grateful to the Gdansk National Gallery for allowing me to use the Bohusz Portrait on the cover of this book; to Desy Safán-Gerard for her beautiful collage/portrait of MM; to Mary Reid for the photographs from Cornwall, and to Giovanna Bloor for family photographs of the Blacketts and their houses. Other images are courtesy of the kindness of John Milner.

Thank you, as ever, to Steph Ebdon, at the Marsh Agency, to Kate Hawes and Kirsten Buchanan at Routledge; and a huge thank you to my husband, Peter Letley, for all his help, support and enthusiasm for this book especially through long, Scottish summers while I completed it; and to our son Alfred who has lived with MM as companion for a good seven years.

A few words by way of introduction to *Marion Milner: A Life*: there has been no previous biography of Milner, but as her biographer I thank those who have gone before me. Although Milner died in 1998, surprisingly little had been written about her and her work. I have, however, drawn gratefully on the study by Naome Dragstedt, work by Janet Sayers, papers and book sections by Michael Parsons and a number of papers from the world of art psychotherapy. It is gratifying to see that works dealing seriously with Milner are increasing – most recently, Elizabeth Meakins *What Will You Do With My Story?* The introducers of the new Milner series – Rachel Bowlby, Janet Sayers, Maud Ellmann, Hugh Haughton and Adam Phillips – are all part of the re-contextualisation of Milner for the twenty-first century, as is the publication in 2012 of Milner's last autobiographical work, *Bothered by Alligators*, introduced by Margaret Walters.

Every effort has been made to trace copyright holders; if any have been missed the publisher and author would be pleased to hear from them. Any errors in *Marion Milner: The Life* are, of course, my own.

ABBREVIATIONS

ALO   Marion Milner, *A Life of One's Own*
BBA   Marion Milner, *Bothered by Alligators*
DWW   D.W. Winnicott
EIL   Marion Milner, *An Experiment in Leisure*
EL   Emma Letley
ES   Marion Milner, *Eternity's Sunrise*
HOLG Marion Milner, *Hands of the Living God*
MM   Marion Milner
MMC   Marion Milner Collection, Archives of the British Psychoanalytical
        Society at the Institute of Psychoanalysis in London
ONBAP Marion Milner, *On Not Being Able to Paint*
SMSM Marion Milner, *The Suppressed Madness of Sane Men*

1

EDWARDIAN HOME

Early life 1900–1927

Writing her last book, Milner feels impelled to face her first memory:

> It seemed quite preposterous, but it did look as if it had come from
> the house in London in which I was born. It is of me, quite naked
> and suspended in a black scarf, which is tied onto the hook of the
> spring scales that my father used to weigh the fish he caught, this
> itself hanging from the ceiling. The black scarf would be my sister's,
> since, according to photos, she would have been wearing a sailor suit,
> then the fashion for children, with its knotted black scarf in memory
> of the death of Nelson. I suppose that when fairly new born, I could
> have been weighed like that, though the 'memory' must surely be a
> construction, because I seem actually to see this baby hanging there,
> so it must really be a dream. If it is a dream, what has this black
> scarf memorial of the death of Nelson got to do with me? What now
> comes to mind is the day my mother called my father 'the Last Straw'
> as well as a time I heard him say to her (rather ruefully) that she
> ought to have married a Highland Scot with a kilt and a red beard.
> Surely then, if my so-called first memory was actually a dream, on
> one level it could have been. It could have been registering the fact
> of us all being born into a family where my mother and father were
> secretly, even half-unknown to themselves, battling with disillusion
> about their marriage, she desperately wanting him to be a hero, he
> very much aware of not being one?[1]

Written retrospectively towards the end of a very long life, this is the view
of a psychoanalyst, a believer in the unconscious, in the 'royal road' of dreams,
and a woman with the wisdom of more than ninety years. In another document,
written in her fifties, she says one of her first memories is of 'being praised
for being so quick in the lavatory' and she comments that indeed she has
never been able to allow enough time (for thinking) ever since.[2] There is also
a more conventional way of viewing Marion Milner's arrival in the world and
the place her parents had in it.

Figure 1.1 Shooting party 1880s with MM's mother and sister

Born on 1 February 1900, Nina Marion Blackett was 'brought up in the kindly security of an Edwardian middle-class home',[3] child of Arthur Blackett, 'a dreamy Victorian Romantic' who loved poetry, fishing and learning. The Edwardian world into which she was born was one of great comfort for the more privileged of the population, with servants available for those who could afford them. Britain remained a predominant economic power with a massive empire. A small group of aristocrats, landowners and, later, industrialists held political and social power. A prevailing air of certainty, soon to be destroyed by the First World War, would have dominated Milner's childhood.

Her father was not a natural for the commercial vigour of the time. From him she inherited her love of nature and, arguably, her early ambition to be a naturalist, the first of her many callings and careers encompassing literary person, educationalist, psychologist, psychoanalyst, artist and poet.

If her father provided the impetus for the early naturalist bent of Milner's personality, the family of her mother, Caroline Maynard, offered an exemplar in the field of education: Constance Maynard (1849–1935) was head of Westfield College, University of London, from 1881 to 1913, having been previously one of the first female undergraduates accepted to study at Girton College, Cambridge. Another Maynard, Henry Langston Maynard, was master at Westward Ho, a school hated by Rudyard Kipling; he then had his own preparatory school at Nethersole. According to his and Milner's relation, Sir Anthony King, he was 'by far the best teacher I ever met.'[4]

The theme of invention also featured large in the Maynard family tree as it was to do later in Milner's own marriage. Caroline claimed descent from Whitmore ancestors, a political family that had represented Bridgnorth from 1621, when Sir William Whitmore first took his seat in the House of Commons, until 1870. Georgina Whitmore married George Babbage (1791–1821), inventor of the calculating machine, predecessor of the modern-day computer, a highlight of family lore and still revered today.

An artistic bent also figures in Caroline Maynard's family: her sister married 'a rather unsuccessful stockbroker . . . [who] had some kind of breakdown' and had a daughter, Dorothy Jones, who had 'considerable skill as an artist, particularly in pastel.'[5] Notable in the family tree on both her mother's and her father's side is the Church. Vigorously anti-clerical and insisting right up until the day of her death that there should be 'no God' in her funeral proceedings, Milner was, however, a deeply spiritual person, profoundly versed in the Bible and its poetry and imbued with more than a touch of mysticism. Through the Maynard connection, she was linked with Bishop William Walsham How (1822–1897), famed as the 'Omnibus Bishop' because of his habit of travelling to London's East End by bus to makes visits to the poor. In 1884, he went on to become Bishop of Wakefield, and, for later generations, was most famous for the hymns he wrote, including 'For all the Saints who from their labours rest' and six other hymns in the Church of England's *Hymns Ancient and Modern.*

The clerical tone is also strong on the Blackett side; Milner's grandfather, Henry Ralph Blackett (1815–1906), was vicar of two London parishes and then, from 1880, of St Andrew's, Croydon. His son, Herbert Blackett (1855–1885), met an untimely death as a missionary in India; Selwyn Blackett (1854–1937), Herbert's brother, was Rector of Wareham for forty years, and eventually became a Canon of Salisbury; their sister, Adelaide (1860–1952), married Charles Scott Moncrieff, Vicar of Blyth; another sister, Alice (1862–1947), married Leonard Dawson, missionary to the Cree Indians in Canada; and their niece, Annie Schafer (1875–1964), daughter of Ethel Blackett, spent her life as a nun in a Church of England convent in Rottingdean. By contrast, Joseph Maynard (1796–1859), brother-in-law of the Omnibus Bishop, joined the Catholic Apostolic Church – also known as the Irvingites after their leader Edward Irving (1792–1834), a deposed Presbyterian minister.

Successful in a number of fields, the Maynards also had their share of competitive triumphs: Henry Maynard was an acclaimed Monte Carlo rally driver, while Frances Maynard became a County tennis player as well as a Lieutenant-Colonel in the ATS in the Second World War.

Milner's brother, Patrick Blackett, fought in the First World War, being a midshipman on *HMS Monmouth* (later sunk by the *Graf Spee* with almost total loss of the crew), then on *HMS Carnarvon*, going on to become one of the most renowned and controversial physicists of the twentieth century. His independent spirit led him to be renounced as a Stalinist apologist for speaking

Figure 1.2 Nina Blackett with her children, Winifred, Patrick and Marion

out against the British and American development of atomic weapons.[6] The strength of his political stands seems markedly different from the innocent apoliticism of his sister, Marion.

Large houses stand out in the family history of the Maynards and the connected families of Whitmore and Sparkes. This has suggested to some previous commentators[7] a class disparity between the Blacketts, originally

Figure 1.3 Arthur Stuart Blackett (MM's father)

small farmers from Hamsterley in Northumberland, and the maternal line in Milner's family. However, Nick Vine Hall from Australia has traced the Blackett line through twenty-two generations to show its royal descent from Egbert, King of the West Saxons (d. AD 839).[8] Whatever the descent of the Blacketts, by the nineteenth century the Maynard family would seem to have been part of a wider, more upper-class tradition.

5

Figure 1.4 Nina Blackett in eighteenth-century fancy dress

Linked with Milner's great-grandmother, Frances Sparkes, was Dudmaston Hall, near Bridgnorth in Shropshire, inherited by William Whitmore (great-great-grandfather of Milner) in 1774 from Lady Wolryche. Whitmore's daughter – Milner's great-grandmother – married Arundel Francis Sparkes, and in this section of the family are two significant houses – Penywerlodd and St John's – as well. The former, in Wales, might well have appealed to Milner's imagination, with its Gothic legends of a haunting by an eighteenth-century man in a red hunting-suit, but it is uncertain whether or not Milner ever went there.

A rare Jacobean house, Chastleton, Oxfordshire, near Moreton-in-Marsh, also has family connections. Chastleton was built in 1607/08–1612 by Walter Jones, a wealthy wool merchant, and inherited by John Whitmore (later John Whitmore-Jones), Milner's great-great-uncle. Originally the house was owned by Robert Catesby of Gunpowder Plot fame; it was mortgaged to Jones, and when Catesby was unable to pay, Jones took over, knocked the house down and built the house then inherited by John Whitmore. Today, virtually unchanged for nearly 400 years, it has almost no twenty-first century intrusions and no concessions to modern commercial trends or comfort. Chastleton was acquired by the National Trust in 1991, and Dudmaston was given to the Trust in 1978 by another distant cousin of Milner's, Lady Labouchere.

Though grand in many ways, the Whitmore baronetcy became extinct in the seventeenth century. Some members of the Maynard family like(d) to think they were connected to the Maynard viscounty; this, too, became extinct in the nineteenth century, with substantial estate and fortune passing to Daisy Maynard, who found fame, and even notoriety, as the Countess of Warwick and the mistress of Edward VII.[9]

Milner's life was rather different from that outlined here: Caroline Maynard may have had the traditional aspirations of an Edwardian mother of her background for her daughters – they were discouraged from going to parties with 'lower class' people and Milner retained the Edwardian upper-class voice patterns until the end of her life – but her own personality and, indeed, unhappiness are more individual than this. Milner's early life was arguably troubled by the conflicted marriage of her parents. As Dragstedt has remarked 'unhappy in her marriage Milner's mother tended to be depressed and not viscerally present to her children.'[10] Looking back, Milner writes of her mother's sadness; as she seeks images in her store of familial photographs she finds *one* of her mother 'actually holding her first born, my sister, and looking quite radiant with happiness; in fact, the only one among the many photos in which she looks like that.'[11] Caroline Maynard was very pretty, and happy memories are recorded of her sketching with her daughters and of her reading the novels of Charles Dickens to them. It is clear, however, that she had a rather stronger bond with her elder daughter, Winifred, than with her youngest child, Moll – as Marion was called in the family. (I refer to MM as 'Milner' throughout for simplicity.)

7

Figure 1.5 The Blackett children – Marion, Patrick and Winifred – and Mickey the dog

Figure 1.6 MM's maternal grandparents at Fleet

In adult life, Milner was told by an osteopath treating her back that she seemed always to have been 'protecting her mother'; at first, she thought she already knew this, and was quite well aware that she had always been upset by her father's irritability with her mother, especially as she was sure it was undeserved – 'I always thought of her as a loving and devoted person.'[12] Characteristically, Milner probes deeper with consummate autobiographical courage:

> The first idea that came was that, when I was about 6, she had made me add to my nightly prayers 'Keep the door of my lips that I offend not with my tongue'. This did suggest that up until then I had been quite capable of using my tongue in ways that could hurt though I doubt whether it was against her, but rather against my-five-years older sister, who used to snub me fiercely . . .[13]

There was also the question of rivalry with her mother; Milner refers to a small drawing made when she was around ten or eleven years old and placed at the start of her nature diary (interestingly, this is not in fact *in* the nature diary, where the first images are of a beautifully observed river bank, finely drawn primroses and a thrushes' nest): 'Saw a drake and two wild ducks' it reads. But the picture shows only one wild duck . . . 'So one of us has to go.'[14] Milner's way out of this impasse was to intensify her identification with her father, doing so by concentrating on the study of Mother Nature, a subject

Figure 1.7 The Oaks, Kenley

that was her father's rather than her mother's interest and was also a bond with her brother Patrick.

Her mother might have survived Milner's attacks; not so her sister Winifred. Milner recalls that aged around six, she deliberately hurt her sister in a 'vengeful act':

> It must have been in the days just after starting the prayer, so I could not use words to express my anger at something my sister had done – perhaps snubbing me. What I had done was to deliberately and secretly smudge with my finger tips an ink drawing she had just done.'[15]

It was only towards the end of her life that Milner was able to consider that her mother had almost certainly 'a sense of deep depression about herself and deep disappointment over her marriage' and it was this realisation from which, perhaps, the young Milner felt impelled unwittingly to protect her.

Milner was deeply attached to her father, so her life changed significantly in 1911 when he had a breakdown: later, in her analysis with Donald Winnicott, she would consider (or Winnicott would consider) this to have been some kind of schizophrenia, but this was a long way in the future (see p. 56). Arthur

Figure 1.8 Peatmoor, home of MM's maternal grandparents at Fleet

Blackett had, on leaving school, been sent, through a relation, to work as a stock jobber on the London Stock Exchange with Conrad Wilkinson Brothers who took him with no capital.[16] He was completely unsuited to this; the Blackett children were always told that 'at the end of a week's work, he would set off walking alone into the country, arriving at a friend's house for breakfast, with a Shakespeare play in his pocket, and having recognised all the different bird songs on his way'.[17] It seems likely that the Stock Exchange job did not provide a very generous or reliable salary. In 1904, the nanny whom Milner had loved deeply left them, and they had to move from their house at Kenley in Surrey, 'which had a lovely flower meadow and a little wooded copse', to a smaller house in Woking, 'which had none of these things'. After her nanny's departure, Milner was disconsolate and cried for some weeks; the situation was saved, she tells us, by that 'memorable day when my brother and I discovered we liked playing together'. Prior to this she had been quite envious that Patrick, as a boy, was excused from housework and she even wondered, in her five-year-old self, 'if THEY had made a mistake and that I was really a boy'. She still had to do her share of housework but then the day came 'when he and I walked together along a sandy bank at the edge of a wood, playing at making bows and arrows'. From then on, the closeness between them grew and flourished until they lost touch to some extent on his marriage.[18]

11

Having married Caroline Maynard in 1895, Arthur would, for the first sixteen years of his married life, set off daily for his city job wearing a black silk top hat, sometimes brushed for him by his younger daughter; then, with no warning, one day in 1911, while getting dressed to go to work, he fell and hit his head on an iron fireplace. At this time they were at Fleet staying with Milner's mother's parents. None of the three children was allowed to see their father for one week – and, when they were allowed to do so, and noticed his clearly bruised head, he enquired only after Mickey, their Irish terrier, who had, in fact, been left at home in Guildford. Milner was most upset: 'This idea that our father might not be entirely in touch with actuality felt like the worst thing that had ever happened to me, and I remember crying and feeling angry with the woman [a neighbour] for drawing attention to it.'[19] For his convalescence, her father went fishing in Scotland, accompanied by his wife, taking with them a male nurse as 'insisted on by the consultant that he saw'. Milner at this time was left alone in the house as Patrick was at Naval College in Dartmouth and Winifred at Godolphin School in Salisbury. It was at this time that she was taken out of a gym class and told she had 'a hunched left shoulder', a condition that seems to have remained with her throughout her life.[20] At the time, it was diagnosed as curvature of the spine; no remedy was suggested, but it was decided that she should not play hockey and that she needed to carry her school satchel on the other shoulder. Disappointed about the hockey at a time when she was due to be in the school team, Milner told her mother about this on her return home, 'crying a bit at the idea of having a crooked back'; this, however, merely prompted her mother 'to be a little impatient', emotionally absent as, perhaps, quite often during her daughter's childhood.

Fortunately, about this time, two of Milner's maternal aunts died, leaving some money to her and her sister because they were thought to be 'not worldly', unlike the other nieces. This enabled Arthur Blackett to retire from the Stock Exchange in 1917 (King says that, on the death of both Wilkinson brothers, he did not have the capital required to continue with the firm),[21] and the family moved to Beacon Hill, 'on top of that dramatic great lump of hill, Hindhead, near Haslemere, which contains within its hump a deep valley called the Devil's Punch Bowl'.[22] The fame of the Devil's Punch Bowl, a natural amphitheatre and beauty spot, dates from around 1768, the year that John Rocque's map of the area was published. It has become a nature reserve with heathland, woodland and small rivers. The First World War carried on, and Arthur's war work was now as a village postman. He had never learned to ride a bicycle but was given the beat of going down to the bottom of the Punch Bowl where the 'broom squires' lived (the gipsies who made brooms and lived at the bottom of a little valley) and read them the postcards from their sons who were soldiers in France.[23] He enjoyed this greatly and, on occasion, was asked to take letters to the big houses on top of the hill where, says Milner, 'my mother was often on calling-card terms'. He also taught himself to make beehives – twenty-five of them – and kept bees until all the bees died one year from Isle of Wight disease, a mysterious illness that began to kill honeybee colonies on the island in 1904, its cause remaining unidentified until 1921.

Recalling this time, Milner singles out the lovely smell of sphagnum moss collected by her father on his long, solitary walks and used for treating the wounds of soldiers in front-line hospitals. A local millionaire built a clubhouse around this time and asked Arthur to be club secretary, an offer he accepted and remained in the post until his death, from cancer, aged fifty-five. He was seen as a 'favourite uncle' by his nephew, Anthony King, who also described him as 'my Mother's favourite brother' and called them 'great pals'. King also recalls his family going over to see the Blacketts at Kenley quite often and 'remember[s] how well he read to us all, crowded into a small room, Kipling's *Just So Stories*'.[24]

It was Arthur Blackett who chose the place for family holidays – Bamburgh in Northumberland, where they went every August from 1904 onwards. Bamburgh is notable then, as now, for its castle, seat of the former Kings of Northumbria, and its association with Grace Darling (1815–1842), Victorian heroine, who is buried there. The young Milner loved the place 'with its superb castle on a rock rising straight from the sea-shore'. It became, she writes, 'a heaven for all of us children, meeting the same families – getting to know every rock pool and the creatures in it, while my mother happily did very good watercolour 'sketches' as they were then called'. From this time comes her earliest memory of her father – apart, that is, from the smell of his Harris tweed jacket. It is of 'his coming up to say goodnight to me, and singing the beginning of the hymn':

Now the day is over
Night is drawing nigh
Shadows of the evening
Steal across the sky
As the darkness gathers
Stars begin to peep
Birds and beasts and flowers
Soon will be asleep.[25]

Bamburgh was clearly a place with many memories of great happiness: Milner's Personal Notebooks contain a section on 'Childhood Memories', what she would later come to call 'beads', moments of charged energy and unconscious power, images with a 'still glow'. From Bamburgh comes: 'the blue cranesbill . . . the smell of horses . . . salt smell, seaweed, miles of wet sand [. . .] the shrimping pool, wandering along below the castle looking for shells' and then the pleasure of 'Filling a pool with lovely things, writing stories, the sea always made me want to write stories' and, in particular, being with her brother

Patrick, at low tide, crabbing.[26]

Mollie Blackett's Nature Diary also records moments at Bamburgh. August 1912 has the following entries and carefully observed illustrations:

> August 1st, A rock-pipit's nest with young at Stag Rocks.
> August 10th, Saw a merlin in the sandhills.
> August 20th, Saw a short-eared (?) owl hunting for mice in the sandhills.
> August 28th, I saw swifts for the last time.

Then there is a small, sepia photograph of Bamburgh Castle.

The nature diaries show a clear talent for very close, meticulous observations and very precise drawings, as she records, for instance, in February 1913, hearing a blackbird singing, seeing wild parsley and dandelion in flower, and finding 'a peacock butterfly indoors on a window', which did not appear 'much damaged but I think must have slept through the Winter.'[27]

There is also a letter from her father to his 'dearest daughter', arguably from this time:

> . . . why are gulls called stupid? [. . .] there is the saying, 'oh he is easily gulled'. Your sketch of the gulls in the park and the waterhens behaviour to them was good. I have also noticed that size does not go for much among birds as far as their treatment of each other is concerned. Bounce & cheek carry some birds a long way.[28]

Milner's involvement with the natural world sometimes caused her to be out of tune with the conventions of her education; retrospectively, she remembers 'sitting at French lessons gazing through the window at the dim line of woods that cloaked the Downs, so deeply longing to be there that my whole body ached with it.'[29] Her papers show an early, somewhat dreamy talent for narrative and story-telling. From the period 1908–1912, there is the tale of 'The Golden Cockle-Shell'; this tells of Margaret Lorna Stilkham, always known as Mossie, who is taken down to the sea one day by her mother. Walking on the rocks, she comes upon a beautiful shell in a pool some hundred feet below. She climbs down but falls, halfway down, and lies quite still at the bottom of the cliff. 'The maid who had charge of her picked her up and carried her home. The docters [*sic*] came but they could do nothing for her.'

One night a pair of wings flies in at the window and Mossie puts them on and sets off in search of the pretty shell. A Queen now enters the narrative, proclaiming that Mossie is a very naughty and spoilt child who must be made good. Mossie's eyes must be shut tight so that she can see everything but not the lovely shell: he is the one who has been chosen to make her good. Mossie finds the shell just where she expects, but when she stretches out her hand

14

to touch it, it vanishes. Mossie, a tearful child, begins to weep; the tears turn to lead and hurt her very much. However, she soon finds the shell, and this time, it does not disappear but moves towards the sea and Mossie follows. Here she finds that all her clothes have gone and she has 'a lovely flowing white dress of soft white stuff' and is able to swim and to breathe underwater. Then there is a magical transformation: she finds herself 'the same size as the cockle, and, on looking at it, she saw that it was a pair of golden cockle shells and inside instead of a fish there was the sweetest little baby boy that ever was seen.' This is 'Cockles'. Cockles instructs Mossie on what she must do: each day she has to clean out a small rock pool, and if she fails to do so, she will be punished; further, he tells her that when she becomes good they can go and live in the place 'where the sea nymphs play, right down at the bottom of the sea'; and Mossie is given a silver shell just like Cockles' golden one and 'the two little golden haird [sic] blue eyed sea babies live together side by side in there [sic] wonderful shells, in the beautiful land where the sea nymphs play'.[30]

Looking back on her education, which included religious training and a time at a boarding school (Godolphin) in Wiltshire, Milner remarks on a crisis in her spiritual life, and she certainly felt disillusioned with the Church and the failure of a 'laying on of hands' to help her father in his illness. She would continue to be out of sympathy with the Church, and indeed with organised religion, and would later refrain from giving her son a conventional religious education.[31]

Milner left school at the age of seventeen; she had spent only one term in the sixth form, there being no further money in the family to pay fees for her to continue. At this stage she had no thought of staying on at school to work for a university scholarship. Instead, in the spring of 1918 she was offered her first job: it was mornings only and involved teaching a seven-year-old boy to read: 'When the boy got the meaning of a word he was so delighted that he would say, "Oh my, oh my!" After the lessons we would go out onto the heath and look for newts; strange how this so small job seemed to determine my future career.'[32]

It did so because when Milner told a friend how much she and the boy had enjoyed their time together, the friend suggested Milner should read the work of Montessori, the renowned Italian physician and educator whose first school had opened in Rome in 1917, shortly followed by others in the United States and Europe, Milner did so and found Montessori's work 'a revelation' from one who 'actually believed that children could be trusted to know what they needed to learn and to do it by a concentrated kind of play, not just any play but using material especially provided so that the play really became work.'[33] It was this preoccupation that led Milner to consider and re-consider the relationship between work and play, a deeply held interest that brought her to the 'psychoanalytic consulting room or playroom, asking the analysand to say, or if a child, to do, whatever came to mind'.

15

Figure 1.9 Patrick Blackett

Having read Montessori books, the next step for Milner was to become a student at a Montessori nursery school training college; she recalls a vivid memory when doing her teaching practice at a slum school in London's Gipsy Hill 'watching a small boy using the Montessori bricks to make a ring which he then tried to get into but found that he was too big'. At this stage, Milner did not make the connection with the Freudian idea of a wish to get back to the womb, thinking the child was simply 'trying to get an idea of his own size'.[34]

After one year at the Montessori College, an older friend suggested that Milner should take a university degree in psychology and physiology, at the same time arranging for her to obtain a grant offered by an organisation concerned with women's post-war training. It was the physiology that most appealed to Milner – apart, that is, from one course taught by the English psychoanalyst John Carl Flügel on Freud's ideas about the unconscious as seen in relation to a well-known book by the neurophysiologist, Charles Scott Sherrington, *The Integrative Action of the Nervous System* (1906).

In *Hands of the Living God* Milner expands on this her first contact with Freud's work when attending 'a brilliant course of lectures by the late J.C. Flügel, in which he drew a parallel between the integrative function of the nervous system as described by Sherrington and the principles of unconscious functioning as described by Freud.'[35] At the time, however, she was more 'enchanted' by physiology than deeply engaged with Freud; amazed by what the body can do she felt, as did Nietzsche, 'the body is a big sagacity'.[36] The result of this was that, when her brother Patrick presented her with Freud's recently translated *Introductory Lectures*, although intrigued by aspects of the unconscious mind, she was not immediately drawn to psychoanalysis; and it was not until her first book that she started to discover the art of the unconscious.

Milner left University College London with a First Class degree in 1923 and began work under Cyril Burt, best known of English educational psychologists, renowned for his work on the heritability of IQ. At the time, Burt was in charge of the Vocational Guidance Department of the National Institute of Industrial Psychology and he was also involved in work with young delinquents.

While engaged in her work with Burt, Milner also started a mental training course called Pelman, a system of scientifically training the mind, a mnemonic method that had become known as Pelmanism, with the Pelman Institute opening in London in 1898. Milner was also influenced much by the essays of Montaigne, and his insistence that what he calls the soul 'is totally different from all that one expects it to be.'[37] In 1926 she began to keep a diary that became the basis of her first book and the start of what was, most authentically, *A Life of {her} Own*, away from parental depression and a family in which she had 'to struggle to be' herself.[38]

2

A LIFE OF ONE'S OWN

A life of one's own: yes, but first there had to be a companion, someone 'who understands music and its queer mysteries . . . [so they may] travel together – exploring, seeing how people live – talking to queer fish by the roadside – sleeping at country inns – sailing boats – tramping dusty roads – getting nearer the truth of things.' And Milner wished for more: 'to get past conventions and hypocrisies'; to grow with him and learn to understand his personality and its intricacies 'like a piece of music'. She also desired a support and 'someone to contend with', wishing intensely to live 'amongst things that grow – a child a garden and quietness'.[1]

In January 1927, Milner notes 'now I want to know what P and D said about me'.[2] D is Dennis Milner: considerably older than she was, he had been married previously, was involved with Bernard Shaw's evolutionary socialists and wrote plays. He was also an 'inventor by temperament', always, when he was well enough, 'constructing new technologies that were much ahead of their time though he never managed to market them'. In the early 1930s, for example, he made 'a new kind of sailing boat, built on our back lawn and actually launched on a large North London lake, only to have it abandoned when the war came'.[3]

In coming to her decision to marry Dennis, Milner had certain reservations, fears of constraint, 'of being tied up, a limiting of my will, no longer a "mobile unit" '; against this, however, it was 'a relief to have someone to specialise on' and on 20 July 1926, she is planning her wedding dress, hopeful that in marrying Dennis, she can 'plunge more into life – and take part in the business of living – home-making, money-making, discovery – even a suburban existence would be exciting . . .'; and after the marriage and the 'sudden disappearance of Miss Mollie Blackett', she is filled with optimism: 'I want our marriage to be the greatest freedom for both of us.'[4]

The marriage celebrated, they set off at once for the United States: Milner had a fellowship – a Laura Spelman Rockefeller Scholarship – to spend the winter of 1927–28 attending Elton Mayo's seminars in Boston. An Australian born psychologist, Mayo, known for his work on 'Revery and Industrial Fatigue' (1924), arrived at the Harvard Business School in 1926 and became Professor of Industrial Research. He is particularly remembered for his involvement with the Hawthorn Experiments investigating the influences on workers' motivation and productivity. Milner writes to her mother on 11 December 1927, having had dinner with the Mayos: 'He is a most charming whimsical and enthusiastic Australian [. . .] four years in this country'; she found him 'most stimulating' and glad that he 'seems to have taken us under his wing!'[5] During the winter of 1927 Milner attended Mayo's seminars; the other two students were research workers being prepared from the Hawthorn Experiments in the Western Electrical Company of Chicago. The company paid for them to interview the staff about anything they wished to talk about; but it seems this piece of research did not continue, possibly, Milner thought, for political reasons.

Arrival in Boston was for Milner a great adventure, a 'much bigger undertaking' than she had, at first, imagined. On 14 October, the day before she and Dennis would move into their first room together, she felt 'a new sense of power, power to enfold and protect with a wide calmness – a sea of life in me.'[6]

Welcomed by Mayo and his wife, Milner also records dinner with the Putnams: 'she is a psychoanalyst and he a neurologist – she is being quite invaluable in leading me into the thick of the medico-psychological world here'; while in the same week, 'on Friday I went to see the Judge Baker Foundation, run by Dr Healy, as a clinic for juvenile delinquents. Healy is the Cyril Burt of America, and was most friendly.'[7]

The interviewing for the Hawthorn Experiment at an end, Milner, with the other research students, spent most of the time studying the work of Pierre Janet, early Freud and Jean Piaget's 'Language and Thought of the Child';[8] and it was at this time that she became increasingly drawn to psychoanalysis; writing once more to her mother, in February, she says she's been:

> going to Dr. Irma Putnam for some experience of being psycho-analyzed: since one can't hope to do much with other people, unless one explores one's own unconscious a bit. I've found it extraordinarily interesting [. . .] and I don't think I could have chosen a better person to go to. She's taking me for a much reduced fee, but even at that its expensive so I've literally bought nothing since we came here – which is great self-control for me![9]

Asked much later in life about this first experience of psychoanalysis, Milner is somewhat dismissive, saying that it was not 'really analysis. In Boston I saw a Jungian two or three times a week for three months. I didn't know the difference then between Freud and Jung. Karin Stephen recommended this analyst. I think afterwards she became a Freudian.'[10] Later still, Milner remarks that this analytic work had centred on her being an introvert in Jungian terminology.

While Milner was pursuing her studies with Mayo and her analysis with Putnam, Dennis continued dramatic work – he had intended to write plays in America; and during their first winter in Boston he came across a book that seemed to offer a wonderful subject for a play – a novel by the Canadian clergyman Basil King, writer of sentimental, often didactic, fiction. He worked on dramatising it, but it was discovered that the copyright had not yet run out and the project foundered – it was subsequently revived by another and scripted as the film *Kind Hearts and Coronets.*[11]

After the winter in Boston, they bought an old Chevrolet and set out across the United States to Los Angeles where Milner was scheduled to study the work of Miriam Van Waters, the early American feminist social worker who, among other initiatives, developed juvenile reform facilities including the El Retiro School for Girls in Los Angeles. It was a splendid journey, sometimes sleeping in the car, sometimes in what 'were then called motor camps, where neat little huts provide just a bed and a cooking stove'. It was in one of these, on the outskirts of Santa Fe, New Mexico that Milner had an experience 'to do with reverie, or rather with concentration, that seemed to me afterwards to be just what I had really, unknowingly, come to America to find out about'. She elaborates: 'It was, quite simply, a way of shifting one's concentrated awareness away from the struggle after logical, discursive statements, which I believed was what I had been given the Fellowship for . . .'[12] She learned she could direct her awareness into bodily movement – in this case, the movement of her hands darning socks – the result being a feeling of great joy and contentment, a precursor of another discovery that came to light when writing her 1932 diary. This was also to do with the body and a change of attention. It had come about when playing table tennis: 'for I had found that by attending to the place the ball should go rather than thinking what I should try to do with my arm to get it there, my arm seemed to know just what to do all by itself'. But during the time in Santa Fe 'it was this simple awareness of my hands, from inside, that I had found myself attending to, and not in a game, but doing something I had previously thought of as a not very interesting activity, darning socks'.[13]

In Santa Fe, too, Milner discovers her love of the primitive as she writes of the adobe houses of the Mexicans, 'low roofed, of sun-baked earth, clustered as if growing on the hillside. A few apple trees still in blossom [. . .] In the crooked roads stray donkeys.' She wonders, why she so loves these things:

> Certainly it is the instinctive life, tilling the soil, breeding animals
> and children, struggling for a bare living with an unquestioning faith
> and dependence on religious rites. But why more interesting than
> the struggles of the down-and-out town worker, the nonconformist
> prayer meeting, or a jazz party?[14]

While the bodily discovery of the darning socks and table-tennis moments foreshadowed Milner's explorations and discovery of 'wide attention', so also did her meeting in Los Angeles with Jan and Cora Gordon, with whom the young Milners spent a considerable amount of time. The Gordons were a very talented English couple known for travel books, teaching in art schools, and accomplished musicianship. They had a long-standing connection with France, and after their marriage in 1909, were renowned figures in Montparnasse.[15] In London Jan became art critic for *The Observer* and published a book *A Step Ladder to Painting*, dedicated to both Milners as people on whom he had tried out his ideas. In 1927–28 their reputation in the United States led them to undertake a tour there; and it would have been then, before a heart condition forced Jan to return home, that they fell into friendship with the Milners.

Jan's views about outline in painting inspired Milner to make her drawing of two jugs that features with important significance in *On Not Being Able to Paint* (see pp. 63, 65). She comments: 'The overlap of their two shapes gradually led me, over the years, to develop the symbol of two overlapping circles which was to become central to my thinking about concentration, reverie and creativity'.[16]

During 1927–28, the Milners travelled extensively in the United States – there are letters and postcards from, among other places, Hollywood, Chicago, Arizona and Amarillo, Texas. On 8 November (?)1927, her diary records their staying at a farmhouse on the edge of a creek in Connecticut. The leaves were blazing in colour, the air was still, their hosts were charming, but she was restless and could find no contentment. She realised then that she wanted a child, her daydreams at this time now 'nearly all of country cottages, of little gardens, of "settling down" with flowers in vases and coloured curtains. I don't think of backaches, dish washing.'[17]

November 1928 finds them thinking about their future; Dennis's play from the Basil King novel is completed, but finances mean, 'blow though it is to the family', that they 'must stay out here another year'; Milner feels she is learning so much, and it is also a chance for Dennis 'to get a footing with plays for the American stage'. One success, she writes, 'would make such a difference to our future when we get home'.[18] It seems also about this time that her husband decided to 'give up engineering' to Milner's relief. However, his health had started to falter about halfway through their two-year stay in the United States; mentions of sore eyes, to the point where he is unable to read, and asthmatic symptoms pepper Milner's letters to her mother. Mentions of 'attacks' are worryingly frequent, and his wheeze becomes 'troublesome'. These matters would gradually become acute asthma, a situation that would lead to Milner's rather pressing need to return to work quite soon after the birth of her son.

Very aware of her own personality, she could see that her wish for a child was a little fraught, She writes:

It seems rather absurd that I, who am hopelessly undomestic and have no money, should think of having children. Of course it would be great sacrifice of all the things I love, freedom, time to myself, time to wander, tramping round Europe, no responsibility . . . Will I feel out of it when I see the country folk, with kitchen dank with drying nappies, while there's sun on fields and sea? Will I feel out of it when I see the swarming kids in tenement backyards?[19]

Would she?

As it happened, in 1931 Milner found she was pregnant, and John was born in January 1932. She had 'not the slightest experience with babies; there had been none in my friends' families and I was the youngest in my own'.[20] In *An Experiment* she recalls 'lying in bed after the birth of my son . . . repeating the name of a book of short stories I had just read, *The Runagates Club*. It was so persistent that finally I let go all my absorption with immediate purposes and simply watched my thoughts'.[21] Even at this point she was developing those ideas that would lead to so much of her work with free association. Dennis, rather wisely in his wife's view, employed a young woman, Star, to help them and 'installed her in our flat while I was in hospital for John's birth'. At this time the only book of guidance for parents of new babies was Truby King's very prescriptive and strictly regimented plan, and, as Milner says, they did not agree with his instructions about rigid four-hourly feeds and just leaving the baby to cry. Her autobiography tells, however, that she 'successfully breastfed J for ten months and the weaning seemed to happen quite easily'.[22] What is more, she was able to make the most of the quiet time in the morning after John's 6 am feed to start to write about the diary she had kept in 1926, to be published in 1934 under her pen name, Joanna Field, as *A Life of One's Own*.

Milner's Personal Notebooks give another side of the picture: the marriage from the outset was troubled by career difficulties for Dennis. In notes entitled 'Intuitions' (30 January 1932[?]) Milner states that he was trying to establish a new 'life myth; and if it is to be working one it must be done entirely by himself'; she must not try to influence him in this, 'e.g. get him into industry because that will mean more money for us'.[23] A letter of February 1931 hints at professional rivalry within the couple, with Milner thinking he can be 'train[ed] up in Yoga' and she should 'let him work with patients'; this would mean he was 'no longer dependent' on her 'for psychological understanding.'[24] As time passed, Milner came to think that Dennis tended to ignore feelings in his intense concentration on the factual and logical and his concern for 'the organised'. Troubled moments increase as in March 1932, she finds that she wishes to hurt him; and then wonders what it is that she might want – 'a gay time with someone else?' No, not this; she wanted to be with him. Possibly, the problem lay with the institution of marriage itself – 'the cursed lot of the monogamous, being dependent on one person' who can then 'hurt you so much'. She is tired of being so reliable but knows Dennis is correct when he suggests that she is inclined to take on too many responsibilities. Even wondering about suicide, she suddenly experiences a change of heart, thinking:

> it's only my sense of self, and of injustice to myself, that makes all this so painful – and if I had no self it wouldn't – and suddenly myself dropped away and I could enjoy the suburban crocuses and the spring air – and realised there's a way of escaping without suicide.

Continuing to ponder, she asks what it is that she wants that 'is not admirable' and answers herself: 'Not to be bothered with John except when I feel like it, not to mind hurting people.' But by July, with John at seven months, she is 'jaded, physically weary, no ecstasies for months, still feeding John, feeling at the end of my tether, worn out with D's leaving everything to me'.[25] She is worrying also about her job, knowing that, by this point, she will need to return to work sooner rather than later – Dennis's health being too fragile to allow for any alternative: 'Fairly soon, because of Dennis's illness, I had to go back to work, not to the Institute of Industrial Psychology but giving evening lectures on psychology to the Workers Educational Association in the East End of London.'[26] This included taking over one of Susan Isaacs' classes in psychology,[27] and in 1933, Milner was asked to undertake research investigating the education system of the Girls Public Day School Trust (GPDST): 'I decided', she writes 'to try and study the system via the girls who did not seem to be benefiting from it and eventually wrote an account of the work in a book, *The Human Problem in Schools*', which was published in 1938.[28] Milner's research on 'difficult' pupils for GPDST was original and groundbreaking; where others saw mental laziness or disobedience, she discovered the imposition of inappropriate adult standards; orthodox education was letting them down. It is typical of her insight that she employed no conventional interviewing techniques but rather the use of a series of images from picture postcards (ranging from a 'Child on Cow' to 'Ski-Ing' to 'Firemen' to 'Joan Crawford') to elicit emotional responses from her interviewees. It was apparently a successful and inspired method, and the book received laudatory reviews: the comments from the *Bulletin of the International Bureau of Education in Geneva* are typical of the positive response:

> This is a book of absorbing interest and of immense importance and value to psychologists, and to parents and teachers of girls. It relates a very thorough piece of experimental pioneering carried out for the GPDST in their schools by Mrs. Milner, a first-class psychologist, formerly investigator to the National Institute of Industrial Psychology.[29]

Milner's work leading up to this book took place between 1933 and 1939; it was interrupted in 1936 when she was advised by a doctor friend who was 'aware of storms in our marriage' to take a journey to Spain, a term off her work in the schools. Later, in her last autobiography, she comments: 'my husband knew of a family in Spain' and 'I was especially ready to accept this suggestion as I was aware of something surging for expression'.[30] This was her book, *Experiment in Leisure*, and it is discussed below.

There had been signs of strain in the marriage for some time: during their American sojourns Milner had found her husband clinging and indecisive, and had worried that they might go on as they were until she was 'too old to find anyone else and then he may find some young attractive girl and I will curse the wasted years'.[31] She had, she later remarks, 'unconsciously assumed' that she must stay with him, and devotedly bear with him because of his ill health. 'Must I? Why?' she now asks. One answer came from her analyst: 'Because Irma says monogamy is the only thing that works? Does it tho'?' Further considering marriage, and her assumption that faithfulness was an imperative, Milner hints that there was some kind of sexual mismatch: 'I do feel the physical is immensely important [. . .] why can I imagine so much beauty in it, and not find it?' Her curiosity impels her to take this further: 'I do not want to miss a "many-splendoured thing" by believing, taking on trust Irma and Mayo.' Later still, she writes: 'In my misery about the asthma situation I have been refusing to learn, I've been clinging to old attitudes and evaluations: crowing to myself over my success [. . .] Just as D. was not content with mediocrity in jobs I am not with mediocrity in love, marriage etc.'[32]

Dennis, too, was showing signs of questioning the need for faithfulness: in September 1929 he was disappointed at not 'getting off with someone more than he has, but then says, "How would one expect to with a newly-married wife?"' Milner alludes to feeling 'restless and depressed for the same reason', wanting to have an affair with one M – 'nothing more probably.'[33] But she was uncertain: 'I have a vague sense that there may be something in the permanent relationship for which it is worth sacrificing the pleasures of affairs.' Had they found it? Are they perhaps in search of 'an Eldorado'? And if this is the case, what does one expect of this Eldorado? A home, stability and – the reason for this – children. At this point, however, there was no prospect of children and the future could look bleak. But then Milner was able to enjoy being back in London, and when walking along Highgate's little suburban roads, where they had bought the Provost Road house in which she was to live for the rest of her life, she suddenly thought:

> Why not enjoy it all like the black in the pattern? We know life is like that . . . quite impossible . . . why not enjoy the pattern and lights and shades [. . .] [then] I was able to enjoy D's little oddities . . . not hate him for – for running after new scents, boisterousness in place of subtlety, devotion, indecision . . .

The weeks leading up to John's birth have more warnings; just before the birth Milner is dismayed by Dennis's 'never speaking of his child himself, saying there was only one subject of conversation in his house'.[34] And, still before the birth, she is irritated by her husband's compulsive social behaviour and 'his lack of awareness of what is really on his mind [. . .] e.g. worry about the baby', exacerbated by 'the definiteness of his observations and opinions, judgments which often seem crude to me when applied to people'.[35]

Shadows, at least, there certainly appear to have been in 1936, and the doctor friend who advised Milner's Spanish sabbatical seems wise. Milner set off to stay in Malaga with Dennis's friends, after a mutually agreed decision. Young John, aged four at the time, was left with his father and Star to look after him. In his mother's absence he wrote her a picture letter, forwarded to her in Spain by her husband. In *Bothered by Alligators,* Milner's ninety-year-old self comments ruefully:

> I felt re-reading this, the awful thing was that I had not the slightest memory of sending back a picture letter [. . .] whenever it was that I first read it, I certainly had no understanding of the message of anger in the letter; and the drawings were just scribbles, totally unrecognisable as being what J said they were.[36]

This was sometime before the profound insights and experiments of *On Not Being Able to Paint,* and at the time, Milner says, possibly a little disingenuously, she 'knew nothing of the notion of an inner world in which there were the psychic representations of the outer world, one in which loved people could be blown up, devoured, drowned etc'.[37]

John, however, was very much present when, living at their house in Provost Road, Milner begins work on her first major autobiographical book, *A Life of One's Own,* 'a deliberate effort to come to terms with daily experience'; starting in 1926, it was 'the record of seven years' study of living', and its aim 'to find out what kinds of experience made me happy'.[38] For us, it is the book in which Marion Milner discovered psychoanalysis.

The book's genesis is fascinating: 'it grew out of the fact that when I was 26 (in December 1926), I began to keep a diary. This was because it had slowly become clear that my life was not as it ought to be.' Externally, all was going well: Milner had interesting work, a full social life and many friends. She had wondered if the trouble might be with her capacity for concentration and, for this reason, had tried a mental training course (Pelman):

> However, the first task it demanded was that I should decide what my aim in life was. As I found that I had not any idea about this, I decided to keep a diary and write down what I thought was the best thing that had happened during the day, in the hope that I might find out what it was that I really wanted.

She had also been inspired by the essays of Montaigne 'and his insistence that what he calls the soul is totally different from all that one expects it to be, often being the very opposite'.[39]

As the text indicates, the results of Milner's diary-keeping 'were most surprising' as it transpired that:

> [the] best things were not at all what one would expect them to be, not to do with successes, either in friendships or work or play, they were mostly very small moments of a total change in the way I was perceiving both the outer world and myself.[40]

Key moments include, in the 'Keeping a Diary' section, a time of 'absentmindedness' when she found herself 'gazing at grey roofs and chimneys, a view typical from a million of London's top-floor windows. I do not remember exactly what I saw but only the shock of delight in just looking.'[41] Thus Milner came to realise that the act of seeing itself was of greater importance than what was seen, while 'the act of writing was a plunge which at once took me into a different element where the past was intensely alive'.[42]

The section headed 'Exploring the Hinterland'[43] (the book takes *Robinson Crusoe* as its structural underpinning) reveals Milner's discovery of her two selves: 'one which answered when I thought deliberately; another which answered when I let my thought be automatic'. This automatic self was occupied with events in her remote past and 'was perhaps bringing over into my present concerns emotions which had no real connexion [*sic*] with my adult life'.[44] This sounds very like a precursor of the process of revealing unconscious patterns and motives through free association in the psychoanalytic setting.

Milner then discovered that it was possible to control the way she looked at things; the first time this idea crystallised for her was with music and her realisation that she could choose to make 'an internal gesture' that transformed her listening into something that 'just happened':

> I described this effort to myself in various ways. Sometimes I seemed to put my awareness into the soles of my feet, sometimes to send something which was myself out into the hall, or to feel as if I were standing just beside the orchestra.[45]

A similar principle lies behind Milner's 'new' way of approaching a painting – as seen in her comments on Cézanne's green apples – green apples, a white plate and a cloth:

> Being tired, restless, and distracted by the stream of bored Sunday afternoon sight-seers drifting through the galleries, I simply sat and looked, too inert to remember whether I ought to like it or no. Slowly I then became aware that something was pulling me out of my vacant stare and colours were coming alive, gripping my gaze till I was soaking myself in their vitality. Gradually a great delight filled me,

dispelling all boredom and doubts about what I ought to like . . .
Yet it all happened by just sitting still and waiting.[46]

Linked with this idea of passively but creatively waiting is Milner's discovery
at the time when she chanced, or so it appeared, on a new perspective, her
'wide attention' opening up new ways of seeing:

> And once when I was lying, weary and bored with myself, on a cliff
> looking over the Mediterranean, I had said, 'I want nothing', and
> immediately the landscape dropped its picture-postcard garishness
> and shone with a gleam from the first day of creation, even the dusty
> weeds by the roadside.[47]

And on another occasion, this time ill in bed and unable to enjoy the idleness:

> I had found myself staring vacantly at a faded cyclamen and had
> happened to remember to say to myself, 'I want nothing'. Immed-
> iately, I was so flooded with the crimson of the petals that I thought
> I had never before known what colour was.[48]

Discoveries such as these left Milner retrospectively 'astonished at what my
diary keeping had shown about the power of the unconscious aspects of one's
mind, both for good and for ill', and it was this that prompted her, she writes,
eventually to become a psychoanalyst; and, with regard to her writings as a
whole, she comments 'with one exception, all subsequent books and articles
were concerned with this aspect of human life, either with my own or with
my patients'.[49]

With the benefit of hindsight, Milner, in an 'Afterword' written in 1981
initially for the American edition, considers the response the book called forth
and the effects upon her of the reviewers' comments that helped her, in
particular, not to lose sight of her discoveries, 'a losing sight that would have
been all too easy in the daily demands of parenthood and the need to earn a
living'.[50]

She first singles out W.H. Auden's comments on the way she was able 'by
the fuse of free-association writing and drawing, to catch the wandering
thoughts of the moment [. . .] It would be unfair to her book which is as
exciting as a detective story, to give away all the methods she tried.' He adds
that her story 'culminates in a mystical experience'; in 1934, Milner felt unable
to accept this description. Other reviewers, too, had picked up this aspect of
the book's underpinning: F.W. Laws for one wrote in the *New Statesman* that
she 'believes mystically in an "inner fact" of individual living which escaped
identification'. Milner writes: 'I thought: this "inner fact" – is it really so
mystical? Isn't it just the astonishing fact of being alive – but felt from inside
not looked at from outside – and relating oneself to whatever it is?' She much

preferred the approach of the reviewer who wrote of her experiences not as mystical but as 'those strange moments of unexpected and inexplicable happiness that are experienced by most sensitive people [. . .] and the slow recognition of the power of the unconscious in affecting thought and behaviour'.[51] Always very interested in the body, that 'big sagacity', and its role in conscious and unconscious life, she was gratified by the remarks of a doctor, James Young, as he quotes Milner: 'Experiencing the present with the whole of my body instead of with the pinpoint of my intellect led to all sorts of new knowledge – and new contentment.' Perceiving with her whole body recalled her transformative moment in the Black Forest when she had discovered that putting something immediate into words could occasion a change of mood: ' So I said "I see a white house with red geraniums and I hear a child crooning." And this most simple incantation seemed to open a door between me and the world.'[52]

Milner then selected the review in the *New Statesman* where Olga Martin was impressed with her experience around ways of concentrating and the effects of wiping the mind clean of thoughts and desires, saying 'I want nothing' as in the moment of discovery with the faded cyclamen quoted above. Martin continues:

> [Milner is] Not content merely to unearth the egotism of childish thinking. In relation to people, as in relation to music and nature the defenses of spiritual virginity must be broken down. It was not enough, she found, to marry and bear a child; unless one is willing to 'immerse' oneself in the destructive element as Conrad puts it, relationships are apt to be sterile.[53]

Stephen Spender in *The Spectator* found Milner's theory of bisexuality of interest; Auden, however, was doubtful as to whether the comments made on male and female elements were of value. Later, Milner as psychoanalyst 'was continually faced with men's fear of their own femininity', particularly if the word is used in the sense of Hamlet's 'a kind of gain-giving as would perhaps trouble a woman'. Olaf Gleeson was another who made this theme central, finding the real value of Milner's book in the author's rediscovery:

> in her curious pilgrimage the secret of that universal symbol, which lies neither at the base of conscious willing nor even of conscious enjoyment, but at the roots of anthropo- and cosmo-genesis. It is embodied in the *ankh* and included in the mystery of the Pythagorean Tetractys.

Others, too, remarked on the difference between Eastern and Western ways of thinking: the Eastern was to influence her thinking:

28

during all the years following 1932 but not to the extent of giving up, or trying to, the Western approach. I was, as always, when any conflict emerged, convinced that I must seek for a marriage between the two protagonists not an either/or solution.

Lastly, Milner appreciated Spender's comments on her quest: he entitled his piece 'The Road to Happiness' and felt she wanted to discover happiness for herself and for others in relation to her. She very soon came to see that this search was but half the story; and Blake, as so often for her, makes the point:

> Man was made for joy and woe
> And when this we rightly know
> Thro' the world we safely go

This was an idea very important to Milner in her work with patients in psychoanalysis: 'the endeavour to give them a setting in which they could discover the truth of this for themselves'.[54]

Milner's store of fan letters gives another perspective: these thank her for giving readers the courage to pursue their own individual aims, say how much the book has meant to them, and tell, in certain cases, how it has led them on the path to becoming analysts. (One analyst who was much influenced is Alexander Newman, who in a recorded interview tells how in adolescence he was given the book as an essential guide for the next stage of his life. It was a long while however before he realised that Joanna Field* was Marion Milner.)[55] One fan found the book a transformational experience and said Milner had 'communicated to me below writing level and the peace of mind that brought to me was beyond description'. The same writer 'felt as Robinson Crusoe must have felt when he discovered Man Friday's footprints'. One letter from 1987 that was particularly appreciated by Milner and annotated by her recognises the correspondent's debt to her thus:

> Particularly your discovery that when you *widened* your focus and *perception of reality* all the hitherto unspoken and unseeing thought-peripheries began to appear and to learn to talk and to surprise. I think one becomes a *hunter* who doesn't push but *waits.* Then all the shy creatures start to appear of their own accord, put their heads up in the landscape.[56]

---

* MM gives various comments about her use of this pseudonym; for instance she tells us she adopted it because she liked the associations of the word 'Field'; and that she felt it appropriate to have an alias when she was working in the schools. Thus *A Life, An Experiment in Leisure* and *On Not Being Able to Paint* all appeared initially under the name 'Joanna Field'.

Milner, who very often answered her fan letters, has written at the top of this one 'very good images', marked the italicised parts and indicated that she has telephoned the writer.

A Life represents a clear stage on Milner's journey towards psychoanalysis and on her development as an assured writer of autobiography. Her next book, written during her leave of absence from her work in the schools (and recorded in *The Human Problem in Schools* – see p. 23), is based not on a daily diary but in 'whatever stood out in my memory [. . .] from the whole of my life, from hobbies, from journeys, from books I had read, plays I had seen, as well as moments of everyday living'.[57]

At this time, Milner also reports another imperative, feeling 'something surging for expression, a kind of continuation of what had driven me to keep the 1926 diary', and she notices the 'deep internal need to write once more'.[58] The book born of this deep need was *An Experiment in Leisure*, published in 1937 just one year before Milner began a Freudian psychoanalysis.

3

AN EXPERIMENT IN
LEISURE

This 'experiment' had been germinating for quite some time; Milner's Personal
Notebooks for 1935 show extensive annotation marked 'M.O.2', her reference
for her own works, as she selects material for her new book; and on 27
December 1936 this is clearly taking shape: 'Leisure – I'm going to make
some notes on how I am managing these holidays – and last summer's too.
Why not call the M.O.2 "some Experiments with Leisure"?'[1]

We see Milner collecting images for her book: an inveterate and frequent
re-visitor of her own notes, she collects images as she gathers objects. The
notebook for April–July 1935 is a particularly rich quarry for her later work.
Thus, she recalls certain of her 'loves' – that of antiques being one such, as
she remarks on her habit of looking 'in numerous shops and market places,
half hoping to pick up some 'old thing'; she mentions 'wooden water-jars
bound with brass [. . .] and a goatsherd's wine-skin in Savoy' – why, she
wonders, are these things so appealing? Why is the old so attractive to her?
Are these things symbols? Are they appealing because they are part of
tradition? Intrigued by such questions, Milner finds herself looking in
ironmongers browsing among gardening tools: 'Is it', she asks, 'yourself you
are always looking for, are all these parts of yourself? Is the world a mirror
in which to find yourself?' These are questions Milner ponders all her life and
they find further elaboration in her later book, *Eternity's Sunrise*, written and
published when she was in her eighties.

Consideration of old things is followed by her 'ache' to find certain creatures
in the natural world – a redshank, a curlew or an oyster-catcher. Marshes and
mudflats are 'entrancing': why? 'For they are sterile – desolate, why is
dissolution lovely? Only yesterday I caught myself wishing to see [if] some
live thing would[?] emerge from the mud.'[2]

Part of Milner's search in this text is for the desolate, the world of the
waste land:

> to find the meaning of 'spiritual disaster'; to discover where the Devil
> lives, to find in modern life what corresponds with the various deadly
> dangers of the Pilgrim's Progress – to find what evil is [. . .] Will I

be able to stand the evil face to face. IN WHAT FORM WILL HE APPEAR NOW?[3]

She is aware that there might well be books to tell her of these things, and, indeed, one reviewer of her previous book had commented that she 'could have got what she wanted from books'; but Milner insists that this is not an option: books on religion are of no help to her – 'as soon as it is abstracted it is dead'. She wishes 'to show a method for approaching such things through organic images',[4] images that, we might say, are a precursor of the 'beads' of *Eternity's Sunrise*.

Becoming increasingly more engaged with psychoanalysis, Milner states: 'Once you become aware of the force of the unconscious, there's no going back and pretending you don't see it.' And she notes in May 1935 how her analytic interests and her general diary 'are insisting in getting into the same books'.[5] Although *An Experiment* pre-dates Milner's first Freudian analysis, she self-confessedly borrows one guiding principle from psychoanalysis:

> that when you give your mind the reins and let it rove freely, there
> is no such thing as irrelevance, so far as the problems of the mind
> are concerned, whatever thought pops up is in some way important,
> however far-fetched it may appear.[6]

Letting her mind 'rove freely', Milner mulls over memories of hobbies, of travel, of an interest in witchcraft, of pagan ceremonial, of her discovery of the inner gesture, a fairy tale in three parts (echoing something of her early fictive excursions such as 'The Golden Cockle-Shell') born of her quest, haunting images of a bullfight, Ibsen's *Peer Gynt*, further images of death and all the many questions that these call forth.

Those responding to *An Experiment* recognise qualities that in many ways show how it looks forward to Milner's later work as it addressed preoccupations in her professional life – 'the problem of how truly to trust "the unconscious", trust the emptiness the blankness, trust what seems not to be there'.[7] One writer picked up on the quest theme, quoting Milner on 'true expression' and the value of 'expressive action' deriving from some 'inner vision' as opposed to 'purposive action determined by some outer goal': 'the inescapable condition of true expression was the plunge into the abyss, the willingness to recognize the moment of blankness and extinction was the moment of incipient fruitfulness, the moment without which the invisible forces could not do their work'.[8]

She quotes another review, this one signed Kenneth Richmond writing in *The Observer*:

> the drive towards self-subjection comes in for particularly interesting
> analysis and discussion, carrying explanation a good deal beyond the

perverted pleasure principle, and the Freudian death instinct. *Experiment* shows that the deliberate suggestion 'I am nothing', the deliberate letting go of all personal concern and fuss actually results in a great gain of personal (or should it be impersonal) stature. It seems a very possible view that the progressive unconscious mind becomes sick to death of the ego and its attitudes and, thwarted and soured by subservience to the posturer, adopts punitive measures.[9]

Re-visiting the reviews (Milner does this with critiques of the works as well as with her personal notebooks and diaries) she selects and extracts this from the *New English Weekly*:

for Joanna Field has the power of making us feel the force of her own experience, which is the more odd, as we don't quite know what we are in quest of, or indeed if there is anything to seek . . . we follow as we do because the writer is living the experience before us, with all the incidental set backs, false trails, patches of dullness and moments of triviality.[10]

Extracted, too, is this one signed by 'Lawes':

Miss Field believes in introspection and in keeping a record of one's spiritual discoveries. She is attracted by quietism and the contemplative life. She believes mystically in an 'inner act' of individual living which escapes identification and in the therapeutic value of a kind of humility.

Meanwhile, the reviewer in the *TLS* in January 1938 remarks that the text is 'the study of an introvert trying to extract meaning from the rich imagery of her personal and collective unconscious'.[11]

A different order of appreciation can be found in Milner's extensive stock of fan letters. *Experiment* continued to call forth comments into the 1980s and 1990s. Thus in July 1978 one fan writes: 'Being a person without much imagination or ability to fantasise you have given me starting points to access myself as I am to go on from them.' From August 1980, another writer invites Milner to stay and comments that the books 'have been like friends I have run to when the world seemed empty of comfort of the kind I thirsted for.' Chapter 16 holds especial 'magic relief' for this reader. One more correspondent, having read *Experiment*, finds herself able to overcome her reticence about writing and says the books 'delight' her and how grateful she is that 'you overcame your own blocks to creative expression enough to convey the experiences so lucidly and poetically – your books give me hope. Thank you for being'.[12]

In concentrating on her many-layered store of images on reverie and the reverberations of unconscious life, Milner is not immune to the upheavals of

33

her times – although there are occasions when this might appear to be the case. In some ways a book of wartime (*Experiment* was, she liked to say, blitzed out of print in the 1940s), it was also written during the time of the 1930s hunger marches and '[it] pointed to the fact that, unless we do manage to solve the problem of how to share the world's resources, the horror-struck face in my Holocaust picture [in *Eternity's Sunrise*] could become a reality'.[13] Maud Ellmann writes that 'in spite of her forebodings about fascism, Milner offers few particulars about the crises of her times'. One could say, too, that she seems immune in her early books, and, indeed, in her notebooks, to the realities of the Spanish Civil War (although there is evidence in her papers of her reading on the subject – for example, a document in the John Milner Papers sent to MM by the Institute of Psychoanalysis Librarian on the history of Spain and of the Civil War). However, Ellmann also brilliantly contends that it *is* possible to read the text as 'a program for resisting fascism – by opposing on the one hand, the authoritarian inclinations of the ego and on the other the appeal of the irrational, so cynically exploited by the Nazis'.[14]

Milner's remarks in her 'Summing Up' to this book are relevant: in thinking about and discovering her personal imagery and learning 'that it was in these images that unrecognized desires expressed themselves', she had been most 'shocked' to find that some of her most powerful images 'were being used by others to foster what seemed to me the most sinister form of egoism – jingoistic nationalism'. She had read in the newspapers 'that pagan rituals', for instance, 'were being revived in Germany, as part of the movement to glorify violence and to discredit the teachings of Christ'. At first this left her inclined to abandon her enterprise, but gradually she came to see that the image could be a force of reconciliation and a mediating power, leading to a more, rather than a less reasonable attitude.[15]

The book all but disappeared:

> [and] the necessary preoccupations with physical survival during the war years, together with the struggles over my apprenticeship for a new profession, meant that the implications of what I felt I had discovered in my experiment became somewhat blurred, indeed I almost forgot about the book.[16]

Thus it was not until 1957 that it re-gained a place at the forefront of Milner's thinking with the response of her friend Anton Ehrenzweig and his thought-provoking review in *The American Imago*.

Ehrenzweig – an Austrian lawyer, sometime judge, with an interest in modern art and modern music – had left Austria and settled in England in 1938. He became a lecturer in art education at Goldsmiths College in London and wrote *The Psychoanalysis of Artistic Vision and Hearing* (1953) and *The Hidden Order of Art* (1967). Milner's personal contact with him began in 1953 at the International Psycho-Analytical Congress in London when they were introduced by his old friend, one Dr Rubinstein; but she only really got to know him well later at the next Congress in Geneva when she 'realised his sensitiveness to what someone else was trying to say, for he came to hear a short paper I was giving to the Congress, in which I showed drawings of two patients of mine'.[17] After this meeting in Geneva, Ehrenzweig lent Milner his 1953 book *Artistic Vision and Hearing*, and this text became important to her in her 1956 Freud Centenary lecture on 'Psychoanalysis and Art' (see p. 154f.).

Milner describes the 'other half' of her exchange with Ehrenzweig as her lending him, after the Geneva meeting, 'a book I had written in 1936 (before becoming an analyst)': this was *An Experiment in Leisure*, and reading it prompted him to write a critique in a paper he read to the London Imago Society in 1957. As a forerunner of *On Not Being Able to Paint* and a most perceptive critique of Milner's text, Ehrenzweig's commentary is worth attention.

An art teacher himself, Ehrenzweig had clear ideas on blocks to creativity and he opens his piece with a comment on 'ego rigidity impeding the free flow of mental imagery'; in this connection he considers that the art teachers' 'task is to make the student's personality more flexible and so to develop his latent creativity'. He follows this with: 'It is our good fortune that Marion Milner, who finally became a psychoanalyst herself, continued her life-long search for creativeness without interruption by her psychoanalytical training.' According to Ehrenzweig (and her writings endorse this) she felt that her 'creative search as an artist [was] something apart from her growing understanding of her id phantasies'.[18] He comments that, after shedding some obstructive clichés in her *A Life* she dealt with 'finding truly potent imagery to replace the abandoned clichés'. He elaborates:

> this change in the character and function of mental imagery represents the crucial creative change in the ego. It needs only to be put into more technical language to make clear that Marion Milner has described a new approach to an ego psychology of creativeness.[19]

Thus she 'scanned the world, her memory and imagination' for powerful images, those with a 'still glow' emanating from their unconscious meanings but whose potency was not wholly explained by their symbolic weight. These were, in the main, 'images of suffering and death' and, as Ehrenzweig states, 'deeply embedded in sado-masochistic fantasy and centred around Frazer's theme of the dying God'. In Chapter 4 of her text Milner tells us how her intense involvement with witchcraft now recedes and she becomes involved with Frazer's *The Golden Bough* and, in particular, with a 'shilling reprint' of the Adonis chapter where she read avidly of how the peoples of Egypt and Western Asia, under the names variously of Adonis, Osiris, Tamuz and Attis, 'represented the yearly decay and revival of life [. . .] which they personified as a god who annually died and rose again from the dead'.[20]

While Milner was aware that her images could be seen as infantile symbolism, this, as Ehrenzweig contends, mattered little in terms of their role as 'creative catalysts'; as they entered the creative process they lost their heavy burden of guilt and gave a 'still glow', leading to a quite different quality of feeling, 'of greatest stillness and austerity'.[21] These are those images comparable once more to those conceptualised as 'beads' later in Milner's work.

Non-differentiation, fusion and the oceanic state comprise an area central to Milner's thinking and vital to her ground-breaking work in *On Not Being Able to Paint*. Ehrenzweig comments on *An Experiment in Leisure* from the vantage point of knowledge of her paper on symbol formation (see pp. 44, 47–48), stressing her view that 'the oceanic fusion between inner and outer world is needed for successful symbol formation; the lack of differentiation in the oceanic state leads to new symbolic equations and to new creativeness'. Freud, remarks Ehrenzweig, would have 'thus described both the source of creativeness in the id – the Oedipus Complex – and the ego condition specific for creativity – the oceanic state'. However, Ehrenzweig firmly distinguishes the imagery of the Oedipus situation from that of the dying god. Thus: 'These two aspects of creativeness do not correspond genetically. The imagery of the Oedipus situation presupposes clear differentiation between the roles of father, mother and child, and is far removed from the lack of differentiation in oceanic fusion.' This is quite distinct from the Dying God theme, which is 'far nearer to the undifferentiated state'; he elaborates: 'Not only does the mother imago – Isis, Kybele, Astarte – stand alone opposite her dead son-lover, but their images are interchangeable indicating a lack of sharp differentiation between them.'[22]

As Ehrenzweig unpacks the Dying God theme, he arrives at the view that 'its voluntary acceptance of self-destruction appears directly related to the structural disintegration of imagery on the oceanic level'. Now he understands Milner anew:

> when she said that the Dying-God theme did not so much represent id phantasy as certain ineffable changes in the ego during the onset of creativeness which she aptly calls creative 'surrender'. What is felt emotionally as a surrender to self-destruction in the image of the Dying God is really a surrender to the disintegrating action of low-level imagery which dissolves the hardened surface clichés while consciousness sinks towards an oceanic level.[23]

He also apprehends Milner's assertion (in her paper on symbol formation) that the first stage 'in the creative use of symbols, must be a temporary giving up of the discriminating ego which stands apart and tries to see things objectively and rationally and without emotional colouring'. He returns to the matter of 'ego rigidity' with which he had opened his critique, now understanding how the interference of the 'free swinging out of the ego rhythm, will also interfere with the successful use of symbols and with creativity in general'. He reiterates his view of the relevance of this to the teaching of art, which can, potentially, 'break this deadlock by resolving ego rigidity and the unconscious anxiety masked behind it'.[24]

Ehrenzweig empathises with Milner in that in her 'artistic beginnings' she did not have the help of an enlightened teacher (this changed and is commented on below with her association with Marian Bohusz-Szyszko). In her Joanna Field persona, she had to face severe anxieties 'after she abandoned clichéd imagery in a catastrophic reversal of ego functioning'. But, as he points out, anticipating some of Milner's comments in *On Not Being Able to Paint* on the importance of these matters for orthodox education:

> The creative surrender is not always so dramatic a gesture. The art teacher will gradually lead his student towards freedom, trying all the way to gauge intuitively the amount of anxiety the pupil can bear and the integration of ego functioning already achieved.[25]

As he remarks, creative imagery does not retain its potency indefinitely; thus the mind is always on 'the look out for new potent imagery' and, in *An Experiment in Leisure*:

> Marion Milner [. . .] takes us right inside this eternal search; image after image is brought up from a rich storehouse of dreams, myths and childhood memories, each with a new promise of final revelation; but in the end we are told the quest was all and the answer nothing. We are left with a fine sense of despair which, however, is a good beginning for the attitude of surrender, a letting go of all purpose and planning and a growing trust in the guidance of the unconscious ego.[26]

Writing of the bullfight she had witnessed in Spain, Milner tells us that, 'blasphemous' though it might seem, she 'had come away feeling as though [she] had attended the most satisfying religious ceremony of [her] life [. . .] I felt purged and fuller and wiser'. She reminds us, too, and Ehrenzweig takes this up, that the facing of this experience 'is a test for a full acceptance of death as part of reality'. It is only fit that in Spanish bullfights the killing of the bull is called the 'moment of truth'. (He comments that Hanna Segal had told him, in an oral communication, that she considered the emotional acceptance of death to be a condition of creativeness).[27]

Paradoxically, Ehrenzweig reports that, in his reading of the text and of the situations portrayed within it, the creative surrender can exhibit a certain 'manic' quality; thus 'the killing of the bull, the sacrifice of the Dying God have no depressive feeling about them; death, once accepted, becomes a feast of cosmic bliss, or liberation from bondage'. His thought here echoes that of Adrian Stokes, who also placed a high premium on non-differentiation, on 'one-ness' as well as on Milner's emphasis on the oceanic as pre-requisite for symbolisation.[28] Sensitively, too, Ehrenzweig reads Milner's child patient's play as enacting the ritual of the Dying God in the symbolisation paper when she attends to a boy's play with the two warring villages, the play itself a reflection of its wartime backdrop.

The preoccupations of war and, as she says, survival were uppermost in Milner's mind in her efforts to protect her young son John; her urgent need to write *Experiment* had come, she comments retrospectively, at a 'cost' – the cost was that her son got no response to his picture letters to her while she was away in Spain – although it was not until much later in her life, indeed towards its end, that she was able to deconstruct some more meanings of her absence from her child's point of view.[29]

On 1 September 1939 in a note headed 'Crisis Week', writing from 'the Van', the caravan in which the family was temporarily living, Milner describes how they had:

> heard all the children were descending on us . . . felt awful . . . went for a walk watching the clouds lying in the fold of the Downs, looking for some philosophic detachment but found none. Then came back to D. in the van and asked him – and he said what he did was simply 'non-existing' – and I realised how desperately I'd been trying to find a way out – when obviously there's none.[30]

John Milner, however, recalls that they were on holiday at West Wittering, near Chichester, when war broke out and that they drove to some Quaker friends near Sudbury in Suffolk where they spent six weeks – he vividly remembers the threshing machine driven by a steam traction engine.[31]

In October 1939, with war having been declared, the family moved to a borrowed cottage in Elsted in Hampshire; they were now required to carry gas masks, and London was not thought to be a suitable place for someone as unwell with asthma as Dennis. It was a good move; John was happy at a small local school, and his father was asthma-free and further engaged on boat-design.

In June 1940, however, Milner writes, after a long gap in her diary keeping, that:

> Because of the bombing fears, Mrs. S., the mother of some friends of J's at the little school, said that, as she had been offered a house in the United States for the duration of the war, she was planning to go with her daughters – and would we like J to go with them?

As the Battle of Britain was raging and they were quite near the south coast, the Milners felt unable to decline this offer and duly set off to get John's passport photograph and to make arrangements. Thankfully, however, the passport photograph was not needed as the neighbour decided not to go to America, and Milner said that, in fact, her family had made the same decision. Soon her work meant that she needed to be in London during the week, and, fortunately, the Provost Road house survived with only minor damage.[32]

John appears to have enjoyed some of the wartime excitement. In a letter headed 'Blitz' he writes to his father:

> I suppose Mummy told you that she sent me away for the last night home because she didn't like me being in London. I heard and felt my first buzz bomb and when we were at Wins [Milner's sister Winifred Burger] the first night of dimout, we were listening to the nine o'clock [.] the siren went and a few minutes later we heard its godforsaken row. Win said out in the passage. The noise stopped. Win opened the back door and bang the whole house shook and the blast blew up the back of my neck. Have the papers told you what the mysterious bumps were yet. When we went and saw Patrick [Blackett] he said they knew what they were but the M.O.D didn't want us to know what they were.[33]

There had, of course, been much darker wartime undertones for the Milner family as in the 'Crisis Week' notes on the evacuees' arrival; and, wish as she might, there was no way out of the war years for Milner herself, whose life, as will be seen, was far from 'non-existing' in this convulsive time.

4

THE ROAD TO
PSYCHOANALYSIS

The year 1939 was the start of Milner's Freudian life – *Experiment* being the last of those texts sometimes referred to as her 'pre-Freudian writings'.[1] She began her training analysis, 'rushed through', she remarks at a later date, 'because of a shortage of analysts to take on the training of students, owing to many being away on war work'.[2] At the same time her creative life took a new and inspiring turn:

> I found myself doing free association or doodle drawings; beginning with something that could only be called a scribble there had emerged pictures that had definite stories even though I had no conscious awareness of what they were about while doing them. I was so surprised at discovering this capacity that, in 1939, the very day war was declared and I knew my work in schools would be over because of the evacuation of the schools, I set about writing another book, making use of these drawings.[3]

This book evolved into *On Not Being Able to Paint* and is discussed in Chapter 6. Milner's arrival in psychoanalysis, however, comes first. Its literary antecedents and development have already been seen in *A Life*, with its discoveries of free associative thinking and image-making; but the road towards analysis had begun earlier – in February 1928, when in the United States on her Rockefeller Scholarship, working with the Jungian analyst, Dr Irma Putnam.

Back in London, working with the Institute of Industrial Psychology, Milner came into contact with Susan Isaacs, pioneer of psychoanalytic research in child development, who asked her to take over her tutorial class in psychology; by this time she was 'really beginning to talk in terms of Freud' to the students. Dennis Milner, too, was led towards Freud because of his very severe asthma. At this time, a number of analysts would not take on asthmatic patients. Through her connection with the Stephen and Woolf families with whom Patrick Blackett was in contact at Cambridge, Milner had asked Adrian Stephen, brother of Virginia Woolf, about analysis for Dennis, but Stephen had been firm that 'he wouldn't tackle an asthmatic'; eventually they found someone outside the Freudian penumbra – a man called Faithfull, a freelance therapist using analytic techniques. For herself, she decided she needed help, in particular, with her work with the 'difficult children' with whom she was involved. She remarks, 'by then I had met Merrell Middlemore [. . .] and she recommended Sylvia Payne and so I decided to start some analysis about three times a week'.[4]

Payne, one of the pioneers of British psychoanalysis, was born Sylvia Moore in 1880, the daughter of a clergyman and one of nine siblings. Initially she wanted a musical future but then turned instead to medicine, training at Westfield College and the London School of Medicine for Women (Royal Free Hospital). Qualifying in 1906, in 1908 she married the surgeon, J.E. Payne, Commandant and Officer in Charge of the Torquay Red Cross Hospital, with whom she had three sons. In 1918 she was awarded the CBE. Her interest in psychoanalysis evolved during the First World War, and it was while working with shell-shocked patients that she first encountered the work of Freud. She started analysis in London with Edward Glover, analysed in Berlin by Karl Abraham and known for taking over many of his brother's institutional responsibilities on James Glover's death in 1926, subsequently going to Berlin herself for analysis with Hans Sachs and becoming acquainted with Karl Abraham. Payne returned to London and was elected an Associate Member of the British Psychoanalytical Society in 1922 and a full member in October 1924. She held many important offices with the Society, was elected to the Training Committee in 1927, becoming Secretary of the Institute of Psycho-Analysis in 1929, and later elected as Business Secretary. She played a crucial part in the Controversial Discussions (see below) and was elected President of the British Society in 1944.

Milner is on record as believing that Payne was able to prevent a split in the Society and had the greatest respect for her inauguration of the Middle Group, discussed in more detail on pages 45 and 46. More informally, she also comments, with wry affection, on Payne's very distinctive attitude towards democracy: 'nonsense – they wouldn't have voted that way had I been in the Chair', she is said to have remarked on one occasion when the vote did not go her way.[5]

In 1940 there emerged a pressing reason for Milner to take her involvement with psychoanalysis to another level: the Minister for Information, Duff Cooper, was implementing the exercise known as Mass Observation, and Milner, with her impressive background and qualifications in psychology, would have been a likely candidate for a role as one of those known as 'Cooper's Snoopers'. Originally a large-scale investigation into the habits and attitudes of Britain's people begun in 1932 in Bolton to monitor public morale, the Mass Observation project was deployed by Duff Cooper to gauge public morale and assess the effectiveness of public information campaigns; hearing the anxiety of her promising patient, Payne simply said, 'Why not train?' So Milner did, and clearly this was preferable to the 'rather pointless work for the government to do with propaganda' so dreaded by the (now) forty-year-old Milner.[6]

She was interviewed by Glover and Payne, and her acceptance is recorded by the Training Committee in October 1940. Looking back on this time of her early training Milner recalls wartime seminars in Anna Freud's house 'and the blackout, going across to Maresfield Gardens and a pea-souper fog when my torch had gone wrong, swimming about and lost in Swiss Cottage or somewhere'. Milner also remembers one with James Strachey, the brother of Lytton Strachey, analysand of Freud's and renowned translator of Freud's work:

> My first patient was interesting (Sharpe was my supervisor) and he was very difficult, a very brilliant Polish boy of 17, a pupil of a famous violinist, and I didn't realise it but he was pretty borderline psychotic. This was my first patient. He responded well in a way to analysis, he came because he couldn't practice. I remember reporting on him to Strachey's seminar and Strachey saying 'Yes, but you haven't said anything about the transference', and I realised that Ella Sharpe hadn't talked about the transference.

Ella Sharpe, analysed by Hans Sachs in the 1920s, began her career as a teacher, and then taught techniques in psychoanalysis. Her clinical seminars were thought to be excellent. It was puzzling that Sharpe had omitted the transference in this instance; it is a topic well covered in her work on psychoanalytic technique, but somehow she had missed it for this boy. Perhaps, Milner remarks, it was the sort of transference that analysts were not ready to deal with at that time: it was not, she says, until Anna Freud's 1951 Amsterdam paper that she 'personally found a bit of theory that would have been relevant for that patient'. There were some seminars also with Edward Glover that Milner hated: 'By then I suppose the split [between Kleinians and Anna Freudians] was beginning', and Milner recalls saying Glover 'seems to be trying to catch us out in terms of politics'; he was like a 'shyster lawyer' and the feeling was of a background of political intrigue.[7]

Milner qualified in the summer of 1943, and as a child analyst in the autumn of the same year. The decision to become a child analyst – one she valued to the end of her life – reflected the character of the London psychoanalytic community. By 1930 40 per cent of the members of the London Psychoanalytic Society were women who brought to the group a high level of interest in children's development. Her full membership of the British Society was granted in October 1944 at a volatile and conflicted time for the Society, a period leading up to and including the Controversial Discussions. The term refers to the discussions between Anna Freud, Melanie Klein, their followers and members of the indigenous group of British analysts that took place in the British Society between 1941 and 1946. The dialogue had started as early as 1925 with Klein's London lectures and Anna Freud's paper on 'The Theory of Child Analysis' presented to the Innsbruck Conference in 1927, and the controversies had been heated, particularly in Vienna.

The discussions centred on the issue of whether the views on child development and psychoanalytic technique for both children and adults that Klein and her group (Susan Isaacs, Joan Riviere, Paula Heimann and others) had developed would be accepted by those supporting the classical view of psychoanalysis as interpreted by Anna Freud and her colleagues from Vienna and Berlin. If this was not possible, then there was the question of whether Klein should be expelled from the analytic community. A variety of issues were involved. The local group of British psychoanalysts – Ernest Jones, Sylvia Payne, James Strachey and others – wished to mediate between the two and to reach a compromise. This was eventually achieved, and three groups were formed – the Kleinians, the (Anna) Freudians and the Independents (initially the Middle Group).[8]

Such is the broad outline; a more detailed account shows how the institutional context may have impacted on Milner's professional life. Milner *did* go to the discussions: 'There was one where we had our meetings somewhere else because there had been a fire at Gloucester Place . . . and I remember only emotional feeling about it really. Sylvia was in the chair for a long time through that.' She continues, appreciating how Sylvia 'handled it very skilfully'. It was not, however, always easy to be working closely with her analyst: 'I remember we used to have tea and it was brought in and I used to take her a cup and I suddenly became self-conscious and I thought this is transference . . .' Melanie Klein, meanwhile, Milner found very beautiful and wished for her to supervise her clinic case. Initially she found Klein rather frightening – until she was able to see her in terms of an image, and that decreased her fear. Later, while not exactly friends, they did occasionally go to a theatre together, such as a performance of Marcel Marceau, and Milner tells us that Klein met her mother at Provost Road, and they got on well. Milner had started her second case supervised by Joan Riviere, an active collaborator with Klein with whom she had been through a 'terrible time' finding her very authoritative and a person who offered interpretations that, although undoubtedly brilliant, were 'rather like those celluloid protractors – I thought she'd laid it down on the material and read off'. This was probably unfair, she knew, but this is how she felt. In an interview Milner recalls Riviere saying roundly, 'If you don't do as I say, what's the point in coming [to supervision]?'[9] Donald Winnicott was at the time much under the influence of Riviere, and it was he who had suggested that, at this juncture, she was the best supervisor for Milner, whose case, however, did not go well, and there was a distressing degree of conflict between supervisor and supervisee.

After this, Milner went to Klein for another case's supervision and for her child patients. She names three child patients: there was the seventeen-year-old musician already mentioned – 'he counted as "my adolescent"'; then the three year old (1944: 'A Suicidal Symptom in a Child of Three'); and then the one about whom she wrote the 'role of illusion' (1952: 'The Role of Illusion in Symbol Formation')[10] – this was about a child patient who was in fact the grandson of Melanie Klein with whom Milner had started work when he was aged four.

A recurrent theme in Milner's recollections of these training and qualifying years is how accelerated her training was: 'she [Payne] made me do my membership only a few months after I qualified. This was the time of the buzz bombs.' Milner delivered the paper 'A Suicidal Symptom in a Child of Three' [Anorexia Nervosa] in the basement of Gloucester Place. The Secretary had rung Milner in the morning asking if they should have the paper. Milner very much did not want to put it off but was anxious that 'if there was a raid then the death of all the analysts would be on my shoulders and Mrs. Newrath said, "well, I'll share the responsibility with you". So I gave my paper.'

There had been other dangers, too, in Milner's child training: 'I used', she said, 'to pedal over to Melanie with the V2s falling and then I decided it was too difficult and told her I could manage on my own.' Thus this supervision came to an end; Klein also decided the patient concerned should go to a male analyst for further work.[11]

As shown, Milner's training took place during wartime and the conditions of wartime London: many analysts either served in the Emergency Medical Service or moved out of London – Klein for one initially moved to Edinburgh to avoid the bombing in London. As Ken Robinson points out 'Émigré colleagues could not, however, leave London easily because as enemy aliens they were not permitted to move freely around the country.'[12] In the first six months of 1939, half of those present at Scientific Meetings were continental colleagues: from September and for the following two years they were regularly a majority.

Things changed in 1941 when members of the Society began to return to London – in particular, when Klein came back to the city in October. To quote Robinson again:

> identities rooted in a common language and practice of analysis were about to be challenged. Instead of being eased by the presence of Viennese colleagues, the existing 'bad conditions' were exacerbated and the Controversial Discussions became necessary for individuals and groups to make and debate position statements.[13]

There is a very comprehensive and fascinating account on the debates around metapsychology and technique by King and Steiner (1991); here I shall confine commentary to those personae most significant to Milner at this point in her analytic career. Anna Freud was to be an important supporter of Milner and, at the instigation of Masud Khan, was to write a foreword to *On Not Being Able to Paint*. At this time, 1941, having come to London from Vienna at the start of the war, Anna Freud remained to carry on her father's work after his death in September 1939. Committed to developing his thinking into the field of child analysis, she also gathered a refugee community around her, and in June 1941, with Dorothy Burlingham, she opened the 'Children's At Rest Centre' and then two more buildings; this initiative became known as the Hampstead War Nurseries. All but four of the staff of these projects were refugees; later, there were also homes at Bulldog's Bank and Lingfield House for the care of child and adolescent survivors of concentration camps.

At this time of a potential split in the British Society, it is interesting that Milner – almost always averse to political confrontation – says that when she had decided to have some Freudian analysis:

> It seemed to be by pure chance that I found myself neither in the analytic stream led by Anna Freud nor in that led by Melanie Klein, for I did not even know that there was a deep controversy both in theory and practice between these two pioneers of the psychoanalysis of children.[14]

Disingenuous though this may be, it is also typical of Milner's apolitical stance, a mask or veneer that was rarely penetrable.

Anna Freud withdrew from the training until 1946, at which point it was through the efforts of Sylvia Payne that she again agreed to participate. Then two parallel courses came into being: the A course for the Kleinians and the B course for the Anna Freudians. Robinson's view here is that the most significant requirement introduced at this time was that the candidates in analysis with a Kleinian or an Anna Freudian must choose a supervisor for their second training case from training analysts who were of neither per-suasion. In effect, this ruling created the three groups mentioned earlier: A, B and Middle – later (and today also) known as the Independent Group, the Group with which Milner is most usually identified.

Those theoretical disagreements and allegiances having most impact on Milner and her work are usefully pointed up in Janet Sayers's *Mothering Psychoanalysis*. It is important to note that in 1943 Susan Isaacs, who was well known to Milner through her work in the schools, was closely involved in the debate. Isaacs' position on Klein's concept of 'unconscious phantasy' was that it could be seen as a natural development of the account of dreams laid out by Freud. All that Klein had done, in her view, was to show how from earliest infancy phantasy representations of our relations with others permeate our whole mental life, not just the superego. There was a degree of agreement on the issues of babies internalising their mother's image to use when the mother is away. Objections arose because Klein emphasised the hostile aspects of this internalisation. Freud, on the other hand, stressed the unconscious as pure wish fulfilment.[15] Milner was eventually to part company intellectually with her former supervisor on this very matter of innate envy, remarking retrospectively that:

it was somewhere about 1954 that I stopped going to Melanie Klein's seminars for analysts because I could not accept her idea of inborn envy. The high degree of envy that I undoubtedly came across in some of my patients seemed to me to be related to far too little allowance having been made in their infancy for their primary omnipotence; in fact, related to the idea of premature ego formation that I had first been driven to consider because of Simon's [her patient's] difficulties.[16]

Next, as Sayers points out, the Scots analyst, W.R.D. Fairbairn:

insisted that infants primarily seek not pleasure but relations with others. Whereas Freud focused on repression of past pleasure into the unconscious, Fairbairn and the Kleinians attended to the here-and-now internalization and projection of mothering and other relations, as though conscious and unconscious thought differed only in terms of spatial location – inside or out – rather than in terms of history and structure.

In this discussion analytic legend has it that 'through it all an air-raid raged outside, with Winnicott having to warn the assembled company to withdraw'.

The following meeting, introduced by Anna Freud, concentrated on Freud's claim that the infant is completely self-centred at the outset – mothering is entirely secondary to instinct gratification. 'But, as critics pointed out, her own war nursery experience showed that babies also early internalize an image of the mother. Why else are they so disturbed at being handled by someone else?'[17]

There were positive results of the Discussions, some of which were of potential significance for Milner: whereas, as Robinson points out, Ernest Jones, founder and president of the British Society, had kept his distance from the Tavistock Clinic, the psychiatric clinic founded in 1920 by Dr Hugh Crichton-Miller, Sylvia Payne took the opposite line, forging links between the two institutions. Payne was equally strong in trying to heal the wounds inflicted by Glover's attack on army psychiatry in a radio broadcast. She herself had found her way to psychoanalysis partly as a result of her Red Cross work with wounded soldiers in the First World War, and now she supported the Society's wish to encourage the interest in psychological medicine that the war had fostered in both the medical profession and in lay people.[18] Those who had served as army psychiatrists, such as Rickman and Bowlby, were welcomed back by the Society; Bion completed his analytic training and others followed suit – Tom Main, Harold Bridger, Millicent Dewar and Jock Sutherland were among the thirty or so people who had worked alongside analysts during the war and went on to train with the Society in the post-war years.

Another outcome of the Controversial Discussions was that they greatly encouraged members to clarify the basic premises on which they stood as psychoanalysts. Robinson writes: 'The papers of Isaacs and Heimann in the Discussions are witness to just how much the challenge of the Discussions benefited from this process of elucidation.' (These papers are: Susan Isaacs, 'The Nature and Function of Phantasy', and Paula Heimann, 'Some Aspects of the Role of Introjections and Projection in Early Development'.) Robinson also singles out for special praise Marjorie Brierley's 'brilliant engagement with Kleinian thinking, a fitting tribute to the woman whose plea for "a self-denying ordinance on personal vendettas" and whose proposal that there should be scientific enquiry into theoretical differences prompted the Discussions'.[19]

Milner's analyst and supporter Payne produced what has been called a 'characteristically straightforward restatement of the basics of psychoanalysis': 1 the concept of a dynamic psychology; 2 the existence of the unconscious; 3 the theory of instincts and of repression; 4 infantile sexuality; 5 the dynamics of the transference.[20] Essentially, this was the British Freudian position before the Controversial Discussions and it now characterised the Middle Group. Payne, a key influence on Milner, was also a significant influence on Donald Winnicott, who was, in turn, a major player in the development of Object Relations theory and practice, a development often linked with the Middle Group. Of course, all three groups are concerned with this aspect of analysis: the Middle Group, however, including clinicians such as Balint, Fairbairn, Winnicott and Bowlby, placed much greater emphasis on the environment than the other two groups, as did Milner herself as she moved away from a more orthodox Kleinian position towards a perspective informed by Object Relations thinking and an Independent way of thinking.

A word now on Milner's early papers in terms of the impact of the theoretical debates of the time and the people involved. Klein had supervised Milner's membership paper in 1943 on the suicidal three year old. She also supervised another case of Milner's detailed in a section of the 1952 paper 'The role of illusion in symbol formation', a paper considered 'brilliant' by Donald Winnicott, presented in its fuller form as a paper in honour of Melanie Klein's seventieth birthday. The section concerned is 'Case Material: A Game of war between two villages', and the boy concerned – disguised as 'Simon' – is, in fact, Klein's own grandson, Michael Clyne. Milner is on record as saying that, despite her misgivings (and presumably issues of boundaries), she 'wouldn't have missed the experience for anything'.[21] She is, according to Grosskurth, scornful of those who say Klein did not take the environment seriously – Milner as analyst in this case is told a good deal about the home background. It is in connection with this paper that we learn of Milner's attitude to her famous supervisor. Klein had disapproved of something she had said, and, staring at her with hooded eyes, had reminded her of a vulture peering out of a thundercloud. After that, she said, 'I wasn't frightened of her any more.'[22]

This case deals with a boy who is suffering from a loss of talent for school work; during his earlier school years, from four to six, things had gone well, and he was always top of his class, but gradually he found himself near the bottom and, on occasion, unable to get himself to school. It is important to remember the context of the play described. This boy had in fact lived through part of the Blitz on London, and had begun this particular play after Milner's own house had sustained blast damage; and he had shown somewhat delayed interest in the damage when he came to the house for his analysis.

The analysis was based on a game of two villages: one comprised all the people, animals and houses; the other comprised toy trucks, cars and 'lots of junk and oddments of exchange'. Thus the analyst's – Milner's – was the maternal space and his space had all the mechanical equipment. She felt that in his play he 'did seem to be working out his conflicts about the relation between father and mother, both internally and externally, and trying to find ways of dealing with his jealousy and envy of his mother in what Melanie Klein (1928) has called the "femininity phase".'[23]

Grosskurth comments that during the supervision Milner was troubled by the scornful remarks made by Klein about her son, Eric, and 'she later wondered whether Eric matured considerably after his mother died.' Grosskurth questions this, being 'inclined to wonder if Klein was *actually* so critical of Eric, or whether she was imposing her own scheme of the predominance of the mother on the material'. It is known that there was some tension between mother and son for some years around this time. Michael was, in the end, passed on to Bion for further analysis, but according to Grosskurth Milner continued to be troubled by Klein's attitude towards her son. Also, according to Paula Heimann, 'Klein was angry with Milner for having produced "a very original idea" on the capacity for symbol making as the basis of creativity.'[24] Milner's next analyst, Clifford Scott – Klein's first candidate to qualify as a psychoanalyst, now usually regarded as an Independent and to whom Milner went in 1949 – shared her bewilderment about Klein's alleged anger.

In this time of rapprochement in the Society following the Discussions it is notable that Milner, with her own strong impulse towards reconciliation, produced her 1945 paper on 'Some Aspects of Phantasy in relation to General Psychology'.[25] Aware that it was, on occasion, said by analysts that no common ground was possible between general psychologists and psychoanalysts – the former, if not themselves analysed, had too great a resistance to those facts about the unconscious mind revealed by the psychoanalytic method of research – Milner sets out to see how far certain ideas 'were based on common ground of agreed theory in the two sciences'. At times referring back to her work with her anorexic patient, for instance, Milner posited some reconciliation on the basis that 'when the general psychologist talks of sentiments and the psychoanalyst of internal objects, we may not in fact be talking the primitive form of the same thing'.[26] She concludes her investigation thus: 'It seems to me that it is in connection with the mental phenomena included under the term phantasy that the general psychologist and the psychoanalyst can most fruitfully meet.'[27]

With all the arguments and turbulent meetings in the world of child analysis in the air, it was only natural for Milner to turn her attention to her only son; her Personal Notebooks of these years give glimpses, but it was not until much later, in her nineties, in *Bothered by Alligators*, that her 'analysis' of him (and his of her) receive full attention. In August 1940, the eight-year-old John is avid for knowledge, asking for information on such matters as whether or not God is a person and, in particular, teasing out facts as to why people become ill or what causes illness; it seemed he was 'really asking, "have I made Daddy ill? Am I bad then? What is goodness and badness, saint, God?"' Later, when his mother suggested that he 'might feel it had been his fault D. [her husband] was ill, he said, '"yes, I have felt that."'

Milner records her explanation thus: 'Daddy is probably ill because he tried too hard, first to comfort his M[other] when his F[ather]died – and obviously as a little boy he couldn't – then he tried too hard to help the poor.'[28]

In October 1940 Milner is thinking further about her relation to John, her concerns and 'a picture of the good mother which I can be'; it is a question 'not in terms of is he or is he not living up to my picture of a good child – manners etc. But is he experiencing all the human possibilities – sorrow, happiness, aggression, sublimity etc. etc.?' She is aware of a need to see 'each contact in terms of give-and-take patterns rather than good and bad patterns' and connects this with the spatula game, 'this take and throw away of the spatula' she had seen at Winnicott's clinic[29] (see p. 51).

Writing from Harting, the Milners' Hampshire cottage, Milner worried about her son, feeling his pain, his tears and rage: 'How difficult it is to put in action with one's child what one really believes – wanting to save him from pain [. . .] of not having enough friends, of loneliness.' But then, as it were recalling her professional self, she notes, 'I might stand back and wait and see how he solves the problem for himself [. . .] [be] able to wait and watch as the analyst does.'[30] And there are painful thoughts, for both mother and son, arising from John's playground experience, 'about whether one is liked or not'. He is seen to be 'a bit lonely, doesn't get on with the village boys'. She tries to think about which parts of her conclusions about living can be put into words for a child of ten to understand. A later note, apparently from the same year, records Milner's realisation that all her son's day dreams are preoccupied with mechanical things – one time he resolved to make a forge, and at the cinema he was most interested in 'the machinery, how they manage to make a long film'.[31] This echoes his father's talents and looks forward to his future as academic, successful engineer and scientist – his mother records that he did *not* like *David Copperfield*.

Looking after her son, and seeing him through his schooldays, was a very important part of Milner's post-war life; however, her career – needed to finance John's education – was also developing fast at the same time. Having obtained

49

full membership of the British Psychoanalytical Society in 1944, she was almost immediately appointed a training analyst; and, by 1946, she already had someone in training with her. From 1945 to 1946 onwards she was very active in the training of analysts, being especially engaged with: teaching seminars on dreams attended by, among others, Masud Khan and Pearl King; acting as a reserve on a panel to teach technical matters; teaching later developments in theory; and also teaching techniques in child analysis. She is thought to have been very active in the Society and a frequent attendee at Scientific Meetings (although, from her notebooks, we might wonder if she was not somewhat inhibited about speaking in such settings). Willing to engage in committee work, she does not, however, appear to have held office. As late as 1972 Milner was involved in negotiations to keep Anna Freud within the aegis of the British Society.[32]

Donald Winnicott had been influential in Milner's decision to train as an analyst, as he was also in her thoughts about her young son's development; but he had become very significantly involved with Milner, and her family even before that time. Their relationship, both personal and professional, is complicated, even contentious at times, but, as part of psychoanalytic history, it deserves its own chapter.

April 18ᵗʰ
Heard the wry neck

Sand Martins

April 19ᵗʰ
Sand martins returned. Small vetch in
flower. Unfinished chaffinches and linnets
nests. Chalk Hill Blue butterfly.

April 26ᵗʰ Two thrushes nests with two
eggs and four eggs and a blackbirds.
I saw a nest in a hedge which seemed
to have no opening. When I touched it
a field-mouse ran out. The nest was
an old thrush's or blackbirds and
the mouse had roofed it in. I put my hand
in and when next I came it was
deserted.

April 27
Heard nightingale near St Martha's.

April 30ᵗʰ
Three linnets nests with 5 eggs 1 egg 0 eggs
Thrush's with one egg. Hedge sparrow's
with a young bird, most probably a cuckoo,
with a hedge-sparrows
with an egg nearly ready to be hatched
knocked out of the nest.

May 4ᵗʰ
Swifts (returned) seen
May 9ᵗʰ
House martin's (returned) seen
May 10ᵗʰ
Heard the turtle dove & found a
starlings nest under eaves of shed
May 11ᵗʰ
Heard nightjar! Blackbird's nest with 4
eggs. Thrush's with 2, empty chaffinches.
Found a starlings egg on the ground.
Flea
May 18ᵗʰ Found early purple orchis, marsh

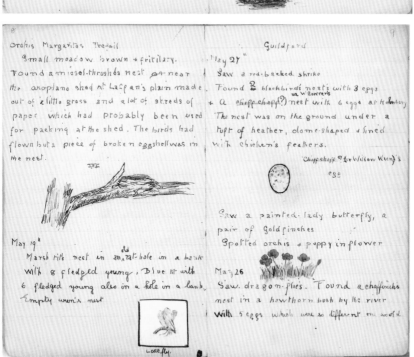

8

Orchis Margaritas Trefoil
Small meadow brown & fritilary.
Found a missel-thrushes nest on near
the aeroplane shed at Laffan's plain made
out of a little grass and a lot of shreds of
paper which had probably been used
for packing at the shed. The birds had
flown but a piece of broken eggshell was in
the nest.

May 19ᵗʰ
Marsh tit's nest in an old rat-hole in a bank
with 8 fledged young, Blue tit with
6 fledged young also in a hole in a bank.
Empty wren's nest

Lace fly.

Guildford

May 27ᵗʰ
Saw a red-backed shrike
Found 2 blackbirds nests with 3 eggs
& a chiff-chaff (?) nest with 6 eggs at Holmbury
or Willowren's
The nest was on the ground under a
tuft of heather, dome-shaped & lined
with chicken's feathers.

Chiffchaff ? (or Willow Wren)'s
egg

Saw a painted-lady butterfly, a
pair of goldfinches
Spotted orchis & poppy in flower

May 26
Saw dragon-flies. Found a chaffinchs
nest in a hawthorn bush by the river
with 5 eggs which were so different one would

Plate 1 From *Mollie Blackett's Nature Diary* (pen and ink drawings)

Plate 2 MM's 15-year old picture of the dragon

Plate 3 MM in 1924

Plate 4 Nina Farhi

Plate 5 MM, Mary Pears (Reid) and friends

Plate 6 MM and Nicola Pears

Plate 7 MM Self-Portrait

Plate 8 The Angry Parrot (from ONBAP)

Plate 9 MM in garden at Provost Road

Plate 10 MM collage: 'The Listeners'

Plate 11 MM collage: 'The Green Baby'

Plate 12 Collage for MM by Desy Safán-Gerard

Plate 13 MM's room shortly after she died; *Suppressed Madness of Sane Men* in front of her chair

5

'A HUGE CATHERINE WHEEL'

Donald Winnicott

Thinking back to her arrival in the world of psychoanalytic training, Milner writes: 'But it was a public lecture, in 1938, by D.W. Winnicott that finally led me to begin a Freudian analysis with Sylvia Payne, and in 1939 to apply for and be accepted by the British Psycho-Analytical Society.'

She continues, 'I do not remember at all what was said in the lecture, but I did get the feeling that, contrary to the impression that some Freudians had given me, the main ideas I was preoccupied with could be accommodated within the Freudian metapsychology.'[1] In 1972, Milner enlarges on this, telling how Winnicott was speaking about his work with mothers and babies and the 'famous spatula game':

> He told how he would leave a spatula on the table in front of the mother and baby, well within the baby's reach. Then he simply watched what the baby did with the spatula, watched for variations in the normal pattern of reaching for it, grabbing it, giving it a good suck and then chucking it away. He told how, out of this very simple experimental situation, he could work out, according to the observed blocks in the various stages, a diagnosis of the problems between the mother and the baby. As he talked, I was captivated by the mixture in him of deep seriousness and his love of little jokes, that is, the play aspect of his character, if one thinks of true play as transcending the opposites of serious and non-serious.[2]

From the start she was captivated by Winnicott's mixture of 'seriousness and funniness';[3] and so impressed was she by the lecture that she asked Winnicott to analyse her husband, to which he agreed, although he later expressed severe misgivings about the decision, saying his meeting with Dennis was the 'worst consultation' of his career.[4] Milner and Winnicott became friendly colleagues from the moment she heard this lecture; Winnicott's biographer Rodman tells that she was on occasion driven to meetings by him and that this driving made Winnicott, embroiled in a very difficult marriage, feel 'less deprived'.[5] Milner apparently could not drive, and significant parts of her social and professional life involve being driven to people and places right up until the end of her life (when she would, even in her nineties, attend weekly Squiggle meetings to discuss Winnicott's work and influence).

Dennis's asthma had proved problematic during their two-year sojourn in the United States, and both were very keen that his condition should be addressed once more. At the time, Rodman tells us, Winnicott was being analysed by Joan Riviere and 'still thought clever interpretations were important'.* 'Yet', writes Rodman, 'he was interested in the potential value of physical contact with patients and would hold Derm (sic) Milner during an attack'.[6] Winnicott believed in what Milner calls 'management' (she later parts company with him on the subject), in doing things for people (and in the physical 'holding' of his patients); it was a tradition he adopted with Margaret Little, a very disturbed woman with whom he worked, who eventually herself became an analyst and has described her analysis with Winnicott in *Psychotic Anxieties and Containment: A Personal Record of An Analysis with Winnicott* (1990). One weekend he visited the Milner house thirteen times when Dennis's asthma was particularly acute.[7]

A letter of 15 July 1940 expresses Milner's gratitude to Winnicott who has done so much for her (by then she may have been in analysis with him herself, although the date that this started is not certain). She comments that this was after the time she started seeing Susan, the patient in *The Hands of the Living God*; and later she refers to how he has helped her greatly about talking at meetings: 'Also having been unable to talk at meetings before, I'm now afraid of talking too much. So give me a kick under the table if I do.'

She now asks for further help. Knowing her request might well be seen as 'transference', she finds herself in this time 'where a bomb may blow any of us up any minute' unable to think 'entirely in psychoanalytic concepts'. She so much appreciates his help that she would like to offer the same to her son: 'you have helped me so much by being the person you are that I would like John to have the same chance'. After Chamberlain had returned to London from Munich in 1938 promising 'peace with honour' with Hitler, Milner, like many, was unconvinced that peace would be maintained. At this time she had asked two people, a cousin and a great friend, Mary Dalston, to stand guardians for her son. By July 1940 the cousin had joined up as a doctor on a battleship and was thus no longer available for the role. Milner's brother Patrick had agreed to be a trustee to deal with financial matters but, wrote Milner, 'I feel the need of someone else, less official, who would say 'hullo' to him occasionally.' Would Donald be willing 'to act as a friend in the background?' This would not be in a professional capacity; Donald would

---

* Winnicott writes in a paper of 1968, 'The Use of An Object', about making interpretations: 'It appals me how much deep change I have prevented or delayed in my patients by my personal need to interpret. If only we can wait, the patient arrives at understanding creatively and with immense joy, and I now enjoy this joy more than I used to enjoy the sense of having been clever.'

need only to 'continue to exist in his world.'[8] There is no record of whether or not he agreed to this.

Before the start of her analysis with him, Milner had also heard a radio talk in which Winnicott remarked that having swollen finger joints might have some connection with a bit of madness. 'Since I noticed my own finger joints had become swollen I rang him to say that I did not think my training analyst [Payne] had understood my mad bit, and could he advise me about who I should go to for more analysis.'[9] To her surprise he said 'Why not him?' despite the fact that he had already sent her the patient Susan, the subject of her great book, *The Hands of the Living God*, and Susan was living in the Winnicott house. He also suggested that Milner's analysis could be done by him in *her* own house since she lived halfway between his house in Hampstead and his consulting room in central London. This unusual arrangement, to say the least (arguably more characteristic of their time than of ours), was further complicated by the fragile state of Alice and Donald Winnicott's marriage and its impact on the patient Susan. (Alice had initially 'rescued' Susan from hospital and the depredations of ECT, and Susan was extremely attached to her.)

Retrospectively thinking about her analysis in her own house, Milner comments that she 'assumed he did this out of kindness, to save me time, since he knew that, because my marriage had already broken up, I was trying to build up my own practice and pay for J's education.'[10] Perhaps, though, there is another explanation: Winnicott's conducting her husband's analysis, and 'managing' his case, in their home(s) in war time may possibly have set a precedent for this setting. Eventually, though, the situation became unbearable. After Winnicott recovered from his first heart attack in 1947, and during the Easter holiday when he dropped in on Milner when she was attending the Cedric Morris School of Painting in Suffolk, he let her know that he had met and fallen in love with Clare Britton, the psychiatric social worker whom he subsequently married. Milner writes, 'So, by now having heard something of his marriage problems when he told me about Clare Britton, I said, "If you don't leave Alice, I think you will die." '[11]

However, Winnicott was soon back at work. Susan was upset, breaking down to the extent that she had to be brought by taxi every day for her analysis, but the situation took its toll also on her analyst:[12]

> As for me, quite soon I found I could no longer manage the situation of having to analyse Susan in her temporary breakdown at the same time as being Winnicott's patient. Obviously I could not abandon Susan, so I left Winnicott and went for analysis to Clifford Scott, whose first comment was that it had all been a travesty of psychoanalysis.[13]

Milner found her analysis with Scott – a Canadian who became President of the British Society in 1953 before returning to his native Canada to pioneer psychoanalysis in that country – very helpful. It was, however, extremely painful to end her analysis with Winnicott. Recalling her last session in 1947, she was unable to stop crying 'at having felt I must stop the analysis, just as I had been, according to my family, unable to stop crying when the nanny, [who left when Milner was aged four] who admitted having spoilt me left us'. Milner, in an interview in 1996, comments that Winnicott at this juncture said something that would never have been said by Freud: he said 'he did not know I felt so strongly about him'.[14] What Milner felt he might – indeed, should – have done was to speak about the transference, making the link with the beloved but spoiling nanny.

Many years later, in 1991, Margaret Little, a colleague and friend of Milner's, wrote to her that she felt she owed Milner a 'massive apology' and a debt 'for not having recognised what giving up your analysis with Donald must have cost you'. Little felt that at the time she was simply unable to 'recognise your generosity', so strong were her own transferential links with a difficult sibling.[15]

Possibly Winnicott had spoiled Milner? Certainly we know that on one occasion she comments firmly that she did not wish to be special; what she wanted was analysis – not special (spoiling) treatment. On this occasion, Winnicott had been smoking throughout the analytic hour and:

> after he had gone away at the end of the session, I found he had left behind, on a little table beside the chair, a most beautiful little crucifix, with the head of the Christ match bent right forward. Apparently I did not know what to make of this and did not mention it in my next session; I think I assumed it was something to do with his marriage, which I knew was childless, and vaguely thought could be unhappy. So I failed to ask, 'Why did he do it?'[16]

An undated letter from Milner to Winnicott tells him that she has been thinking about her three analyses and 'doing mental accounts', and feels 'there's something more to be said about my analysis with you'. She wonders if she can see him just once and 'perhaps get it said'.[17] Unpublished 'Notes from a talk' between Milner and Winnicott on 20 July 1950 shed some further light: 'He says the mistake was in that first interview I was asking for P.A [psychoanalysis] and he took on Dennis. The crucifix was very wrong, only he would not have done it to anyone else, it shows how he felt about me.' Milner says she found this little comfort at the time, remarking that 'somehow . . . I don't want him to be fond'.[18]

Fond, however, he most certainly was. One of Milner's close friends has said that the trouble with her analyses was that she caused each of her analysts to fall in love with her – 'thus remaining outside the experience – deeply lonely but formidably independent.'[19] Did Donald fall in love with her? We don't know. She was a very private person in this and in very many other ways right from the moment when she remarked roundly that she did not wish 'to be *legible*'. When asked outright whether or not he was in love with her, Milner replied she had noticed a 'light in his eyes' when he had taken her to the station at the start of the war.[20] There is an unpublished letter of 22 March 1943 that suggests they were very close: Winnicott tells her that he has read her recent letter four times:

> In regard to you, th'other way round, you know that I am not easily romantic. I seem to have chosen another method which is to choose certain persons in whom I believe I can see wonderful things. I frankly tell you that I very easily see in you something very loveable, and tantalisingly unfathomable, and I think of you as tremendously valuable to me as well as others who have the sense to know.

This very personal letter continues: 'I feel that our relationship, which is bound to be pretty close, is made a lot richer by my knowing what words are imprisoned behind your eyes, or were.' He is devoted to the point of saying, he 'could not have too much of you, but as I cannot eat you I shall probably want to choose from among the possibilities which leave life manageable as a going concern.'[21]

There is a companion letter to this from Milner to Winnicott in the Wellcome Collection where she alludes to his remarks about leaving life 'manageable as a going concern' and remarking that perhaps 'your choice does make it manageable for you. I'm not so sure for me. You see, I'm not good at being platonic, really.'[22] The transference missed by Milner in the crucifix incident seems curiously absent or, perhaps, all too strongly present; and the loving friendship between Donald and Marion continued. Some believe that to her life's end Milner reproached Winnicott for his analytic failure of her. Alexander Newman, psychoanalyst and President of the Squiggle Foundation for a number of years, believed that Milner, his colleague and, indeed, friend, hated Winnicott and had 'for years [. . .] because he let you down, and further, how much you hate us who have promoted his work'. Newman resumes in this vein later in the same month, commenting that 'no matter how many Saturday seminars' Milner attended she was 'unlikely to learn anything'. In his view, she simply could not forgive Winnicott for being unable to help her – moreover, 'you cannot learn from a man – neither DW or me – or your son'.[23]

This view of Winnicott, from letters of the 1990s, is, of course, well after his death in 1971; she clearly had ambivalent feelings towards him but was selective in her representation of him in the decades to come. Christopher Bollas, in supervision with her in the 1970s, recalls her praising Winnicott and stating he was a very devoted and creative analyst, and he was surprised when she offered quite different views of him in the 1980s, wondering almost naively why he had come to her house to analyse her.[24] It seems reasonable to assume that Milner held quite distinctly different views of DWW and this, as we see in *Bothered by Alligators*, remained unresolved in her life time.[25]

So, what did Milner gain from her analysis with DWW? Early on in their connection she values and is grateful for his helping her find her voice in intellectual discussions. Later, in a 1996 interview, she states: 'The main interpretation that I remembered he made was that I had been spending the rest of my life trying to deal with my father's schizophrenia.'[26] Looking back, she wonders if he might have been right, commenting justly that it all depends on how you understand the term. Certainly, the events around her father's breakdown are distressing as Milner recalls telling Winnicott that 'once, when we were living at Hindhead, my father, who sat at the head of the table in his Windsor chair, and was standing beside [it] just before a meal, lent forward and kicked his heels up in the air'. Winnicott had commented that it was all right had Milner thought this funny (which she did) 'but it might have seemed a bit mad.'[27] Possibly this 'antic' kicking resonated with Milner's perception of Winnicott's returning from seeing a mother and child at Paddington Green and jumping gaily over the electric heater.[28] His analytic view of her relation with her mother was also instructive: 'Although my mother was a most predictable person both in character and devotedness, her breast abscess changed things. Then did this mean that I would never have any "continuity of being"?'[29] Milner was less sure about his take on her first book: was he correct in seeing this, *A Life of One's Own,* as an instance of her 'for ever starting again'? She was doubtful: 'for as I see it, writing that book initiated change in my inner world that has been going on continuously ever since'. In fact, Milner could not avoid wondering if Winnicott's talk of a fresh start that gets nowhere 'is his own wish to have actually been born a woman'. Writing *A Life* showed her that she was 'very glad to be a woman, and not the boy I had secretly thought I was'.[30]

Milner's insight into Winnicott is acute also as to the aetiology of the crucifix matter, at the time considered by her to be a sign of his deeply unhappy marriage. The clue comes to her when, working towards the end of her life on her last book, she read the poem included in Adam Phillips's work on Winnicott and sent by him to his brother-in-law. The poem is 'The Tree', the intensely painful underside to Clare Winnicott's robustly optimistic view of her late husband's parents who believed there was 'no doubt that the Winnicott parents were the centre of their children's lives, and that the vitality and stability of the whole household emanated from them. Their mother was vivacious and outgoing and able to express her feelings easily.'[31] 'The Tree' bespeaks a different story:

> Mother below is weeping
> Weeping
> Weeping
> Thus I knew her

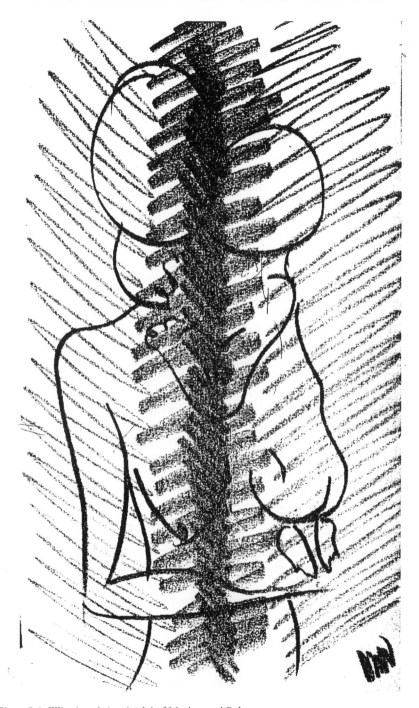

Figure 5.1 Winnicott's 'squiggle' of Mother and Baby

Once stretched out on her lap
As now on dead tree
I learned to make her smile
to stem her tears
to undo her guilt
To enliven her was my living[32]

In an interview with Angela Baum at the time of the exhibition of DWW's drawings and squiggles in 1976, Milner says that, in her opinion, the poem relates to the Mother and Baby drawing (see Figure 5.1). She then re-visits the matchstick crucifix, wondering if it might not be that it 'was an early version of the poem and that he, with his so great intuitive gifts, had, perhaps only implicitly, guessed that my problem could also be largely to do with a secretly depressed mother?' It was even possible that the poem touched on something that had been left out of his own analyses, something as yet not consciously known, but with the crucifix perhaps 'his first attempt to bring it into consciousness.'[33]

Milner often reminds us (and herself) that she is one of those people 'who Freud reminded us exist' who 'think in pictures'.[34] Her thoughts on Winnicott typically centre on an image – especially one of a mother and baby, understandably; the image relates clearly to the ideas of the depressed mother so central to both her own and Winnicott's being:

> [it] has this black central column, making it impossible to see the contact of the mother and baby's bodies, though the baby's beautifully drawn left arm is shown as if holding on to the mother's neck. Whether it is actually supporting her, or hanging on to her for dear life, is not clear – perhaps both. The baby's feet are also beautifully drawn and tucked under its bottom, but the mother's right forearm and hand, which should be supporting the baby's feet, are shown as having lost all solidity, and a gap is left between her arm and the baby's feet.[35]

For the memorial meeting for Winnicott in 1972 Milner was asked to describe the highlights of her contact with him in matters of theory; this she found almost impossible – so what she wanted to say about him 'must centre around certain visual images.' These are images that become for her metaphors of D.W. Winnicott: the first one is from a night when she is in France in 1957:

> I saw a crowd in the market-place of a little town, all gathered around an arc lamp where a trapeze had been set up by travelling acrobats. The star performers were there [. . .] Below them was a little clown in a grey floppy coat too big for him, just fooling around while the

others did their displays. Occasionally he made a fruitless attempt to jump up and reach the bar. Then, suddenly, he made a great leap and there he was, whirling around on the bar, all his clothes flying out, like a huge Catherine wheel, to roars of delight from the crowd.[36]

To the whirling clown and the Catherine wheel, Milner adds a shared joke, and DWW's own favourite images, Tagore's line, 'On the sea-shore of endless worlds children play'.

In the same paper of 1972 ('Winnicott and the two-way journey') Milner – who is, as Caldwell and Joyce comment, in 'continuing dialogue' with DWW throughout much of her analytic life – compares his thoughts on 'creative apperception' with her own ideas about 'those sudden moments when one's whole perception of the world changes – changes that happen, sometimes apparently out of the blue, but sometimes as the result of a deliberate shift of attention, one that makes the whole word seem newly created'.[37]

One such moment comes to her when starting to write her paper in honour of Klein's seventieth birthday. She starts with an image, explaining then that, in fact, the whole image does not come into the paper:

> and the third one [holiday] John and I went up to Savoy, and there he was about 15, and we started climbing mountains and he was at a terribly grumbly stage, and I remember one day he said he didn't like climbing, it was hard work and things, and we went up on a hot day through the woods and he was grumbling and then we came out onto the high alps and he was ahead of me and I could see him up against the skyline and suddenly absolutely still and when I got up to him he said 'what's that', and it was cow bells. Of course it was something he had never heard – it's like Scarlatti in the air – and he was a changed boy after that – he saw the point of mountains.[38]

Milner and Winnicott held images in common; a last one comes from his paper on cultural experience ('The Location of Cultural Experience') where he is talking 'about how the baby comes to be able to make use of the symbol of union and can begin to allow for and benefit from separation, a separation that is not separation, but a form of union'. Here he refers to one of Milner's drawings 'showing the interplay of the edges of two jugs'. He said 'the drawing conveyed to him the tremendous significance there can be in the interplay of edges'.[39]

The jugs drawing is included in *On Not Being Able to Paint* and is discussed below; central ideas from Winnicott's review of the text in *The New Era* of September–October 1950 can conclude this section on the interplay of these two creative thinkers. In her paper 'The Role of Illusion in Symbol formation' Milner had interrogated Klein's view that 'Symbolization is the basis of all talents' and, in so doing, she had encompassed illusion and fusion, the need for a frame and concentration; the case material, the 'game of war between two villages' had shown the boy patient struggling with bisexual conflict, jealousy and envy of his mother and, in particular, his school difficulties:

> Thus one way of trying to describe the situation was in terms of the idea that the school, the place in which he must seek knowledge, had become too much identified with the destroyed mother's body, so that it had indeed become a desert [. . .] In fact, one could describe the situation here in terms of the use of symbolism as a defence, and say that because the school had become the symbol of the forbidden mother's body this was then a bar to progress.[40]

In doing the work with this boy patient Milner came to notice that on the days when he could make use of the 'pliable medium' offered – that is, the toys in the playroom – he somewhat settled down, no longer needing to treat his analyst in a persecutory manner, treating the toys 'as external to himself, but not insisting on their separate objective existence'.[41] The analyst, as the toy(s), becomes for the patient just this 'pliable medium', 'this pliable stuff that can be made to take the shape of one's phantasies'. The patient in his case had been able 'to use both me and the playroom equipment as this intervening pliable substance . . .' This patient had been able to do with analyst and with toys 'what Caudwell says the poet does with words, when he uses them to give the organism an appetitive interest in external reality, when he makes the earth become charged with affective colouring and glow with a strange emotional fire.'[42]

As Milner ponders the implications for technique of this case she considers with the deepest insight the patient's gestures towards the end of his work with her:

> near the end of his analysis, this boy told me that when he was grown up and earning his own living he would give me a papier-mâché chemical clock which would keep perfect time and would be his own invention [. . .] I thought that he was telling me something else as well. I thought that the malleability of the papier-mâché provided him with a way of expressing how he felt about the curative factor in his analysis. It was his way of saying how, in the setting of the analytic playroom, he had been able to find a bit of the external world that was malleable; he had found that it was safe to treat it as a bit of himself, and so had let it serve as a bridge between inner and outer.[43]

Clearly Winnicott greatly appreciated his connection with Milner, and the emotional bond between them was strong. Milner's papers – those she retained and often annotated and re-annotated from their long contact – give further insight, significant clues as to the nature of their interchanges. First there are those questioning Kleinian ideas; from the 1950s Milner has kept a comment by Winnicott on Klein's paper 'A Study of Envy and Gratitude' that stresses his view that, much as Klein can tell us about envy, it 'cannot be carried over in a statement of earliest infancy' and the word *envy* 'is not something we can apply in earliest infancy'.[44] He reviews *Envy and Gratitude* in 1958 on the same grounds, adding to them a central and characteristic objection: 'there is no description of an infant that leaves out the behaviour of the person caring for the infant; or in an object relationship, the behaviour of the object'.[45]

Also in the Milner/DWW papers private collection is a typescript of a letter from Winnicott to the Kleinian analyst Roger Money-Kyrle, a letter that later finds its way into *The Spontaneous Gesture*. In this letter Winnicott is annoyed with Money-Kyrle, feeling there is a 'party line' involved to which he is 'allergic'. Reading between the lines, this line would seem to be a Kleinian one. Thus Winnicott writes firmly: 'when people like Marion Milner or myself for that matter write papers, we do not write in order to show each time that we have grasped Mrs. Klein's contributions to theory but we write them because of an original idea that needs ventilating.' In the same letter he somewhat acerbically comments to Money-Kyrle: 'if you think that someone like Dr. Segal, who is just starting analysis of children, is in the same street as Marion Milner who has vast experience, there is something fundamentally different in our attitudes.'[46]

Also from the 1950s Milner has preserved an offprint of a paper by Winnicott on 'The First Year of Life', published in *The Medical Press* on 12 March 1958 somewhat flirtatiously inscribed 'A Marion de Donald'. A letter of 27 November 1952 (typescript, also published in *The Spontaneous Gesture*) identifies his own views with those of Milner, finding a 'definite overlap' with theirs and some of Money-Kyrle's. The letter, hand-inscribed by Winnicott 'For Marion Milner's entertainment', goes on to discuss his concept of the 'good enough mother' as opposed to the 'good mother' of 'Kleinian jargon' [DWW's phrase].[47]

Interestingly, too, there is a typescript of a letter from Winnicott to Charles Rycroft of 25 June 1953 about a draft article, 'Some Notes on Idealization, Illusion and Disillusion', that Rycroft has written.[48] Here the coincidence of views of Winnicott and Milner is very clear. Indeed, he is able to write: 'Mrs Milner and I are so interwoven in our development on this subject that it is very fortunate that neither or us is interested in the matter of priorities.'[49] In October 1955 Milner suggests that research could be developed on 'Communication between adults and children' and that there is, too, a large work of communication to be done in terms of that between analysts and the public; 'people', she writes, 'are so stuck in their misunderstandings of early Freud that someone like Kathleen Raine, for instance, can still refer to the Freudian unconscious (in a letter to me last week) as containing only bad things.'[50] Milner's respect for Winnicott is undoubted in a letter of 23 April

1954 when she asks if she may nominate him as President of the British Psychoanalytical Society.[51]

Throughout their professional and theoretical interchange, there is much respect in the 1950s, 1960s and, 1970s; this comes to a peak in Winnicott's honouring of Milner's work in *Playing and Reality* where he 'Pay[s] tribute to the work of Milner (1952, 1957, 1969) who has written so brilliantly on the subject of symbol-formation';[52] and in the cross-fertilisation of their ideas seen in Milner's ONBAP. She is herself anxious about his influence in the book, writing in an undated letter that she is concerned that it seems 'full of things I've pinched from you' and worrying that on re-reading the text she finds 'several phrases which I've definitely pinched from you, and that's real thieving. But I'll give them back.'[53] Winnicott's review of ONBAP shows no sign of reproach for any such 'thieving' as he recognises and appreciates Milnerite ideas; importantly, his piece for *The New Era* opens both magisterially and very sensibly:

> Let no one think that this book is just about painting or not painting. Yet it had to have this title because in that way the writing of the book started. The real purpose of the book only becomes clear to the author in the course of her experience of writing, in fact the book is itself an example of its main theme. This theme, which gradually becomes clear to the reader, is foreshadowed in an early quotation: 'Concepts can never be presented to me merely, they must be knitted into the structure of my being, and this can only be done through my own activity.' (M.P. Follett, *Creative Experience*)[54]

Let us see how *On Not Being Able to Paint* does just this.

6

ON NOT BEING
ABLE TO . . .

Milner had addressed blocks in learning with her GPDST pupils and blocks in schoolwork with her early patients; now, on the day the Second World War was declared, she turned her attention to her own creative blocks and produced in *On Not Being Able to Paint* what has been described by another esteemed psychoanalyst as 'One of the high points of psychoanalytic writings on creativity'.[1]

A 'Sunday painter', as she styled herself, Milner had tried various ways of learning to paint and read books on the subject – all had resulted in a vague but undeniable sense of disappointment. So she starts a new 'experiment' with free drawing instead of the habitual intention to draw something particular. Here is the result of her first effort to draw without any conscious intention: one day, filled with anger with a certain person, she turned to free drawing and produced the angry and somewhat hateful figure of 'Mrs. Punch'; she was similarly surprised by the results of her efforts to draw a summer's morning and summer's beeches: instead of these bland images she created a blazing heath fire and a raging storm.

In the next chapter of ONBAP she frees herself from the constraints of conventional perspective, moves away from detachment and separation. At first this seemed something of a retreat, a retreat from being a separate person But then again, it felt more like a search, 'a going backwards perhaps, but a going back to look for something, something which could have real value for adult life if only it could be recovered.'[2]

Having questioned the orthodoxies of conscious intention and of perspective, Milner turns now to those conventions of outline and awakes one morning with a change in perception: she 'saw two jugs on the table; without any mental struggle I saw the edges in relation to each other, and how gaily they seemed almost to ripple now that they were freed from this grimly practical business of enclosing an object and keeping it in its place'. Experimenting with the 'play of edges', Milner finds a freedom from 'the emotional need to imprison objects rigidly within themselves'.[3] (This is, however, different from her firm belief in the need for a frame in the psychoanalytic session, which

Figure 6.1 Heath fire

Figure 6.2 Beech trees

Figure 6.3 Two Jugs – an image shared with DWW

provides 'an area within which what we perceive has to be taken as symbol, as metaphor, not literally'.)[4]

Colour offers the next intensification of experience as Milner learns about transitions – for instance, 'where the yellow lichen on a barn roof had tempted me into letting the yellows and reds merge, unprotected by any felt division, so that you could not say exactly where one colour began and another ended'.[5] Gradually she finds out about the feeling of colour as 'moving and alive': 'it happened that when I closed my eyes and tried to recall the colour combinations seen in nature, the memory did grow and glow and develop in the most surprising way.'[6]

This required a certain amount of 'watching and waiting' – not always easy for Milner, who found part of her mind 'still wanted to keep colour firmly within boundaries and staying the same'. There were, she found, two ways of feeling about experience: one a common-sense world of objects that stayed the same and was bound by outline; the other a world of change and process in which there was no set line between one state and the next. She comments: 'But though I could know, in retrospect, that the changing world seemed nearer the true quality of experience, to give oneself to this knowledge seemed like taking some dangerous plunge . . .'.[7]

A favourite Milner metaphor, the plunge here also evokes the plunge into free association in psychoanalysis, that hard-won ability to trust the space; and here she is reminded of another of her favourite referents, Cézanne, who is reported to have said upon looking at a picture: 'Shut your eyes, wait, think of nothing. Now, open them . . . One sees nothing but a great coloured undulation. What then? An irradiation and glory of colour [. . .] a coloured state of grace.'[8] The disquiet Milner felt about this plunge into colour was, she came to see, to do with 'fears of embracing, becoming one with, something infinitely suffering, fears of plunging into a sea of pain in which both could be drowned'.[9] One cannot help recalling the intense pain of Winnicott's Tree poem and fears, often found in the analytic room, of being subsumed in maternal depression, an experience well known to Milner herself (see pp. 56–57 and pp. 179–180, 183–185).

Chapter 5 faces the fascinating, though fraught, topic of 'the necessity of illusion' as Milner unpacks the 'spiritual dangers' involved in the process of coming to see as the painter sees; again, it is a 'plunge', 'a plunge that one could sometimes do deliberately or when one falls in love'.

Influenced here by the philosopher Santayana, Milner homes in especially on his words: 'In imagination, not in perception, lies the substance of experience, while science and reason are but its chastened and ultimate form.' Thus, she comments, the substance of experience is what we bring to what we see. She expands on this, coming to understand certain very vivid experiences in a new way. Thus: 'They [these ideas] threw light, for instance, on the persistent feeling about parts of the country that I loved most, that these were haunts of the gods, places where undefinable presences were about.'[10]

Santayana's words also pointed to a false dichotomy: the effort to decide which was more 'real' – thoughts or things, imagination or perception – was to ignore 'the true nature of the relation between them'. Of love, she endorses Santayana's comments:

> Whenever this ideality is absent and a lover sees nothing in his mistress but what everyone else may find in her, loving her honestly in her unvarnished and accidental person, there is a friendly and humorous affection, admirable in itself, but no passion or bewitchment of love: she is a member of his group, not a spirit in his pantheon.[11]

These, and other idealisations, are, Milner comes to apprehend, 'the vital illusions by which we live'; however, there were dangers in accepting the necessity of illusion, were there not? Even if, for example, it were true that, on occasion, one did not need to decide which was oneself and which was other:

> It might become so alluring that one did not wish to return to the real world of being separate; like the man in the folk tales who, coming home alone at night, chances on the fairies at their revels and joins them and is never seen again; or only returns so many years later that his whole world is changed and nobody knows him.[12]

One of her free drawings did, in fact, address this problem (it was called 'Rats in the Sacristy'); but now, having at least 'found a way of thinking about the connection between madness and sanity'[13] Milner was able to look at the drawings themselves. Part II of the text is sub-titled 'Crucifying the Imagination', echoing Blake (as so often a seminal influence in Milner's work), and begins by addressing the influence of Jan Gordon – whom she had met while in the United States in 1927–28 – and the idea of 'an imaginative body as well as a physical one'.[14] This and like ideas informed her search for the meaning of her free drawings. Significantly, her own interpretive comments are strikingly close to those that might be made by a psychoanalyst:

> I had, of course, already recognised that they were about feelings or moods, that the blasted beeches and heath fire and Noah's Dove drawings represented states of mind, they were not records of external facts but of internal ones. But up to now it had seemed that they were records more concerned with psycho-analysis than with painting. This was mainly because the majority of them had emerged at a time when I was undergoing the process of Freudian psycho-analysis myself.[15]

Up until then in Milner's life, however, it had not been pressing to look at the drawing as a whole in connection with problems of learning to paint (although there are links with Milner's findings on learning blocks in her earlier work in the schools – see p. 53) or with 'the question of how both one's gods and one's devils could take up their shrines in the external world'.[16] With this in mind, Milner was aware that there was, in the free drawings, some kind of monster as well as 'a harmless and innocent one' and that 'I myself was identified with the innocent one', who might be 'a sort of Mickey Mouse' or a 'young donkey, silly and innocent' who 'was usually threatened by some sort of danger from the unpleasant one'.[17]

Gradually, through the free-drawing images, Milner shows us step by step how she becomes aware of some kind of reversal – 'the trick' that our minds employ 'of trying to get away from the necessity to admit unpleasant things to oneself by putting them outside and feeling it is others who are bad, not oneself'. A linked aspect of this was the realisation that the 'attacking creatures' in the pictures – monsters or insects of varying shapes and forms – 'must really be within myself'.[18] An image of a centipede arising in the picture 'Freedom' is helpful here: initially this figure had given Milner such a shock she had turned away from it, fearing it was the product of madness:

> But now, having learnt considerably more about how the mind makes use of images, I was able to see what was happening; my mind was trying to tell about the angry attacking impulses that are an essential part of oneself, but the existence of which I had persistently tried to deny.[19]

Clearly 'the expression of hidden aggressive impulses in an indirect or symbolic way was part of the ABC of psycho-analysis', but what is so interesting for Milner and for us is that here she shows 'a pictorial dramatisation of that very process' that she had observed when trying to see 'action' in nature: 'When consciously observing the chair growing defiant and the piano beginning to gnash its teeth, I had surprised in the act, as it were, a process that usually goes on secretly without our knowledge.'[20] It is a process that, for Milner, comes to account for a significant part of 'not being able to . . .'. After all, the many imagined dangers deriving from unadmitted angry and greedy feelings could readily cause a severe contraction of the imaginative body, making it nigh on impossible to imbue external objects with life or action. Further, 'Once one began this game of endowing external objects with a spiritual life there was no knowing what might not happen, the spiritual life might turn out to be an infernal one.'[21]

The question became more subtle and difficult when trying to draw not just objects but real, separate people:

> To feel the real separate identity of another person, as compared with an orange or a jug, and express this in terms of paint, must raise even greater difficulties. And when it was not only a question of drawing other people, but the give and take of living with them, did not the same thing apply? To recognise the real spiritual identity of other people in everyday contact, in fact, to use one's imagination about them, might seem equally fraught with dangers, it might seem much safer to mind one's own business. Also one's capacity to allow for the spiritual identity of others in daily life, one's capacity to allow them to be themselves, must be linked up with one's capacity to allow oneself to be oneself.[22]

Allowing oneself to be oneself has, of course, to include accepting the less pleasant aspects of the self and being true to these; Milner's Personal Notebooks for the time of writing *On Not Being Able to Paint* show her pondering these ideas as she notes in one entry: 'I'm not playing this game of "how nice we all are" "what a wonderful time we are having"' and 'it's only a game, this being so charming – underneath there's the perpetual break in to [a] *Donald Duck* tirade of fury and frustration & "who's going to forgive God?"'[23]

In her excursions into understanding blocks in painting Milner comes here to see how a denial of the interplay of characteristics in the self can potentially turn nature into something not loved but hated – 'the peaceful summer morning could turn into a raging fire or a blasting blizzard'.[24] Some more of the drawings dealt with that anger fuelled by issues around authority – 'the theme of rebellion against an imposed authority and imagined destruction of it'.[25] One such was of a blazing castle on a hilltop with shadowy figures in the foreground; another was of a 'Skeleton Under The Sea' a 'landscape of jagged ice mountains, in which the dim shape of an ice demon had frozen sky and earth into an agonised tension of lifelessness'.[26] Similarly, the well-known (to Milner enthusiasts) image of 'The Angry Parrot' again showed themes of rebellion against authority but also the feeling of an urgent need for their protection. The 'story' of this image, of an angry, terrified bird, a powerful grey woman and a precious egg refers on one level to the psycho-analytic situation itself – in that there is a common anxiety that analysis will result in the foregoing of something previous one is clinging on to. But Milner felt there was more to the image than this – 'for I suspected that if I only knew what the parrot was so afraid of losing I would also be able to see more of what current educational practice was leaving out'.[27]

The egg comes in Milner's discussion to stand 'for one's own separate identity'; but it was more than this: 'something deeper than that, more to do with the danger of losing one's whole belief in any goodness anywhere, it was this that the parrot was so frightened of and angry about.'[28] Two further drawings, the angry ape and a three-faced figure, 'showed not only a fury of rage against frustrating authority, but also a process of denying such rage'.[29] Eventually, building on and refining these ideas, Milner sees the parrot's egg partly as 'a symbol of the necessary illusion of no separateness between subject and object' and this, for her, is an illusion that must not be too soon 'shattered' lest this is ' felt as undermining the very foundations of one's hope of eventually achieving a true objectivity'.[30] The bridge from innocence to experience needed, Milner indicates, to be accomplished in the child's own time, not imposed prematurely.

The text turns now to further monstrous creatures – not only the angry but also the hungry. In a section 'Preserving what one loves', Milner considers Jan Gordon's idea that in painting one takes possession of one's subject: 'You have enclosed it in your mind, you have absorbed it spiritually and are going to transform it into art. This sense of your spirit enveloping the subject comes naturally and instinctively.'[31] Milner embellishes this idea, commenting that she had already felt there could, perhaps, be 'an imaginative connection between this spiritual enveloping of what one loved and eating'. Indeed, she had found a diary note mentioning 'those feelings of wanting to eat a landscape' and commenting: 'That's partly why I want to paint, in order to preserve.'[32] The impulse to eat in order to preserve was not, of course, without problems; for while eating may satisfy the desire to possess a thing, it does not preserve it: 'it rather destroys this identity in order to merge it with one's own.' Thus, there are free drawings with teeth, drawings depicting a kind of imagined cannibalism. One, in particular, showed no whole people – only parts of people – and 'called itself "Drawing without a name"'. Milner, characteristically respectful of the unconscious process here at work, is careful to give the draw-ings their own (unconscious) agency of interpretation. Her respect for what Freud, after Groddeck, called '"the forces by which we are lived"' is consum-mate.[33] Later in *Bothered by Alligators*, she speaks firmly about how her later life collages had named themselves (see pp. 181–182). She is concerned, too, that the baby's greedy kind of loving 'could have injured the life-giving breast', once more invoking Blake: 'The caterpillar on the leaf/Repeats to thee thy mother's grief.'[34] A further image suggests that the eye, too, can devour, thus showing the potential impact of this kind of thinking for the visual arts. A drawing turning out differently from Milner's expectation takes this idea further. Intending to draw an outdoor café scene from memory, a figure emerged who 'insisted on being given the title "The Pregnant Butcher"', and she realises that this is surely 'expressing the idea of giving the object new life as an artistic creation, in fact, the idea of the artist as creator'.[35] But this, together with certain other images, revived the anxieties about the destructive aspect of the artist – the artist is also the butcher. There is a potentially sinister aspect of creation; and these ideas can go some way towards explaining how it is that the question of whether or not a picture is 'good' can seem a matter of life and death.[36]

Another picture addressed the 'despair about the potential destructiveness of one's primitive love, and its attendant hate would drive one to set up a terrifying god within almost as a second line of defence'. This idea could 'clarify one's basic assumptions about education' and, following here a Kleinian influence, Milner comes to the view that: 'If all this were true then one of the functions of painting was surely the restoring and re-creating externally what one had loved and internally hurt or destroyed.' And she realises now that this was also part of the current psychoanalytic theory on the subject, theories posited, as Milner says, by Melanie Klein 'on the basis of Freud's discoveries, described in his paper "Mourning and Melancholia", and through her own work with children'.[37] It is, incidentally and, I think, importantly, here that Winnicott usefully positions Milner's originality as a thinker on art: his review of ONBAP has this to say:

> Psycho-analysts are very used to thinking of the arts as wish-fulfilling escapes from the knowledge of this discrepancy between inner and outer, wish and reality. It may come as a bit of a shock to some of them to find a psycho-analyst drawing the conclusion after careful study, that this wish-fulfilling illusion may be the essential basis for all true objectivity. If these moments of fusion of subject and object, inner and outer, are indeed more than islands of peace, then this fact has very great importance for education.

Winnicott, in his review of this text, is appreciative of Milner's emphasis; he writes:

> If I understand the author aright she wishes to make a yet more fundamental statement about creativity. She wishes to say that it is for her (and perhaps for everyone) the primary human predicament.

This predicament arises out of the non-identity of what is conceived and what is to be perceived.[38]

Thus, Milner in writing *On Not Being Able to Paint* had come to see, and to share with her readers, her previous two works (*A Life* and *An Experiment*) in a rather different light. Thus:

> It was now possible to see more clearly the relation of this study to earlier ones. In two earlier experiments I had especially studied moments of happiness and significance. In this one, by trying to study difficulties and failures of significance, I was coming to see that certain inescapable facts of the human predicament had not been sufficiently taken into account in the earlier studies.

Certainly there were facts to do with that 'primitive hating' derived from the discrepancy between subjective and objective, between our dreams and quotidian reality, but they were also linked with how traditional education 'can perpetuate this hate, by concentrating so much on only one half of our relation to the world, the part of it to do with intellectual knowing, the part in which subject and object have perforce to be kept separate'.[39]

How could a creative way be found out of this predicament, a way 'that gave due recognition both to the need for separation and no-separation'? To give some answers, Milner turns to the method by which the free drawings were produced. A wise comment from Follett, known for her books on politics from the perspective of Gestalt psychology in the 1920s and 1930s, introduces this section sub-titled 'Incarnating the Imagination': 'as we perform a certain activity our thought towards it changes and that changes our activity'.[40] It is a comment that can be very helpful to those with many kinds of creative block: for the writer, for instance, write it freely and the attitude to process and creation will change. Milner's first task here was to ensure, as far as she was able, that the free drawings were not willed, not planned. The effort, similar to that required for free association in psychoanalysis, was 'to keep one's hand moving and one's eye watching with a peculiar kind of responsive alertness the shapes that it was producing. In fact, it was almost like playing a game of psycho-analyst and patient with oneself'.[41] When free drawing was achieved, this resulted in a 'mood of reciprocity' where 'there was an interplay of differences that remained in contact' – the differences were essential as Milner had discovered from the early drawings of heath fire and blasted beeches (see pp. 63–64). Blake would have agreed, as he wrote: 'Without contraries there is no progression.'[42] It was also vital, as in a psychoanalysis, to be able to accept chaos as a temporary but necessary, if necessarily discomfiting, stage. Perhaps, we could say that the self as painter in this text has much in common with both the analyst and the analysand.

In the next section, 'Refusal of Reciprocity', the author turns to the two kinds of attention operating in her experiment: there is 'the wide embracing kind of concentration' and there is 'the analytic narrow-focused kind of attention'. To apprehend 'the unique quality of a person or a picture' the first is essential, but Milner considers these two kinds 'could also be thought about in terms of the antithesis of male and female ways of being'.[43]

Problems of difference continue in focus in the section 'Ideals and the Fatal Prejudice', with thoughts on the 'discrepancy between dream and actuality'; by now Milner was certainly aware that this was 'again a central part of psychoanalytic theory' and knew that 'the childhood spectacle of the parents together and oneself shut out could become a kind of prototype of the difficulties to do with the recognition of difference'.[44] This discrepancy was one of those difficult facts of emotional life, a key apprehension of the 'gap' and an awareness of the disillusion resulting from the knowledge 'that the inner dream and the objective fact can never permanently coincide, they can only interact'.[45]

Brilliantly here Milner finds a way forward, a way out of the gap as chasm: long aware that the failure to accept the inevitability of the 'gap' could result in much futile effort and straining, she now finds something new:

> at times, if one could bring oneself to look at the gap, allow oneself to see both the ideal and the failure to live up to it in one moment of vision, and without the urge to interfere and alter oneself to fit the ideal, then the ideal and the fact seemed somehow to enter into relation and produce something quite new, something that had nothing to do with being pleased with oneself or having lived up to an ideal or miserable because of having failed to.[46]

Milner invokes Alice in Wonderland who, in Carroll's world of nonsense, discovered that 'when she wanted to get somewhere, found she had to walk in exactly the opposite direction'.[47] Similarly, in the next section, on 'Rhythm and Freedom of the Free Drawings', Milner becomes aware that to allow a developing rhythm its evolution one must be willing to accept 'a temporary throwing to the winds of the dominating will', and this was, again, 'a kind of plunge which one's ordinary consciousness could dread'.[48]

Thinking about order and its different forms, Milner again refers to the Angry Parrot image and 'the principle of limitation, outline, patterning, the ordering principle which could be both hated for its restrictiveness and yet loved because utterly needed for one's very psychic and physical existence'.[49] Looking at a relevant image (here, 'If the sun and moon should doubt'), she expands on this hatred:

> if the hate of the restricting and frustrating parent figures becomes too great and is therefore denied they are then felt in imagination to be either destroyed or turned into avengers [. . .] Then all belief in

one's own creativeness can fail; one can psychically go out just because of having lost belief in any non-willed order. But by its emphasis on control through an inherent rhythm this drawing did suggest that there was a way of mitigating the original hate of the imposed order.[50]

Her images at this stage indicated two kinds of order – that imposed and the inherent; and, with her positive bent, Milner discovers a 'third way' – 'a controlled exuberance, controlled by an inner sense of rhythm and repetition and form'.[51] The inherent form of control goes a long way towards solving the Angry Parrot's dilemma: the inherent form reduces fear and hatred thus: 'It reduced fear of separation and of the chaos that would happen if one lost contact with the external controlling force: but it also reduced the need to hate the controlling force for its interference.'[52] The parrot in the image can deal by itself with the 'tumultuous waves of feeling' – it can, to quote Joseph Conrad, 'in the destructive element immerse' without fear and 'need no longer be a kingdom divided against itself'.[53]

Here Milner's application of her discoveries to the wider educational world is most acute: what she sees as spontaneous ordering (as opposed to the conventional ordering of authority) does not lay down rules or make prescriptive comments. Instead it offers activities by means of which both love and hate become attached to the good or bad things 'through the spontaneous pattern-making associative powers of the organism in action'. Milner is confident (here) that 'All parents and teachers know about this activity method of control, they give unruly children something to *do*, so that the disruptive impulses become changed by fitting into a context beyond themselves.' The 'freedom' the author now finds is not simply that of feeling all restraint has been banished; it is the freedom 'resulting from having entered into active relationship, from having recognised the necessity of difference and from having allowed two differences, dreaming and doing, a maximum of interplay',[54] which could be a way of talking about a very good analysis.

Milner throughout her life placed great importance on the body, often calling to mind Nietzsche's axiom, 'The body is a big sagacity', In Section 13 she turns to 'The Concentration of the Body', opening the chapter with an epigraph from the *Book of Common Prayer*: 'With my body I thee worship'. Follett, Jan Gordon, and Dunoyer de Segonzac, French painter, print maker and draughtsman, had drawn Milner's attention to matters of concentration, body awareness and the sense of 'grace' involved in the creative process. When the free drawings were successful, it was in terms of an achieved dialogic interchange: 'although certainly a condition of the spirit, it essentially encompassed the body.' A diary note expanded this idea, telling us that once there was an awareness of the object as a whole, there arrived a response 'like the feeling that exercise gives, particularly dancing or skating'. In drawing a tree, for instance, Milner found that 'the spread of the branches and leaves gives an awareness of my shoulders and arms and fingers and I feel its roots in my feet'.[55]

Milner's view of the creative process is, it might be said, essentially spiritual, with the condition of the spirit encompassing the body. There are also 'body dreams' deriving from all our 'inhibited bodily impulses', those so often controlled: 'in our social life after childhood, we do not jump for joy or kick and stamp with rage, we do not prance for pride and exuberance of life.'(Possibly this physical exuberance links with Milner's father and with the gay clowning of Winnicott that she so enjoyed.) However, we do, in Milner's view, get to know about these feelings in dancing, for instance, but also in painting, which 'taps this rich source of body dreams' and finds in 'what painters call the action of the picture a most potent way of affecting our feelings'. A drawing again clarified this idea, as it 'touched on the idea of consciousness suffusing the whole body and also on the effects of that narrow non-embracing kind of attention which cannot by its very nature encompass a wholeness'.[56] It is this narrow version of attention portrayed in the image used here that for Milner recalled 'all the years one could spend at school in dog-like obedient' concentration on the face of the teacher, 'shutting out feeling and impulses and trying to be what is expected of one'. (This compliant but non-creative obedience recalls, perhaps, or parallels, Winnicott's notion of the false self in that this obedient, monologic attention 'which shut out wandering thoughts and rebellious moods' was deeply uncreative, making it 'impossible to create a picture' and, more, 'impossible to create oneself as a properly balanced whole of integrated moods and desires within a body'.[57])

As Milner thinks about the 'state of total body concentration' involved in creativity, she once more re-visits the Angry Parrot image, seeing how the parrot's dilemma now clarified some of the possible negative effects of conventional scholastic education and the ways in which a pupil is expected to acquire the art of concentration through school learning. The parrot's fear of losing the egg was:

> in part a fear of losing for ever, through submitting to the intellectual academic kind of learning, the capacity for this other kind of total concentration, the kind which envelops the whole body, and at the same time can be spread out in spiritual envelopment of the object.

Without this Milner felt she could become merely a parrot – 'saying only what one had been taught to say'.[58]

Section IV of the text moves on to 'The Use of the Free Drawings', subtitled 'The Image as Mediator' and opens with the matter of 'The Role of the Medium'. She comes to appreciate that the relation of the subject to the external world is 'originally a relationship of one person to another [. . .] in the beginning one's mother is, literally, the whole world'.[59] 'True dialogue' here, as in other spheres, did not always win over – there could be, for instance, a dictatorship, a situation when the self was 'seduced by objectivity', a seduction shown by those drawings (heath fire and blasted beeches, for instance) exemplifying an untenable, 'gap', 'the possible discrepancy between what one could imagine one was feeling about the object looked at and what one really felt'.[60]

As has been seen, this whole text is underpinned by psychoanalysis and nowhere more pertinently than here, as Milner suggests that the medium itself, the chalk, pencil and paper can itself become an 'other', both pliant and undemanding, situation:

> in which the other gave of itself easily and immediately to take the form of the dream, it did not stridently insist on its own public nature, as I had found natural objects were inclined to do. So by means of this there could perhaps come about the correcting of the bias of a too docilely accepted public vision and a denied private one. And apparently it could come about just because there was this experience of togetherness with one's medium lived through together.

As in analysis, because of this experience, it becomes possible to re-possess, re-claim or even, as it seems, discover as for the first time some of 'the lost land of one's experience'. Psychoanalysis works, similarly, 'through the analyst acting as a pliant medium, giving back the patient's own thought to him, in a clarified form, rather than intruding his own needs and ideas'.[61]

Milner is now able –with the aid of an image entitled 'Ego Island' and a story of a desert island, a castaway and a broken boat – to re-state ideas about free drawing and psychoanalysis in terms of illusion. Could one say, she asks, that, by finding a piece of the outside world, whether art material or analyst, 'that was willing temporarily to fit in with one's dreams, a moment of illusion was made possible in which inner and outer seemed to coincide'? Were these not moments when the bridge could be re-established, the broken boat repaired, and the self 're-awakened at least to the possibility of creative life in the real world'? Milner asks, with some urgency, if it is not a legitimate hypothesis to suggest that these moments of 'achieved fusion between inner and outer' would at least restore the self to a life of potentially creative action.[62]

Free drawing and psychoanalysis both offered this opportunity – free drawing because one could draw anything one liked; it was, after all, only a drawing and could, if desired, simply be discarded. In analysis the analysand can say whatever they like because it is only saying and the analyst is trained not to react as they might in reality – they can serve as the bridge that makes, in John Donne's words, 'dreames truths and fables histories'.[63] Milner, however, wanted more; in her art she wished 'to ensoul nature': 'I wanted painting to be both a means towards and a record of true imaginative perception of significance.'[64]

Further, painting for one who thinks in pictures, involves images and other questions that need to be answered. The ideas explored in *On Not Being Able To Paint* embodied a form of knowledge that traditional education of the academic kind largely ignores – this academic education has a strong linguistic bias as against 'thinking in pictures', those 'intuitive rather than logical reflections' about living. Again, thinking back to the angry parrot and his dilemma, Milner could now see more of what the 'over-academic kind of education' might be leaving out. Its defect was not merely that it was cut off from ordinary living: 'there was too little recognition of the essential role of the bridge between lived experience and logical thought: that is, the role of the intuitive image.'[65] This was a serious 'gap' in conventional education, and Milner suggests here that this might be one of the reasons for the increasing demand for psychoanalysis, which could mitigate the over-academic bias on the intellect as against the intuitive.

'Painting and Living', the next chapter, brings together Milner's ideas explored so far in the text, describing how she has found a certain kind of new experience deriving from the interplay of two fundamental differences – these could be conceptualised in different ways: 'imagination and action; dream and reality'; the incorporated environment and the external environment.[66] Some of this material was already familiar to her from her education and especially her study of the history of philosophy. However, she had also found a new way of thinking about the distinction. This is specifically in relation to the third set of differences – that between the external environment and the incorporated one (or to put it in another way, between the inner and the outer). This way of thinking about the subject stressed, for example, the issue of changeability – 'some of the drawings seemed to show that, unlike the external environment, the incorporated one did actually change according to one's feelings, and particularly in response to one's unadmitted feelings'. As an aside here, a literary response to this notion might be to draw attention to that matter of pathetic fallacy long familiar to our poets when the landscape or features of the natural world seem to reflect particular human emotions. Here Milner exemplifies the idea thus: 'If one had been full of unadmitted hate, it could apparently become a desert land with only dead bones in it, since the destructive wishes could be felt as fulfilled merely by thinking them.'[67]

Much of the theory in this area was known to Milner as psychoanalyst, as becomes clear in the text's Appendix; but there were ideas unknown to her before this experiment:

> what I had not known, until the study of the method of the free drawings had forced me to see it, was that this hate that is inherent in the fact that we do have to make the distinction between subject and object, if we are to develop at all beyond blind instinct, is overcome in a particular way through the arts.

The arts let us 'deliberately restore the split' and bring together subject and object in a new unity. The bringing together of inner and outer – something we 'blindly' enter into when we fall in love – is 'consciously brought about in the arts'; thus in the experience we call the 'aesthetic on the cause of the primary hate' (i.e. the separation of inner and outer, of subject and object), 'is temporarily suspended' – and once more, it can be said that such is the case with a good analysis and its negotiation with what Milner a little later refers to as 'landscapes of the inner world'.[68]

Thinking of the artist's task, she moves on to considering not just what a person seeks to find in the external world but also what they might seek to give; Blake once more provides the frame of reference:

> When two people meet in relationship the Prolific [. . .] in one cannot give unless the Devourer in the other is ready to receive; and the Devourer in one cannot receive unless the Prolific is willing to give at the moment his products are required and what is required.[69]

Milner's Personal Notebooks elaborate on this: 'People can't paint because they can't *give*. Creating is giving – [this] argues that there must be the devourer – the public – even tho' the artist may think he paints to please himself.'[70] In analysis, and Milner would agree here with Winnicott (see p. 52), the moment for interpretation has to be correct, apposite, ego syntonic – an interpretation cannot be heard, held and processed unless the analyst has gauged the state of receptiveness in the analysand.

It is important to consider that the outside world wants what one offers, or can offer; and Milner links this idea with one of the tasks of maturation – that life task in the transition from childhood to adulthood 'of finding a particular niche in the social world, or finding the gap or need in the social structure into which one can pour one's energies and find that they are wanted'.[71] In painting, Milner suggests, one does 'create one's own gap'.

Thinking about her dilemmas around and motives for painting, including the relation between painting and living, she comes across an old diary note to this effect: 'If one paints in order to possess, make one's own, it's not only perhaps a greedy thing to do, but also a kind of stealing the fire of the gods, stealing immortality . . . .' It did, to be sure, suggest that it was something of risk 'not to rest content with the conventional view of reality [. . .] also it expressed the thought that to try to re-make what one loved, in order to have it permanently there and under one's control, was an attempt to cheat mortality'.[72] And the greatest disillusion in all these matters is the fact of death itself – the greatest 'discrepancy between one's wish and the external facts'. She concludes on the side of life: 'giving life to the portrayal of one's subject [. . .] one is actually creating something' and it may even be that 'it is perhaps ourselves that the artist in us is trying to create'.[73]

Chapter 17, 'Painting as Making Real', takes off from certain ideas of Follett's, insisting, however, on what he leaves out, namely 'how the poet and artist in us [. . .] by their basic capacity for seeing the world in terms of metaphor, do in fact create the world for the scientist in us to be curious about and seek to understand'.[74] Further, the free drawings 'had shown how essential for anything but *blind living* was the emotionally coloured image . . .' Through these drawings and her self-analysis of them, Milner became 'able to live reflectively rather than blindly'.[75] Through the drawings she moves to the idea of 'contemplative action', finding that one crucial result of her study was that she could now 'begin to learn how to paint'. To do so she had had to shed some intellectual ideas from the climate of the era in which she had grown up – namely, nineteenth-century views of painting as pure representation; also, nineteenth-century (and earlier) views on 'the efficacy of thought by itself as an omnipotent God'.[76]

Milner's struggle was not only personal, she feels, and not only to do with painting: it was 'a struggle to slough off the old caterpillar skin of an outworn ideology about the relation of thinking to doing, of mind to body'. All the time going on around her had been 'a revolution in man's attitude to his own thinking' that she had been 'failing to see the significance of'.[77] Incidentally, she tells us that it was only now that she became aware of a further split between inner and outer and an effort to keep them apart: noting the date of a particular drawing including an Indian war drum looming in the sky, she realised 'it had been only a matter of days between the making of the drawing and the bursting of the storm of war over the whole of Europe'.[78] Thus the storm that Milner had been treating in *On Not Being Able to Paint* as a private and inner matter was also a public and world one. As we saw, she began work on the book on the day war was declared, and her Personal Notebooks show her working on, refining and developing her ideas in this text, coming, for instance, to see one particular free drawing, the 'Bursting Seed-Pod', as emblematic both of her epoch and her relation to it 'a state in which the upward thrust of life was giving birth to new ideas, and these were bursting through the seed-pod of the old world that gave them birth'.[79]

In painting Milner had discovered something unique and irreplaceable, 'a bit of experience that made all other usual occupations unimportant by comparison'. Sometimes, when painting something from nature, there was 'a fusion into a never-before-known wholeness; not only were the object and oneself no longer felt to be separate, but neither were thought and sensation and feeling and action'.[80] In this process it was clear that something very special had occurred to her sense of self, something, I would suggest, analogous (again) to the experience of psychoanalysis and its meeting of two selves, conscious and unconscious.

And, again, Milner thought there could be implications for educational theory: there could be less weight placed on the objective powers; indeed, were attention paid to their opposite there could even be a strengthening.

Figure 6.4 Bursting Seed-Pod

Was it not, she wonders here, possible that orthodox methods of education had:

> increased the hate resulting from the primary disillusion, not only
> by not giving enough scope for the aesthetic way of transcending
> that hate, but also by not giving enough scope for the social way,

the way of spontaneous co-operation in enterprises undertaken for the good of everybody who is taking part in them?[81]

There are, Milner finds, revolutionary ideas afoot about creativeness – specifically, that it 'is not the result of an omnipotent fiat from above, but is something which comes from the free reciprocal interplay of differences that are confronting each other with equal rights to be different, equal rights to their own identity'.[82] This idea and its derivatives now explain further layers of meaning to Milner as artist of the 'Bursting seed-pod image' (see Figure 6.4): now she could see this as a 'picture both of the epoch I was living in and my own relation to that epoch'.[83] Her postscript draws the reader's attention to one of the book's enduring strengths: it 'is not the retrospective account of a creative experience which had happened independently and was written about; it is itself an attempted embodiment of the process of creating.'[84]

Winnicott had been influential and appreciative of *On Not Being Able to Paint*, and the text shows a certain cross-fertilisation of ideas in the areas of creativity and the body, transitional space and inhibitions to creativity, but it was Masud Khan – that talented, maverick, tragic, discredited figure of the Independent Group – who suggested a second edition, this time with a foreword by Anna Freud.[85] This edition appeared in 1957 with a psychoanalytic appendix as well as Anna Freud's prefatory words with which Milner was very pleased.

The first edition of 1950 was aimed mainly at a market of teachers and published in the Heinemann Education Series; the second edition gave Milner the chance of formulating some of the ideas discussed in psychoanalytic terms.

Masud Khan can appropriately, given his instigation of the second edition, have the first voice among many appreciative reviewers and commentators: towards the close of his influential review in the *International Review of Psycho-Analysis* he writes that one fact is clear: 'that in the publications of Ella Sharpe, Melanie Klein, Ernest Kris and Marion Milner psychoanalytic researches into art have come of age'. Their work, he contends, means that there is now 'a very firm body of theory and vital technique of research to offer all those who are interested in the mysteries of aesthetic experiences and activity'.

Khan arrives at this view, and exhorts all, 'especially the psychoanalysts, to read and re-read the book' with 'a passionate attitude of surrendered attention', with praise for the book as 'not only the product of a sensitive human being but also that of an able clinician'. For Khan, the third volume of her trilogy (following Milner's discovery of psychoanalysis in *A Life* and *An Experiment*) is crucially informed by her further analytic experience. Confession now, he rightly contends, changes to communication in ONBAP, so that 'the reader can participate at all levels of experience reported'.

To make a recovery of creativity through a regressive return to an earlier state was a given and hinted at before in Milner's earlier works. What Khan suggests 'was needed was a technique that would render the processes involved accessible to observation'. Milner's free drawings required a similar technique to that of free association in the consulting room; and, for him, it is Milner's 'great achievement' that 'she could create a technique for aesthetic research which would afford the same vantage point of observation that Freud's discovery of transference and free association in the analytic set-up, has supplied for the clinical understanding of human personality and its pathologies'.

He approves also of her explorations of the 'dialogic relation' and the 'mood of reciprocity of the free drawings', and links these ideas with the trend among post-war psychoanalytic writers to concern themselves with 'the problems of an individual's differentiation from its early beginnings into a separate entity and achieving a personal identity'. He names Clifford Scott, E.H. Erickson, W. Hoffer and Winnicott[86] among clinicians thus concerned.

The esteemed art psychotherapist Rita Simon comments usefully on the many insights she gained from Milner's book; for her the most 'nourishing' to her developing idea about the therapeutic value of art lay in Milner's contention that here were two unconscious influences upon art that referred to different stages of maturity. This idea became clear to Simon when she read the appendix to the second edition where Milner 'discussed the use of pictorial symbols in terms that anticipated Object Relations theory, as well as the Kleinian view of a need to make reparation to objects destroyed in phantasy'. Crucially, Simon insists; 'Milner saw art as not only the work of the depressive position but also aris[ing] from a more primitive impulse to create symbolic images, thereby expressing the primary need to distinguish Self and Other, without which the depressive position and its reparative efforts cannot be achieved.'[87] Simon valued Milner's book in her work as an art therapist, and her further comments on this subject are referred in Chapter 9.

Among many other reviews and letters about this text, Henry Wilson in the *BMJ* approves it as 'an absorbing mental adventure story'; the *Manchester Guardian* points out 'Miss Field delves deeply into the creative process and into her own interests'; the *Listener* finds it 'a fascinating attempt to find a new route to an old destination', somewhat missing the point, however, by remarking that, 'To the artist it is a completely unnecessary book, since it laboriously arrives at the very point where he starts.'[88] Certain artists, Heinz Koppel for one, were appreciative; Koppel writes in a review in an issue of *The New Era* in 1958, re-visited by Milner and highlighted by her as follows:

> This is a penetrating enquiry into the nature of creativity. It also tells the story of a battle which has to be fought in the painting of a picture. Reviews of the first edition did not mention this side of the book, and as a professional painter I feel I must point to its importance.[89]

The art historian/critic Eric Newton applauded the book in a letter of 14 May 1950: 'what is important is that you've got hold of a set of truths – or threads leading to truths – that haven't been got hold of before, and indeed couldn't have been guessed at until 20th century psychology suggested where to look for them.'[90]

Congratulatory letters came from academics, too, such as Professor W.R. Niblett of the Department of Education at the University of Leeds, who singled out Milner's concept of the imaginative body 'as distinguished from the intellectual mind' as very rewarding and heartily agreed with her suggestion 'about the need in schools for encouraging undirected thinking in children. The roaming mind, the relaxed mind, is the only mind which will be able to create in a succeeding period of concentration.'[91]

Praise, too, comes on 6 November 1950 from Dorothy Burlingham, who had found the book both 'fascinating' and 'exciting' – her own four children having been brought up to draw as they pleased 'without correction'; Milner's text had 'made [her] think about the drawings of the insane. Nijinski's drawings while in an asylum come to mind.' Burlingham had some reservations about free drawings if the person were not well balanced; 'I can imagine that boarder-line [sic] cases [. . .] might lose too much contact with reality. On the other hand, I can imagine in guidance work that both, analyst and patient, might be greatly helped through the medium of such drawings.'[92]

W.R.D. Fairbairn provided an extensive Critical Notice of the book in *The British Journal of Medical Psychology* of March 1951, recognising its difference from the previous volumes in the trilogy and understanding that it 'embodies an inquiry of a somewhat different nature – one arising out of certain misgivings that she experienced in connexion with the results of a 5-year scientific study of the way in which children are affected by orthodox educational methods.' He appreciated also the trilogy as a whole for its 'special interest as representing a special pilgrimage towards an overtly psycho-analytical standpoint'.[93] The Jungian analyst Michael Fordham has a piece entitled 'A Reaction' following Fairbairn's in the same issue of the *British Journal of Medical Psychology,* where he situates the text in a Jungian framework; thus he says he had always had some difficulty in understanding 'introverted sensation' as defined by Jung in *Psychological Types* (1923); but, after reading Milner's book, he re-read the Jung and:

> found that it gives a clear account of the relation of subject to object which Joanna Field also describes. This function is decidedly odd because the object is used to express inner contents; the object contains, in the form of an image, a statement of how it affects the subject, with the emphasis strongly on the subjective end of the perception. This image, according to Jung, has an historical content.

He continues that it is this content that led Milner, it appears, 'to find in psycho-analysis the means of integrating the irrational content in a valuable way'.[94]

The American response was also positive; for instance, a psychoanalyst from Berkeley wrote from California of the 'urgent need' for *On Not Being Able to Paint* and 'for a course on the psychoanalytic approach to art at the University of California'. With a later edition, from 1983, Jeremy Tarcher, book publisher in Los Angeles, comments that ONBAP has 'made *The Village Voice* best seller list' and there have been reports that it is 'one of the leading sellers at stores with an intelligent young professional clientele'.[95]

Others were pleased, in particular, with Milner's ideas about symbolism: as Janet Sayers has shown in the new introduction to this text, Adrian Stokes, one time analysand of Melanie Klein, had written appreciatively of her work with the patient Michael. Her view is that 'states of illusion of oneness are [. . .] a recurrently necessary phase in the continued growth of a sense of two-ness'. Both Stokes and Milner likened this illusion to falling in love.[96]

Correspondence shows that there was some connection between Milner and Stokes from 1954 when she writes to tell him that she had 'devoured' his 'colour and form' and had lent the book to Bohusz, the Polish professor of Painting from Vilnius University whom she said she would like Stokes to meet. A month later she informed Stokes that she was 'struggling with an extra chapter [the analytic section]' and says how delighted she had been to hear of his approval of *A Life of One's Own*.[97]

Janet Sayers writes of Stokes after the war returning to 'writing about the healing outwardness of art', detailing the architecture of Venice to illustrate the 'intoxication' of the early Italian Renaissance with 'showing outer form . . . stabilizing an inner content as outer shape'. He had mentioned psycho-analysis before, she states, and now did so increasingly. His stress came to be less on the outwardness of art; rather he emphasised oneness, thorough art, of inner reality with outward object-otherness. In this, Sayers comments, he was less in tune with Freud or Klein than with 'the work of post-Kleinian psychoanalysts, notably Marion Milner and Wilfred Bion', both of whom were regular members of the Imago Group founded in 1954 with Robert Still to discuss applied psychoanalysis.[98] Other members included Donald Meltzer, Roger Money-Kyrle and Erich Gombrich and Richard Wollheim.

Milner, who, in one interview with Pearl King, says she maps out her life according to conferences, presented her ideas on inner and outer and their interplay at a psychoanalytic conference in Geneva in 1956 where she began to get to know another important colleague, friend and intellectual discussant, Anton Ehrenzweig, also a member of the Imago Group. (His response to *Experiment* has already been seen, see pp. 34–38.) She says: '1955 [sic] was Geneva [. . .] I met Anton at that lovely castle and that was very important for me because Anton became an important friend.'[99] She read his book

Psychoanalysis of Aesthetic Hearing and Perception, and he read *An Experiment*. His critique is in *American Imago*.

The American analyst, writer and mystic Michael Eigen is another colleague and friend, linked to Milner by *On Not Being Able to Paint*, a book that branches out into friendships and across countries for her. Correspondence in the Milner Archive at the Institute of Psychoanalysis shows that Eigen and Milner had been in some sort of contact since 1975, when they had met at a conference.[100] It was not until 1983 that his major piece on the appendix included in the second edition appeared in the *International Review of Psycho-Analysis*.

Eigen's stress is on the appendix so I will take the opportunity to consider them together. In the appendix Milner tells us that, in the process of writing the book, she had discovered what for her was the meaning of 'psychic creativeness' – it is 'the capacity for making a symbol. Thus, creativeness in the arts is making a symbol for feeling and creativeness in science is making a symbol for knowing.' In this last section she wishes 'to put forward the hypothesis that, from the point of view of psychic creativity at work, the logical terms in which the capacity for symbol formation is thought about are perhaps less important than the pre-logical'.[101]

In the original edition the intended audience was of lay persons, so she had limited the psychoanalytic concepts: here she focuses on 'The anal aspect of the parrot's egg', anality obviously being of great importance when investigating the 'human capacity to make things'. From her work with blocked children and adults, Milner had found that these individuals had a very idealised notion of what their products should be; clinical evidence had backed this up, particularly in the case(s) of poets and artists suffering from inhibition deriving from 'a catastrophic disillusion in their original discovery that their faeces are not as lively, as beautiful, as boundless, as the lovely feelings they had in the giving of them'.

The way, Milner contends, to help patients with a fixation point at this stage:

> was, not by interpreting to them the phantastic nature of their ideal-
> isations, not by showing them their mistakes in so idealising their
> own body products; but by showing them that the idealisation was
> not a delusion, in so far as it referred to the intensity of their own
> orgastic sensations, it was only a delusion when they clung to the
> belief that the 'mess' was itself as beautiful as the feelings experi-
> enced in making it.[102]

Eigen notes that it is 'the moment of undifferentiation' that Milner emphasises, as he does also when Milner expands on the 'grey lady' and the 'angry parrot'. It is of interest that Eigen had already noted his disquiet about Milner's concept of wholeness in 1977 in the *Psychoanalytic Review* where he wrote: 'Unfortunately the functional concept Milner uses to articulate "wholeness" – undifferentiated union – remains vague and undoes itself.'[103]

Milner's next appended section is on 'Infantile Prototypes of Creativity', to which she brings once more her psychoanalytic expertise to our experience as infants when we discover, with some disillusion, even fury, 'that we have not made everything', and, upon finding this out, we 'transfer this belief to our parents and feel that at least they have'.[104] The infant's 'doubts about the goodness of wishes towards the external parents' can lead to doubts about goodness of the creative forces inside itself. Eigen here notes Milner's re-working of the meaning of the infant's masturbatory fantasy at this stage.

At this point of putting together the appendix, Milner has accumulated a wealth of clinical experience and is able to say with some confidence: 'Clinical material suggests that the symbols used for thinking about the creative process in oneself are derived, variously, from the stages of interest in different aspects of bodily experience.'[105] She contends that it might therefore be possible to work out the kinds of symbols used at different developmental moments, for instance:

> the stage at which to open one's eyes was felt to be a fiat of creation, a saying 'let there be light', which resulted in there being light [. . .] For there seems to have been a time when even the faculty of consciousness itself was felt to be entirely creative, to be aware of anything was simply to have made it . . .[106]

In the process of free drawing and thinking through her ideas in her book Milner found there were, in the words of Section IV's title, 'Changes in the Sense of Self': something new emerged, and this was summed up in the phrase 'contemplative action' in contrast to practical action. The essential fact about this mood was that it involved Milner in relinquishing a wish to make an exact copy or reproduction of anything seen, however tempting might be the pull towards 'mechanical copying'. When resisted, and she had broken free from this wish, not only did a new entity arise, but there was also 'a kind of blanking out of ordinary consciousness', a phase of 'complete lack of self-consciousness'.[107]

Both writings in psychoanalysis and mystical texts had something to say on this subject: the former wrote of 'states of elation, as blankness, as oceanic feeling'; the latter, such as in the central concept of the *Tao Te Ching* as '"emptiness" as a beneficent state'. Analysts, as is well known, relate this experience to 'the satisfied sleep of the infant at the mother's breast', and Milner recognises this – but as a starting point of her thinking here. She then extends her ideas, asking if it might not be the case that such moments are an essential prelude to the emergence of 'a new psychic creation':

> May there not be moments in which there is a plunge into non-differentiation, which results (if all goes well) in a re-emerging into

a new division of the me-not-me, one in which there is more of the 'me' in the 'not me' in the 'me'?

What Milner stresses is that a good free drawing brings into focus 'the fact that there is some force or interplay of forces creating something new.'[108]

Part of the set of ideas highlighted by Milner in this appendix, and also taken up by Eigen, is the matter of 'Rhythm relaxation and the orgasm' – she relates moments of non-differentiation to orgasm; the study of techniques for bodily relaxation shows that 'the release of any particular muscle is largely achieved by the apparently simple act of directing attention to it, letting consciousness suffuse it.'[109]

Milner comments that the subject of the capacity to make one's attention suffuse the whole body, and the relation of this both to genital and pre-genital orgasm, would require a discussion beyond the scope of this text. However, she does note that such a discussion would need, critically, to include a commentary on colour, with its clear links with highly charged emotional states – green with envy, seeing red, feeling blue, to name but three.[110]

Eigen voices his misgivings about Milner's use of ideas of non-differentiation; he recognises that 'we are always on shaky ground' when approaching this area – the critic may well be charged with being too 'well-defended' against such states. He situates Milner's work as part of a reaction against a Cartesian subject-object split in which 'the mind is free' and 'the body is a machine', with each interacting 'as two radically different orders of creation'. Freud, with his important tenet that the ego is 'first and foremost a body ego', had overturned this view; and as Eigen states, both Freud and the philosopher Merleau-Ponty are part of a 'larger movement which has been re-evaluating the epistemological role of the body.' I quote from Eigen:

> For the larger part of the history of western thought, the body has been a second class citizen. It has been associated with the ephemeral, animal or machine, something to be used and transcended. There were materialisms, but either idealism swept the day or the two were locked in holy wars. It was, paradoxically, the scientific investigation of the body as machine which played an important role in establishing the body as an organizing centre of subjectivity. Spontaneous ordering processes were discovered at every level of life [. . .] Therapies proliferated on lived bodily awareness.[111]

His reservations about Milner's *On Not Being Able to Paint* are based on a certain vagueness; her stress, he says, 'is on the experiencing subject with regard to subject-object interlocking and the lived body' but he finds 'her distrust of intellect and celebration of non-differentiation exploits difficulties she glosses over.'[112] (This celebration is very important in relation to Nina Farhi's extending of Milner's work and is discussed in that connection in the chapter on *Hands of the Living God*.) Eigen continues: 'It is as if she fears something will get lost if she thinks too clearly', and locates a certain 'sleight of hand' in the shift in levels of discourse in her writings – a shift unacknowledged, he thinks, in her text.

Unpublished correspondence in the Archives of the British Psychoanalytical Society indicates that Milner was not entirely happy with this critique (although there is no record of *her* letter to Eigen); a letter from the Independent Group analyst John Padel about Eigen's article says he has spent some time 'trying to understand what he's grumbling about' – and says it seems to be 'something to do with the concept of differentiation'.[113] On 30 November 1983, Eigen writes that he fears his paper had offended Milner 'as I half-expected. It is a provocative paper. But I also hoped a helpful one. I may be wrong.' He would, he adds, be 'quite sad' were he to have wronged her, since Milner's work 'had a sustaining effect for me and I've valued our letter contact. Too bad we murder each other to grow. I keep Winnicott's use of object paper in mind. [. . .].' He had meant his paper 'as an appreciative critique'.[114] Milner, however, does not seem to have received it in this way. A further letter from Eigen of 3 December 1983 says: 'Clearly you did not feel well mirrored or helped and that's food for thought. My appreciation for your work is steadfast.'[115] Later, in 1994, he remarks in an interview with Antony Molino that his article had 'apparently precipitated antagonism from Margaret Little who, unbeknownst to me at that time, had used the concept of undifferentiation to couch an awful lot of her own work'. Little had also let him know that she felt he had 'hurt Marion with this paper'. Their connection was maintained despite these mutual misgivings, and Eigen's work continues to pay homage to Milner's influence.[116]

The remaining sections of the appendix come outside Eigen's critique. Section VI is on 'Painting and Symbols'; here, Milner comments on the frame – an entity that 'marks off an area within which what is perceived has to be taken symbolically, while what is outside the frame is taken literally'.[117] In the original edition of *On Not Being Able to Paint* she did not make very much use of the term 'symbol' because, at that time, she 'was still confused by the classical psycho-analytical attempt to restrict the use of the word to denoting only the defensive function of symbols, to what Ernest Jones called "pure symbolism"'.[118] In the meantime, having written and published a paper on symbols, and reached the view that she was not able to limit her use of the term in the manner of Jones, she now felt able 'to accept the idea that a work of art is necessarily and primarily a symbol'. Further, she realises now that 'a mental image is a symbol'.[119]

In psychoanalytic terms, the artist's seeking to preserve lost objects and experiences, his 'recreation of a lost object', is, for Milner, certainly part of the function of art; however, for her, it is a secondary function – the main function is the 'creating' of objects at a developmental stage earlier than the depressive position. Milner's thought chimes with Stokes's view that the artist is concerned with the 'out-there-ness' of his work.[120] Here Milner draws an important distinction:

> Certainly for the analyst, at certain stages in analysing an artist, the importance of his work of art may be the lost object that the work re-creates; but for the artist as artist, rather than as patient, and for whoever responds to his work, I think the essential point is the new thing that he has created, the new bit of the external world that he had made significant and 'real', through endowing it with form.[121]

Section VII expounds Milner's views on 'The Two Kinds of Thinking', that is, the logical kind involving a separation (differentiation) between what a thing is and what it is not and the non-logical involving 'a willingness to forgo the usual sense of self as clear and separate and possessing a boundary' – it is the case that, in the field of aesthetics, logic can give a false view.[122]

In her journey of learning to paint Milner found that to be authentic every mark on the paper should be her own, not a mechanical copy – and she had also found people to teach her (Bohusz for one, see pp. 89–92) who did see that this was the essence of painting.

Significantly, the final section of ONBAP, while recognising the validity of the term 'phantasy', regrets that that most expressive word 'reverie' has fallen out of the language of the profession: 'For the word "reverie" does emphasise the aspect of absent-mindedness', and this, in turn, brings in the very important need for a 'certain quality of protectiveness in the environment'. There has to be a safe physical setting for absent mindedness – this is one where 'we are freed, for the time being, from the need for immediate practical expedient action; and it requires a mental setting, an attitude, both in the people around and in oneself, a tolerance of something that may at moments look very like madness'[123] – an environment, in other words, of a good frame both for painter and for patient in analysis.

7

INFLUENCES, FAMILY
AND FRIENDS

1950s–late 1970s

During the years of writing *On Not Being Able to Paint* and afterwards, Milner had attended Cedric Morris Summer Schools at Hadleigh in Suffolk. She loved these, the excellent food and good company but found Morris's emphasis on 'extreme realism' in art not entirely to her taste preferring the more 'playful' approach of the Polish-born Bohusz.[1] She writes:

> and finally, I owe a deep debt to Prof. M. Bohusz-Szysko, in whose painting classes I have been able to begin the task of learning how my own observations, however small their scope, do make sense in the total setting of the difficulties facing both the modern European painter and the student of aesthetics.[2]

Bohusz, born in 1901 near Vilnius in Russian Poland, had served with the Polish Army in the First World War, and was an artist trained in Krakow involved also in education and in the teaching of art and mathematics. He joined the Polish Army again at the start of the Second World War and was captured early on in the war by the Germans and imprisoned for over five years. On his release he journeyed to Italy to work with the Polish forces in that country. He arrived in Britain on 11 November 1946, landing in Glasgow and progressing a few days later to England, little knowing that he would remain there for the next thirty years.

In 1946 members of the Polish forces arriving in Britain who did not wish to return to Poland were gathered together in camps of the so-called Polish Resettlement Corps. Bohusz, characteristically, managed to gather in one camp all the artists and students he had known; at first, this was near Sudbury in Suffolk, and then at Kingswood Common near Reading. There was an art school set up there under the direction of the Association of Polish University Professors and Lecturers Abroad, an institution of which Marian Bohusz was appointed head some eighteen years later.[3]

Milner regularly attended Bohusz's weekend classes in London, from the early 1950s accompanied not only by her own analyst, Sylvia Payne, but also by one of her supervisees at this time – Masud Khan, whom she introduced

Figure 7.1 John Milner at Oxford

to Bohusz. She comments, 'Masud would drive me across Hyde Park on Sunday mornings down to the class in Knightsbridge.'[4] Bohusz's classes were held at the Polish YMCA in Kensington Gardens Square, and the cost, for those who could pay, was £1 (no fee for those unable to pay). She attended for four years, probably (the dating is uncertain) starting in 1953 – also the year of his 'Portrait of Mrs Milner', which appears on the cover of this book – and she was clearly impressed by him both as teacher and as artist. In March 1954, she writes to Adrian Stokes that she would very much like Stokes to meet him, saying how much she approves of Bohusz's use of colour and praising his picture 'Deposition'.[5]

Milner appears to have been very close to Bohusz: a letter of 1 June 1961 expresses his chagrin at being unable to get to London to see her because of ill health – angina and doctor's orders. He is 'longing awfully' for her but it is impossible: 'as you see,' he writes, 'we have some malicious ghosts near us who are jealous and try to spoil our meetings.' As late as 1967 they are still seeing each other as, at the very least, loving friends; in October of this year it seems he had forgotten an appointment with Milner at a time when she was 'not strong enough' for such disappointments – she had gone to his studio to find him absent.[6] It is likely that the spiritual quality of Bohusz's work would have struck a chord with Milner; as Dr John Taylor wrote, 'because Marian is a mystic, all his pictures are, in a sense, icons. They call for contemplation.'[7]

Their personal situation was destined to change when in 1963 Bohusz met Cicely Saunders, founder of the Hospice Movement in Britain. Saunders writes: 'It was not chance that brought me to the Drian Gallery at the end of Marian Bohusz's 1963 exhibition and began the co-operation and the series of special gifts that have filled the hospice with vibrant colour.' Their relationship grew:

Figure 7.2 MM at the Drian Gallery, 1971

Cicely was 54, he 60. Unlike her previous two Polish husbands, Bohusz 'was in good health, vibrant and full of life'. 'He was a wild, mad artist, bless his heart', Cicely once said. Although Bohusz had been separated from his Polish wife for many years, he was not actually divorced; he and Cicely bought a house and lived together in an apparently congenial arrangement with two of their friends. Bohusz was to become artist-in-residence at St Christopher's Hospice which became his permanent gallery. His art still decorates its hallways, chapel and garden. Soon after the death of Bohusz's wife, he and Cicely married, she in her early sixties and he in his late seventies. They had already been together for seventeen years and were to have another fifteen before Bohusz's death at St Christopher's in 1995.[8]

In 1971 (from 27 January to 19 February) Milner was to have her own solo exhibition at the Drian Gallery in West London with works arguably influenced by Bohusz's art and teaching. The exhibition was praised, for example, by the critic Richard Walker who singles out such qualities as the exceptional and bold use of colour. He writes of:

> a serene, balanced art, gentle strength immediately apparent in the abstracts underlying the figurative. Reticent richness of colour is the most obvious vehicle for the pervasive serenity often lacking in the work of psychiatrist-painters or painters with conscious psycho-logical orientation. In fact, it doesn't *look* like the work of a psy-chologist and this, of course, I intend as a compliment.[9]

These paintings and this exhibition look forward to Milner's bold use of colour and playful quality in those collages that distinguish her artistic life in its later decades.

Painting was not the only interest pursued by Milner during the years before the 1971 exhibition. The archive of her papers is remarkable for the range of activities with which she was involved. Dance figures prominently throughout the period 1951–1960 with annotations by Milner on a number of related subjects. There are programmes for ballet, modern dance, Spanish and Indian dance productions; information about the Arthur Murray School of Dancing; newspaper cuttings; and instructions manuals such as the *Woman's Own Pocket Guide to Better Dancing*.

Performances attended in London during the 1950s include flamenco and singing by Rosario and Antonio, with Cedric Morris as her companion; the Yugoslav State Company with dancing in 'Slavonic Rhapsody'; the Bulgarian State Song and Dance Company, created in 1951; the Japanese Ballet of Miho Hanayagui; pieces staged by Javanese dancers; Antonio and his Spanish Ballet Company at the Palace Theatre in 1955; and, for the Christmas season 1956, José Greco and his Spanish dancers at the Royal Festival Hall.

In 1954 the great American pioneer of modern dance Martha Graham visited London, and Milner was much taken with the film *A Dancer's World* presenting and presented by the Martha Graham Company. She kept a notice from Contemporary Films Ltd of this fascinating film about 'one of the greatest figures in American dance'. Milner has also retained (she seems to have discarded very little) a typed programme sheet of the London Ballet Circle's presentation of a film show featuring, once again, the work of Martha Graham, and also acrobats from Shanghai, an eclectic combination. There is a record of Milner applying for membership of the Arthur Murray Lifetime Club and also of a 1951 New Year Festival of Folk Dance at the Royal Albert Hall. Detailed illustrated pamphlets on Spanish songs and folk dances and on Yugoslav folk dance suggest she is likely to have tried out and practised some of the dances.[10]

Opera and theatre programmes also bespeak an ongoing engagement with current cultural events; visits to performances at the Royal Opera House, Covent Garden, are recorded in December 1958 (*Ondine*) and March 1960 (*La Rendezvous* and *Petrushka*); and in 1961 she attended performances of the Leningrad State Kirov Ballet in *The Sleeping Beauty* in June and the ballet *La Fille Mal Gardée* in October.

Also a devotee of the theatre, Milner the collector retains a playbill for October 1960 for Chekhov's *Platonov* at the Royal Court Theatre and one for Jean Anouilh's *Beckett* at the Globe Theatre, Shaftesbury Avenue, in 1961. Her lifelong enthusiasm for Shakespeare took her to Stratford-on-Avon in 1958 to see *Twelfth Night*, and the archives of Milner's interests contain typed records of reading of a number of Shakespeare's plays with colleagues and friends right up until Milner was in her nineties.[11]

As has become apparent, Milner consistently throughout her life attended to the body and its experiences, and it is no surprise that there is a rich archival collection 'Meditation, Relaxation, Posture' containing material on topics such as 'Foot Efficiency', 'The Balanced Co-operation of Body and Mind' (this is developed from the work of F. Mathias Alexander) and 'Exercise for Low Back Pain'. The year 1963 yields leaflets on 'Experiences with Dynamic Relaxation and the Relationship of the Discovery of the Reichian Bioenergetic View of Vegetotherapy'; and, from the *Journal of Nervous and Mental Diseases*, a piece on experimental meditation.[12]

One significant friend from the late 1960s was Mary Pears (now Reid), an educational psychologist and a person whom Milner described as one of her most important 'non-psychoanalytic friends'. Sharing a love of the English countryside, nature, the seashore and poetry, as well as an interest in yoga and Reichian therapy, they also shared the love of Joel Shor, a research psychoanalyst from the University of Southern California Law School and the Research Division of the Southern Californian Psychoanalytic Institute. After a time in England, at the time of his return to the United States, Shor asked Milner to look after Mary Pears in his absence. This she did, and they became great friends.

Pears describes Milner as a friend as 'fun', 'tolerant', 'wearing her scholarship very lightly', 'very faithful and reliable' and 'marvellously eccentric'. Attending Reichian therapy sessions and events, Milner said she 'heard music in her feet'. Participating in Gestalt groups together, Pears says that Milner, as a senior professional and much-respected analyst, 'never pulled rank', and they took happy holidays together in Oxfordshire and Cornwall. Arriving one day in her eighties, laden with books and a haversack, Milner insisted on taking a sea swim after removing 'an awful lot of underclothes'. Another time, Pears with her second husband, Kenneth Reid, took their friend for a picnic to Box Hill; while watching birds, and being told that a certain one was a 'tit', Milner, with her typical naturalist's care for detail, responded, 'Of course, but what sort?'[13]

From the early 1950s Milner was involved with the Braziers Park School of Integrative Social Research at Ipsden near Oxford. The seventeenth-century house, still standing today, was bought in 1950 by Norman Glaister, sociologist, pacifist and psychiatrist, who set up the school. One of the oldest of the secular communities in the UK, it operated on commune principles and aimed to explore group dynamics and communication.[14] A paper by Glaister, retained by Milner and very likely written for a conference attended by her in 1951, expands on his approach:

> Our research is distinctively *integrative*. Our approach is designed to bring together the objective and subjective aspects of experience, over-separation of which seems to be one of the main defects of our current civilization. We are ourselves material for study, and the student-teacher relationship is one of mutual learning and teaching.

The attitude towards conflict and controversy would have appealed to Milner's personality, perhaps especially the 'positive methods used in our approach to controversial questions' and the committed effort to get around an entrenched position of the 'repetition of contrary assertions'. Glaister continues giving further insight into 'The Braziers Approach':

> The mutual contradiction is irreconcilable, but where both parties are [word missing] since it is usually found that the *positive* assertions on both sides are based upon partially accurate observations of actual happenings, and are not inherently incompatible; very often indeed, if both sides can be brought to consider the whole mass of evidence in spite of any preconceived hostility, they find the total result more satisfactory than any previous partial findings, and a real enlargement of understanding is achieved.[15]

Glaister's paper recognises the debt owed by the Braziers approach to Quaker peace philosophy and Quaker thought on conflict resolution, while the Braziers' philosophy also has links with Freudian ideas on group behaviour. A letter from Robert Glynn Faithfull, a key member of the Community and son of the therapist who treated Dennis Milner in the 1920s, comments on the Freudian link and invites Milner to a weekend event entitled 'Dialectic of Arts' introduced by Harold Walsby.[16]

Walsby was a revolutionary socialist who, in the late 1930s, developed a theory of ideology explaining why the Left, although claiming to represent the interests of the majority, remained in the minority. Walsby and others, including George Walford, founded a study of ideologies known as 'Systematic Ideology'. The group that formed around Walsby is generally considered as a breakaway group from the Socialist Party of Great Britain; and during the Second World War, it was deeply engaged with the investigation of impediments to mass social consciousness among the working class. Walsby's book *The Domain of Ideologies* had been published in 1947, and he is recorded as having lectured at Braziers Park in 1951, 1959 and 1965. There he was also involved in art tuition and music. The Braziers Park brochure retained by Milner shows that students could participate in music, drama and dance during their time at the school.[17]

As well as Cedric Morris's summer schools at Hadleigh, Milner joined summer schools in 1950 and 1951 on Wilfred Trotter's *Instincts of the Herd in Times of War and Peace*. Trotter, a neurosurgeon and social psychologist, is best known for his work on herd instincts on which subject he published papers from 1908 onwards. He was connected with Freud in that he was a member of the Council of the Royal Society that granted Freud honorary membership on his arrival in England in 1938; and, later, he was involved in consultations about Freud's terminal cancer. Additionally, he was the brother-in-law of Ernest Jones and the surgeon under whom Bion worked as a resident in his medical studies before his ground-breaking work on groups and group dynamics.

An important group in Milner's life at this time was the 1952 Club, a private group of analysts who wanted to meet and discuss their ideas outside the British Society. Pearl King writes that this started initially in her flat and was called 'a middle group seminar', and it then became known as the '1952 Club'.[18] Charles Rycroft had insisted that they have a name without any political significance.[19] The 1952 Club comprised Armstrong Harris, Masud Khan, Barbara Woodhead and Pearl King as well as Rycroft. Milner was among those they decided they would like to approach to give papers; thus, in the early meetings, a discussion was led by Masud Khan on her 'Aspects of Symbolism in comprehension of the not-self'. Pearl King also tells us that the Club had a fiftieth-anniversary dinner in 2002 and that it continues to meet eight times a year.

The year 1954 saw the formation of the Imago Group. Janet Sayers writes of how, in January of that year, Adrian Stokes presented a paper on 'Form in Art' to a gathering of artists and analysts who, in the following month, had transformed themselves into the Imago Group,[20] initially known as the Imago Society. The members 'aimed to discuss areas of mutual interest from a Kleinian perspective. Membership was open to practitioners and non-practitioners who had experience of analysis.'[21] Co-founded by Stokes and the composer Robert Still, it included Richard Wollheim, Donald Meltzer, Wilfred Bion, Roger Money-Kyrle, John Wisdom and Stuart Hampshire.

Phyllis Grosskurth sees Imago as a sign that Kleinian ideas were beginning to be discussed in a context wider than the purely psychoanalytic, and she reminds us that Stokes himself had been analysed by Klein from 1932 to 1936 and again in 1938. The philosopher Richard Wollheim explains why he believes Kleinian concepts can be applied to the study of art, a view upheld by many Imago members:

> By concentrating upon the content of the work of art, Freudian criticism laid itself open to the objection, often urged against it, that it ignored the specifically aesthetic aspect of art; for if products of identical content are treated identically, how do we distinguish between say, a Leonardo and a day-dream or a child's game with the same motivation? Kleinian criticism has deliberately set itself to redress the balance. A work of art is defined in terms of the possession of certain formal characteristics and those characteristics are then analysed as the natural correlates of certain ego-processes.[22]

Figure 7.3 John Milner's wedding, 1960

In the early 1960s, the world of groups and the more public group activities and meetings gives way for Milner to important family matters. A letter to Winnicott of 9 September 1960 describes a visit to Santa Sophia in Istanbul: 'Under the centre of the dome [. . .] is a little cross on the floor. The guide said "you must wish". I wished for John to find a nice girl.' Only five minutes after reaching her home, Milner had her son on the telephone saying he had much to tell her – that, on Saturday he had become engaged and 'the girl would be turning up in a few minutes – she's gay, intelligent, perceptive, just his age. They plan to get married at Christmas. I must light a candle to St. Sophia.'[23]

John, a successful academic at City University where he worked up until his death in February 2013, had met his future wife Karen de Lechler at a friend's wedding in Bristol. Karen's family was a colourful one: her mother, Lizzie, had originally gone to Paris with one Paddy Dunky; the British Consul persuaded them to marry, but on returning to Southampton, Lizzie later became interested in an army officer by the name of Vaughan. A fight ensued and Paddy lost an eye. Lizzie married Vaughan who became a brigadier. John Milner tells how he and Karen went with their first-born son Giles (born September 1962) to Dublin to meet Paddy. Before this time Karen had never met her father, having been brought up by her mother and her stepfather. They occasionally saw Paddy after this but this does not seem to have been encouraged by Paddy's then wife. Karen's first job was in the Army, in intelligence, found for her by Vaughan. She and John lived in London, in the modern house in Canonbury where he resided until his death, and were a most popular couple among visiting academics and scholars, particularly those from Eastern Europe.

They were, however, a couple ambivalent about psychoanalysis and its world. Milner once suggested that Karen might seek a meeting with an analyst. The response was unequivocal: 'I do not want to see a bloody analyst.' There is some evidence that Milner considered Winnicott might be a suitable person to whom her daughter-in-law might speak. (I do not think this ever happened.) John, too, had something of a chequered history with analysts and recalls stopping his own analysis and using the money to buy his house. (Dennis Milner had left him enough money to pay the deposit, the residue of his estate going to his third wife.)[24]

The relationship between Milner and her daughter-in-law was, at times, tense; it seems to have begun well enough and to have been congenial for some twenty years, during which the couple and their young children (Quentin was born in July 1964) would enjoy time at Harting in Hampshire or at Milner's sister Win's house (inherited by Milner on Winifred's death in 1969) near Sissinghurst Castle, where Quentin Milner says they would go nearly every weekend when children.[25]

Later, John Milner says, they had a hard time 'seeing the point of one another',[26] and things seem to have come to a head in the 1980s after the death of Karen's mother. Sadly, Karen herself died in 1992 leaving Milner to make anew her relationship with her son and grandchildren.

Aside from family matters, Milner developed her psychoanalytic life. The year of John's marriage saw the publication of the first, and much celebrated, book by one of her best-known, most controversial and maverick supervisees – the Scotsman, R.D. Laing. In 1958 Milner was one of those to see the manuscript of his seminal book *The Divided Self*; and from 1958 onwards she was one of his two supervisors from the Institute of Psychoanalysis; the other was Winnicott. Laing, although very brilliant and charismatic, was not the most regular attendee at lectures and seminars, and his qualification was called into question. His biographer John Clay tells how a report was asked for. Milner responded:

> In my opinion to delay his qualification because of his [non-attendance at] seminars would reflect on the psychoanalytic society by suggesting we are incapable of being flexible enough to meet the needs of a specially brilliant student; in this case a man who during the time he missed most of the seminars was deeply preoccupied with the creative work of planning an independent research project and getting financial support for it.[27]

Milner refers here to the project at the Tavistock Clinic with schizophrenic families that Laing was setting up. She resumes in positive vein: 'I found him a pleasure to work with because I never feel he is distorting the material to make it fit into a preconceived theory or formula, he never gives ready-made or clichéd interpretations.' And, what is more, she does not confine her praise to his work with psychotic patients: 'I would', she writes, 'certainly trust Dr Laing with patients of a more orthodox psycho-neurotic type (even though I have not seen his work with such problems) because I feel he will always be able to learn, and learn quickly from his patients.'[28]

Laing's son Adrian gives a further view of his father's controversial qualification at the Institute:

> two polarized schools of thought emerged. Marion Milner and Donald Winnicott, Ronnie's supervisors, and Charles Rycroft, Ronnie's training analyst, together with John Bowlby and Jock Sutherland, were in favour of Ronnie's qualification. Fanny Wride and Ilse Hellmann, the training committee [. . .] were adamantly opposed to the idea that someone with Ronnie's temperament should be allowed to call himself a psychoanalyst.[29]

Eventually, on 24 October 1960 the Training Committee relented and wrote that they could see no useful purpose in delaying Laing's qualification.

Milner and Laing shared a divided or ambivalent relationship with institutions – not just with the Institute of Psychoanalysis but with all organised entities; both, to some extent, worked outside many orthodoxies. In any event, Milner had a prolonged and positive connection with Laing's work; as early as 1964 he had openly expressed his political attitude towards schizophrenia, and in August of that year, he writes in his paper for the First International Congress of Social Psychiatry: 'I do not myself believe there is any such "condition" as "schizophrenia". Yet this label is a social fact, a *political* event.' Milner has marked this on her copy with an affirmative check. Of a person thus labelled, Laing writes that they are 'degraded from full existential status as a human agent and responsible person, no longer in possession of his own definition of himself, unable to retain his own possessions, precluded from the exercise of his discretion as to whom he meets what he does.'[30] Laing's arguments against labelling people 'schizophrenic' strike a chord with Milner (this was to be an issue in her treatment of 'Susan' in *Hands of the Living God*), and she follows the fortunes of his book through the 1970s up until its re-consideration in 1982 in the *British Journal of Psychiatry*. Milner had read *The Divided Self* in manuscript in its earlier stages and, as Laing was finalising the text, he had asked colleagues to comment – Rycroft and Winnicott, as well as Milner, were approving.

Milner, as his supervisor from 1958, had been very supportive of Laing's, at times wayward, brilliance. Other analysts are on record as appreciating *her* qualities as supervisor. Pearl King had been to Milner for supervision from 1946 to 1950, and then, on the death of her analyst, Rickman, in 1951, went to Milner as her second analyst; King was well pleased with their work.[31] In an interview with Jeremy Holmes, Charles Rycroft names Milner (together with Winnicott) as an important influence on him: she was 'very helpful and my first case did very well, that's always very nice', he says.

In an interview with Peter Rudnytsky, Rycroft comments that his supervisions with Milner were 'very helpful – quite an education'. Jenny Pearson, his wife, also tells how Rycroft went into analysis with Milner for writer's block, specifically for an inability to move into writing fiction.[32]

Other analysts are similarly appreciative. Roger Kennedy, whose first training case Milner supervised in the late 1970s, says she was a significant influence on his paper 'The Dual Aspect of the Transference' (in his book *The Many Voices of Psychoanalysis*). She was, he says, very straightforward, down to earth and very good with dreams; he found her 'calming'. A characteristic example of Milner's work with him was in connection with a religious, Jewish patient, when Kennedy had said, 'I don't believe in God'. Milner had responded roundly, 'That is not important. What is important is what God is for her.' He also recalls her pragmatic advice about the couch – the unwilling patient, anxious about the degree of separation occasioned by its use, could sit on the side.[33]

Figure 7.4 MM 'The Hens' (on the right)

Christopher Bollas was supervised by Milner from 1976 when he asked to work with her on his second training case. He writes:

> my impression of her then – and through the years – was much the same although I was to come to know that she had a sort of 'set routine' for each visitor. She would usually pass by the ground floor room where she had a few of her collages, one that I think she called 'The Hens' which was a portrait of Melanie Klein and Anna Freud.

For reasons of confidentiality, Bollas cannot comment on the case, but he does say that this patient turned out to be quite unanalysable, someone who 'wanted to remain in analysis so that it could be clearly established over time that I would not be able to read the mind and I was to be tested by being fed wild tales along with bits of the truth'. Milner, he comments, was 'bemused' by this, and his account is typical of her individual idiom:

> after a while she would begin the supervision by saying, 'So what has our friend done this week?' as the accounts given were usually tales of remarkable encounters. She would often giggle, often say, 'whatever are we to make of this?' and would say 'I have never heard

of anyone like her before' and she quite meant it. She was struck with my ability to tolerate this situation and we talked some about my having worked with autistic children at the beginning of my career and she talked about her work with 'Susan' and how strange it can be that an analyst is both so crucial to a patient and yet at times so cast aside and rather helpless.[34]

'Susan' was the patient, herself a 'divided self', about whom Milner was to write her great book *The Hands of the Living God*, discussed in the next chapter. Her connection with Laing was helpful to her in this enterprise, as was, of course, her professional relationship with Winnicott and another luminary of these years, Masud Khan, who at this time, before his tragic decline of the late 1960s, was an extremely attractive and gifted young man.

Milner was not only involved with Khan through Bohusz's painting classes, where he had seen her as 'a person with an incisive capacity for concentration and indefatigable in her resolve to paint an apple as it was'; she was also part of his professional life. They had first met in the winter of 1947 when she gave seminars on dreams, and, says Khan, 'what a hash she made of them!' And yet, of all the seminars and lectures he attended during the years of his candidature, 1947–1951, 'only those by three persons stay vividly in my memory: by Winnicott, Milner and Bion'. His comments on her manner of teaching might also apply to features of her writing and its idiom (her use of unchecked quotation for example):

> her lectures lacked such qualities as a reliable knowledge of the relevant literature, or an organised presentation of clinical material. She was a youthful and shy person with gleaming eyes, and distressingly modest, every now and then she would say something that would make one listen with body and mind and then scamper away into conversing randomly.[35]

Khan's first psychoanalytic paper 'Notes on the Dissolution of Object-Representation in Modern Art' was given to the Society on 5 June 1951 and was influenced by both Ella Sharpe's and Milner's ideas. The artistic emphasis of his interests is also to the fore at the 22nd IPA Conference held in Edinburgh from 10 July to 2 August 1961. Before this, Clifford Scott had visited Khan and the ballerina Svetlana Beriosova in London; and, later, they had all booked into the Caledonian Hotel in Edinburgh with a group of delegates. While there, Khan had planned a meeting with Scott, Winnicott and Milner; and he was active as a speaker. On 1 August 1961 Milner led a discussion group with him on 'Psychoanalysis applied to art' chaired by Charles Rycroft.

Socially involved also with Khan, Milner had attended his first wedding to Jane Shore (he was later to marry Svetlana) at the Kensington Register Office on 16 July 1952. But it was in the 1960s, at the time of the decline of his second marriage, to Svetlana, that he is at his most confiding to Milner, writing to her of 'the private nightmare I am living through at home at present. One can only wait.'[36]

Around 1966, at the same time as Khan was closely involved in editorial work on Milner's behalf, he involved her in a complicated professional situation, itself a kind of nightmare. He asked her to take over the treatment of Miss B., one of his patients, an artist and sculptor. Milner accepted the referral, believing the treatment to be near completion, and the analysis began. Quite soon, however, she found out that Miss B. was engaged in an ongoing sexual relationship with Khan thus rendering her analysis a long way from completion. In fact, the patient remained with Milner for a number of years. It is thought likely that Milner was not Khan's first choice of analyst for this patient: he had initially approached Robert Shields but had later retracted his offer. Roger Willoughby suggests that in this matter Khan 'placed greater trust in Milner's silence'[37] – silence, perhaps, that was more in the nature of Milner's personality than disclosure or confrontation.

There is no doubt however that, as Willoughby suggests, Milner had been put in an extremely difficult position in the matter of Miss B., caught, as she was, between her duty to her new patient, 'her relationship with Khan (who had been her supervisee and was now a friend, current colleague and simultaneously her editor) who she saw as needing help, and her obligations to the profession and the public'.[38]

Despite the exigencies of this situation, Milner respected Khan in the days before his downfall; she is quoted as saying to a Khan patient, 'There is only one person who can do the magic Masud can in one or two consultations, and that is Ronnie Laing.' It is not certain whether or not this patient is in fact Miss B., but this seems likely. In any case, we know she was later referred to Milner, of whom she says, 'It was not an intense analysis but I loved it and I loved her and I learned the freedom of my own voice. We didn't talk much about my complicated feelings for Masud. I felt awkward about it and possibly she did too.' When the relationship became abusive nearing its end, the patient commented, 'The situation was past enduring and without Marion Milner I don't know how I would have held together.'[39]

Miss B. is arguably instrumental in matters of Khan's editorial career. In early 1969, he became aware that he might not automatically become editor of the *International Psychoanalytical Library* and the *International Journal*. For some time he had been Jock Sutherland's associate editor and he had good reason to suppose himself the favoured son and successor. This did not, however, proceed smoothly. Khan told Miss B. that he would resign were he not given the post. Inevitably, Miss B. reported this to Milner, who contacted Khan, letting him know that it would be a great loss to the Society were he to resign; he was needed 'in every way, brains are in such short supply'.[40] Brains he undoubtedly had, but the situation did not go well, and on 13 January 1969, he writes to Milner that he is 'very hurt and desolate with it all' and he is deeply upset that the two people 'I have served with the utmost devotion and loyalty and effort, Winnicott and Jock [Sutherland] have both failed to endorse my identity in the British Society'.[41]

Khan's role was clear in relation to Milner's next book: in 1966 he was working with her on the manuscript. She had presented some of her material as a case at the 1952 Club, persuaded by Khan, and she then invited him to come to her house and see the material. Delighted, he expected some 'sort of rough, huge sprawling manuscript'; instead it was a 'novel and amazing' experience:

> she took me downstairs to a room laden with books [. . .] and then dug out four or five paper shopping bags that were crammed full of bits and pieces of written stuff, drawings, etc. Each scrap of paper was an EVENT in itself. Most of them were written over in all directions, upside down and sideways with a particular bias towards illegibility. I stood there and gaped. She was perfectly at home in this massive, seething and still world, and knew exactly what was what. It dawned on me that Marion is an antiquarian of unintegrated states, and that suddenly gave me hope about the venture of publishing a book . . .[42]

8

SERVANT OF A PROCESS

Hands of the Living God: *the most beautifully written book on psychoanalytic themes that has ever appeared in English . . .*[1]

Looking through reviews of her great book later in life, Milner singles out and extracts words from her friend, colleague and sometime supervisee, Masud Khan, in appreciation of *Hands*: he says the text describes 'how the analyst becomes the servant of a process, one of self-healing [as she] sees all psychic processes as elements for (self-curing process.)'[2] Appropriately, it is Donald Winnicott who introduces the book on its first publication in 1969.

Winnicott opens his foreword roundly: 'Schizophrenia is about something. But what is it about?' This is a question Milner ponders deeply throughout her work, in the contact with R.D. Laing in the 1960s, in her deep reading of Searles, Bion, Rosenfeld and others, and nowhere more astutely than in her work with Susan, the named patient in *Hands of the Living God*. Winnicott flags up how Milner allows us, her audience, to take:

> [the] opportunity to look at a schizoid person without the involvement that makes thinking so difficult. By some miracle of detachment she has been able to keep track of the myriad details of a long treatment and to collate these in such a way that she and the patient do together give us a vicarious experience of the schizoid processes. All we have to do is to settle down to an involvement not with a patient but with a brilliantly objective and complete case-description.[3]

In the 'settling down' Milner gives some warning: should the reader be a lay person, they will need to give value to 'pre-logical, non-discursive modes of thinking in that part of our minds of which we are not usually conscious'. In short, the putative reader will need to be receptive at least to the idea of 'the forces by which we are lived', those forces that Milner found so crucial in *On Not Being Able to Paint* that were discussed in Chapter 6.

Central to Milner's thought in her work in that book is the idea of non-differentiation and the place of the oceanic in creative life; fittingly, *Hands* proceeds from 'a background of preoccupations both with the nature of creative process and the nature of internal perception'.[4]

Susan was a very disturbed twenty-three-year-old with a deeply difficult history of a non-separate mother, a period of ECT in which she felt she had 'lost her soul', an abusive connection with a neighbour and multiple impingements (in Winnicott's sense) on her continuity of being. The severity of her disturbance and the levels of her distress meant that the more conventional approaches to treatment in which Milner had been trained did not 'fit' this patient. Milner is also concerned about the paucity of appropriate places in which such a patient might be able to find sanctuary; she writes: 'I thought I wanted to show to anyone who would listen the urgent need of places other than mental hospitals where certain kinds of mentally ill people can be sure of a roof over their heads.'[5] And, Milner adds, since she could not contribute financially to this endeavour, the book was to be her offering to this cause. Published in 1969, and recording a treatment from 1943 until 1958/1960(?), *Hands of the Living God* shares something of the history of the psychoanalytic treatment of schizophrenia and also that of the psychotherapeutic community movement.*

Traditionally there has been much debate about the efficacy of psychoanalytic treatment for schizophrenia – Freud was sceptical about the success of treating such patients although, of course, many of the very early analysts were attached to or linked with hospitals for those termed insane. Milner, as has been seen, was closely bound up with Kleinian theory and clinicians; and Kleinians, and now post-Kleinians, are among those more recently who consider schizophrenia amenable to analytic intervention and treatment. Richard Lucas in a 2003 paper on 'The Relationship between Psychoanalysis and Schizophrenia' contends that 'After early optimism of a psychoanalytic approach, interest has waned other than in the field of first-onset psychosis.'[6] Milner is less than sanguine about the efficacy of the treatment for Susan and, after some months' work, comments on the lack of changes in her patient and her own 'growing misgivings about whether analysis could help her at all, or at least the only kind of analysis that I thought I knew how to give

---

* I am aware that this section begs the question as to whether or not Susan can correctly be called 'schizophrenic' and that the term is alternated with the milder 'schizoid' – certain commentators have (erroneously, I suggest) commented on a kind of 'insouciance diagnostique' in Milner's apparent acceptance of the psychiatric label. See Roberto P. Neuberger, 'An Imaginary Trauma?', *Journal of Lacanian Studies*, 2006. Christopher Bollas (email communication, July 2012) comments that at first Milner 'stated that it puzzled her that people saw Susan as schizophrenic and later that Susan was upset with her over the use of that term [. . .] I do know that Marion had no interest at all in diagnosis and would have taken anyone into analysis without nomenclature.' This is characteristic of the British Society members of which, unlike their central European or American counterparts, had no real interest in diagnosis.

her'. The analysis Milner has in mind here is that based on her experience 'with patients suffering from identifiable and organized neurotic complaints': clearly Susan was not one such, and Milner's learning to date did not answer in this case. It was, she tells us, only through the insistence of Winnicott that she felt able to carry on with the work[7] and begin to see what Susan called 'going crazy' could be 'partly her way of describing that very lessening of her own rigid organization which would in fact have to happen before she could find a better one'.[8]

Milner comes to realise that what she actually says, or her interpretations, did not have much impact: but if she 'could keep to this warm "holding" mood, [this] did seem to reach her', and sometimes on such an occasion Susan 'would suddenly begin to laugh at herself, and after that would say "goodbye" naturally instead of stalking out in an angry silence'.[9] Susan's analyst needed to realise that interpretations about the patient 'as a hungry infant going for what she wanted' were decidedly premature; first they had to establish a safe enough environment that would reliably hold Susan whatever she might do.

Over the years of this long analysis, Milner learned that Susan had considerable difficulty tolerating the idea that at times 'the conscious logical part of her ego might have to be abrogated temporarily during the sessions'.[10] At the outset Susan fought against even the idea of dependence 'on the unconscious forces by which she is lived'. Susan's creative urges, and Milner's work with these, find a parallel in *On Not Being Able to Paint*, in the patient's 'desperate search for that self-surrender which would lead to new life'.[11]

For much of the early stages of their work together, Susan was extremely critical of Milner's technique, and Milner herself suffered from constant misgivings about her approach. A transformative change came about only when Susan read *A Life of One's Own*, at which time she remarked, 'it was so like her she felt I must have thought she had been reading it before'.[12] This said, they still came up against a block – Susan's continued inability to grasp the idea of unconscious mental activity; she would revert often to her question, 'But in what part of my mind do I think these things?' Then Milner shifts her approach so that instead of verbalising what she thought to be Susan's unconscious fantasy or wishes, she 'began trying to keep her to the point of herself seeking to find an exact word for what she was feeling'. The difficulties with this process led Milner to consider there was some 'defect' in Susan's thinking and, in time, to connect this with blocks about considering any kind of symbolic thinking; in turn, this went back to a situation during her schooling when she reported issues with 'symbolic or metaphorical expressions' – the 'mouth or head of a river', for example. Problems with symbolism were linked with difficulties with separateness; this resulted in a block in recognising the duality that 'makes it possible to accept that a symbol is both itself and the thing it stands for, yet without being identical with it'.[13]

One day Susan came to a session quoting from the Bible the words 'and Mary pondered all these things in her heart'; this urged Milner to mull over the words and come, gradually, to the view that the pondering was required of her, as analyst, and that, crucially, it would need, as Winnicott would agree, to have a profoundly physical aspect: 'what I said was often less important than my body-mind state of being in her sessions.' Further, before there could be much change in Susan, there needed to be a change in Milner, who had to learn to 'wait and watch' rather than 'be seduced into this working too hard for her'.[14]

Milner's new approach chimed with her own creative endeavours during the period up until 1950, the publication year of *On Not Being Able to Paint*, a time when one of her prevailing preoccupations was working on blocks against psychic creativity. In *A Life of One's Own*, as Milner reminds her reader in connection with Susan's response to that text, she had discovered the positive effects of a 'wide unfocused stare' as opposed to 'a narrow, deliberative concentration'; and this, she remarks in a footnote, was to become key in the analysis of Susan who, after some years, discovered that she herself had the capacity to produce doodle drawings.[15] Milner had made just such a discovery near the start of the Second World War, at the time of the inception of *On Not Being Able to Paint*. Links with her previous book continue in *Hands*; just as Milner had needed to pay 'body-attention' in her painting so that she perceived whatever she was trying to paint with a whole body attention, so in working with Susan she needed to achieve what she calls 'full body-attention' when listening to her.[16]

A major breakthrough comes in the work when, having asked most presciently whether she '*must* lose' herself (and Milner having replied that it is not unheard of to have to lose oneself to find oneself), Susan begins to draw, the start of a sequence of an extraordinary 4,000 drawings in nine months. Milner comments:

> There was one noteworthy coincidence. Her drawings were practically all 'doodles', she said, that is, made without any conscious intention about what she was going to draw. In fact, she began them about two months before my book about my own doodle drawings was published. I had not told her anything about my book, and I had never suggested to her that she might want to draw as part of her analysis.[17]

Milner's learning from her work towards *On Not Being Able to Paint* had led her to a deep appreciation of the need for periods of non-differentiation, temporary states of fusion, of not being separate, arguably states of a very early developmental stage. Two drawings redolent of this state recalled the time when Susan was actually part of the mother's body and suggest 'that what she was unconsciously demanding of me, and nothing else would satisfy her, was an eternity of unbroken fusion and continuity of existence'.[18] The drawings allowed these thoughts to be elaborated in the analytic work. Milner had discovered that the pliability of the medium, the paint and the paper could provide a kind of 'other' with which one can achieve a very subtle interchange, a kind of ideal fusion. The finished picture could, thus, as in the case of 'a very subtle and witty portrayal of my own feelings towards Susan', help towards psychic integration.[19]

Chapter 18 of the text, Part III, the years 1951–1957, elaborates this and other core matters in Milner's handling of this case. These are years marked by 'an increasing enrichment' of Susan's personality, and the analytic work of the period revolves around one particular image brought by the patient on 7 January 1952; it is of a mother and child (see Figure 8.1) and prompts Milner to consider this 'symbol of fusion of mother and child' with an awareness of how 'the child's external world is the mother's inner world'.[20] Working with the drawings and their sheer quantity, she recognises Susan's need:

> for a continued contact with a bit of external reality which was 'other' and yet completely responsive to what came from her; the paper became as it were a substitute for the responsive ideal mother, receiving the slightest movement of her hand and giving it back into her eyes, a hand-and-eye co-ordinated interchange . . .

The materials here and the picture produced equate to a Winnicottian transitional object* – Milner suggests this, I think, as she comments that the painting offers 'a relation to an ideal mother-me who would be with her whenever she needed, since there would always be a pencil and paper handy to be held and touched'.[21] Her drawings thus were 'constantly creating a bridge between me and herself'; and even when they were not seen or interpreted by Milner, offered a substitute for 'the mirror her mother had never been able to be'. They also provided access to deep levels of self-knowledge from which ECT had cut her off.

Benign bridge and mirror as the drawings were, they also carried an aggressive component:

> for, through the confusions and obscurity of the drawings she was surely unloading into me not only what she felt was her own 'craziness' but also all her mother's; thus it could be said that the flood of drawings was partly intended to drive me mad as she felt she had been driven mad.[22]

---

* It is notable that when Milner was absent and unable to meet with her patient (when she was on holiday, for instance) she received letters from Susan. There is evidence, for example, that this was the case on occasions when Milner was at Hadleigh in Suffolk and Susan in hospital. This maintaining of a connection by letter would have been unusual for British psychoanalysts of the time. It is comparable to the maintaining of email contact between clinician and patient during absences. The letters can, perhaps, also be seen as a transitional phenomenon. (These papers are not open for general access.)

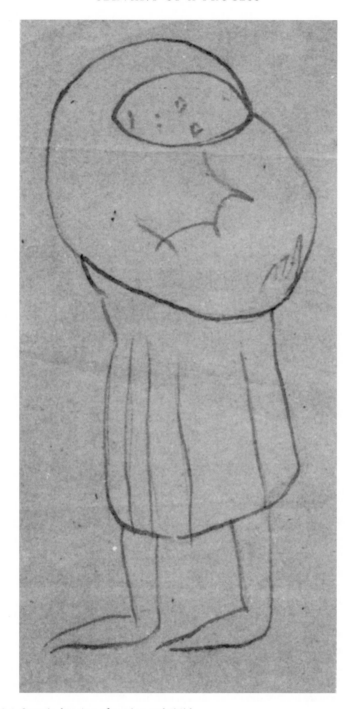

Figure 8.1 Susan's drawing of mother and child

Here Milner references Searles[23] and reflects on how easily Susan could have been driven crazy by the fluctuations in her mother's attitude towards her, changes from great idealisation to seeing everything as her daughter's fault.

Despite employing a number of psychoanalytic concepts in her work with Susan, including those from both Klein (the paranoid-schizoid position and the depressive position, for instance) and Anna Freud (the concept of 'identity with the aggressor'), Milner still felt 'some essential instrument for my thinking was missing'. Re-considering a previous transformative change in her patient, Milner recalls, *in her own life*, moments of 'an internal act of some kind of surrender; for here I remembered how Susan had said that her high moments at N.I [the hospital where she had had ECT] had also come after a deliberate act of self-surrender'.[24]

Milner is typically generous in calling on her own experience to expand the insights and horizons of her patient; similarly, as in *On Not Being Able to Paint* and as in her 'dialogue' with Michael Eigen (pp. 84–87), here she records, how she had:

> become increasingly interested in trying to understand more about the whole process of fusion, merging, interpenetrating [. . .] for I had been slowly coming to the conclusion that the acceptance of a phase of some kind of fusion was necessary for all creative work whether the work is within the psyche or in the outer world.[25]

Fusion for Milner is not, as in many of the psychoanalytic textbooks of her time, just an attempted escape to the memory of being an infant at the mother's breast; it is 'one end of a constantly alternating polarity which is the basis of all psychic creativity, and therefore of symbol formation and psychic growth'.[26]

These ideas link not only with her previous book and with Eigen but also with Adrian Stokes whose paper entitled 'Form in Art' Milner had read in 1952 and found much in it that helped clarify her own thesis.[27] Her view of the necessary fusion in creativity coincided with his: 'As well as the vivid impress of self-contained totalities we reach, at the instance of aesthetic sensation, the "oceanic" feeling, upheld by some of the qualities of id "language", such as interchangeability, from which poetic identifications flow.'[28]

Milner was very much in touch with the thinking and papers of Stokes during this period of her analysis of Susan as she was also with the work of Margaret Little. Little was analysed by Ella Sharpe from 1940 to 1947 and became a member of the British Psychoanalytical Society; she sought further analysis with Winnicott at the time of a psychotic breakdown in 1949. Best known for her work on counter-transference, she was, like Milner, also a painter and a poet. From the late 1950s Milner was very much aware of Little's work, and affectionate letters show that they remained friends, with plans for Milner's visits to Little's home to the fore until Little's death in 1994.[29] As might be expected, Milner gives respectful reference to Little's work in *Hands*. To quote from a footnote to Chapter 18:

> there were other papers in the British Psycho-analytical Society which continued to enrich my thinking on this theme of the role of the state of fusion of subject and object, particularly Margaret Little's work on how the illusion of unity affects the transference and the countertransference . . .[30]

This 'unity' or fusion, however – as Milner so sensitively knew from her work with the boy and his wartime soldiers onwards, discussed on page 48 – required certain conditions in the environment; a 'protective framework' was mandatory. Susan's symbol and Milner's painting once more fertilise each other:

> Not only through Susan's constant use of the symbol of the frame, but also through my own studies of painting, I had become very interested in the role of the frame of a picture, that which marks off a different kind of reality from that of everyday life, just as the frame of the room and the fixed period of time mark off the analytic session.[31]

She reports here becoming very involved with the 'internal aspects' of the frame and with how to reach those concentrated states of mind in which 'one creates one's own inner frame' – this, for Milner, is vital in creating both ideas and works of art, and, one might say, in forging something new in the relation of analyst and patient. Milner did not, however, see one crucial refinement of these ideas until one of Susan's post-ECT drawings declared its meaning: 'I had not yet seen that one of the earliest roots of such a capacity might be the experience of being held in one's mother's arms.'[32]

Why was it, Milner asks herself, that Susan should bring this particular image after nine years? Milner cogitates deeply on this question, wondering, after a while, if it were not possible that Susan was indicating 'she herself could now take responsibility for what she knew she needed to find again, in some token way, the encircling arms, the re-discovered sense of the hands of the living god that she had had however precariously in N.I.'.[33]

This rich and many-layered image helped Milner become aware that, as analyst with Susan at this stage in the work, she needs herself 'to achieve, knowingly, a partially undifferentiated and indeterminate state'.[34] This was a state of a kind of emptiness, 'an empty circle' with no pressing need to find interpretations; it could be seen as a 'good self-loss', a relinquishing of self-images; relating to this was something else of which Milner had become centrally aware in her studies of painting: that there must be 'moments in making a picture when one seemed to have lost all the original inspiration and nothing good was emerging, a kind of despair that always came, if the picture was to be any good at all.'.[35] This despair Milner also saw reflected in the post-ECT image brought to her nine years into the analysis, an image which, in some way, threatened her sense that she could do anything to help this patient.

There was another danger here: a patient so subtly and extensively demanding as Susan could very easily tempt the clinician into 'the omnipotent saviour role'; as an aside, I would compare Susan with Berke's – and later the playwright David Edgar's – Mary Barnes in the Kingsley Hall Community in the 1960s, with her extremely demanding regressions, and deeply challenging creative products. Mary's deficits, at times, called forth some narcissistic responses in her community and in those influenced by Berke's well-known work with her.[36] Milner, though, knew very well indeed that 'no one in this kind of work can ever cure another but only help to release the self-curing forces'. She did know, too, that she 'had not been sufficiently alert to interpreting the omnipotent image that she so constantly tried to foist on to me.'[37]

At this point, 1957, some fourteen years into Susan's analysis, the issue of Klein's work on envy comes to the fore: *Envy and Gratitude* was published in this year and with it Klein's view of envy as one of the deepest causes of psychic illness – 'envy being seen in terms of an extra amount that certain people are born with and which interferes with any dependent relation to the not-me source of goodness'. At this point Milner parts company with Klein: certainly Susan did say she was envious at times, but this could not be seen as primary; Susan was, too, aware of how destructive envy could be, how much it was part of the repertoire of her own personal devil who 'tramples underfoot what isn't his', as she had expressed it in one session.[38] But Milner was more inclined to consider this in two ways, neither of which 'required the hypothesis of an extra amount of inborn envy'. First, Milner's, in my view, more enlightened hypothesis was that envy was 'the result of having to recognize the me-not-me distinction prematurely, being forced into emerging from primary omnipotence before the infant psyche is ready to contain the pains of recognized separateness'. Second, the destructiveness bespoke a need to 'obliterate the too exciting stimulus, the image of the too tantalizing mother who does not adapt herself consistently and therefore provokes a level of excited desire for a longer period than can be tolerated'[39] – a chilling description of Susan's mother.

Susan and Milner's work in this area lead inevitably to some consideration on Milner's part of Freud's death instinct, aiming at 'destroying connections' and 'reducing all to the inorganic'. This central chapter ends on a creative note: Milner, while appreciating much about 'the deflection of the death instinct outwards' had not hitherto 'been able to see at all clearly was that this urge to be nothing, when recognized and accepted, could surely become part of the process that leads to a new birth, both of self and of other, a new birth that has to be preceded by a psychic "death."'[40]

Involved in this new birth was the question of how Susan was to find a way of expressing her feelings, once she was able to react to Milner, who, in 1955, wrote about just this issue in a paper called 'The Communication of Primary Sensual Experience' sub-titled 'The Yell of Joy'. This paper focused on the conflict between Susan's wish to share her feelings by communicating them and her 'striving after a totality of experience, fusion, primary unity'.[41]

One especial conceptual tool for Milner's thinking at this time was the paper by Ehrenzweig, 'The Creative Surrender', commented upon above in relation to *An Experiment in Leisure*. In this paper Ehrenzweig, not himself an analyst, had put forward the idea that:

> [Milner's] preoccupation with the mythology of the Dying God was not only to do with sadomasochistic fantasies and attacks on the superego [. . .] but also an intuition of the ego state that is a necessary phase in all creative experience; that is, the learning how to let go, recurrently, the usual activities of conscious discursive thought.[42]

The notion of alternating ego states and their interplay was at the centre of Milner's 1956 paper on 'Psychoanalysis and Art', where she uses Susan's images of alternating circles as examples, together with pictures from Blake's *Job*, as well as further (earlier) ideas of Ehrenzweig.

In thinking about the interplay of different mind states, Milner found herself drawn towards the term 'manic-depressive swing'; this had problems, however, with terms such as 'manic' and 'mania' hardly being true to Susan's moments of 'surrendering herself to an ideal something'; in a sub-section of the text, 'Being a Saint', Milner considers Susan's aspirations; what kept surfacing in their work was 'her tremendous ideal of loving self-surrender'[43] – all those whom Susan most loved and admired were people who dedicated their lives to something; at one point, Susan said she wished to be a saint.

Interestingly, Milner turns here, as frequently in her texts, to Blake: to Blake's *Job*. Milner's engagement with Blake goes back a long way. His combination of the visionary, the other-worldly, the poetic and self-states on the edges of insanity clearly appealed to her. Additionally, Milner has been seen as a mystic, as was Blake.[44] (This is discussed in more detail in Chapter 11.)

Milner reminds us how, in *Job*, Blake gives a final twist to the story by showing the start of his inner catastrophe, that is, after the loss of all his children and possessions, when he shares his last crust with a beggar. Milner had thought a great deal about why it was at this moment that Blake chose to show God giving Satan the power to affect both Job's body and soul. At first she thought it was to do with Job's denial of his destructive wishes with Satan standing for his split-off rage; then she began to wonder if, perhaps, Susan's ideal of self-dedication might not contain within some seeds of disaster; might this kind of concern with one's self-image cut a person off from

113

'plunging into the regenerative sea of self-loss, of undifferentiation, of not-being?' Then there was something else to be taken into account: cloaked in Susan's wish to be a saint, might there not be:

> [a] striving after a psychic state that did not have its roots either in the neurotic structure of a savage superego, nor in undigested infantile shocks, but something that would be a true 'state of grace', a state of being that could be the true achievement of maturity?[45]

If this hypothesis is maintained, might it not thus be that Susan had an intuition about the nature of psychic creative process, embedded in her wish for complete self-giving, that psychic emptiness has to be achieved over and over again, a 'wiping out of all old ideas', before there can be a re-birth? This, in turn, could link up with what Blake called 'the annihilation of the selfhood'.[46]

All these fertile ideas, however, had no very marked affect on Susan's symptoms, and her analyst, again, asked herself what it might be that she was leaving out. Milner – allowing, we might say, herself to free associate around this question – remembered how a certain rhyme had been circulating in her mind as she wrote *Hands*. This was the long 'nursery saga' of the old woman trying to bring her pig home from market and her many efforts to get over the animal's refusal to move:

> She asks the dog to bite it, but it will not; nor will the stick beat the dog, nor the fire burn the stick, and so on, through seven more refusals to move: the water, the ox, the pitcher, the rope, the rat, the cat, the cow. But the cat will not kill the rat unless it gets milk from the cow, and the cow will not give milk till it gets hay from the haymakers. However, when the old woman asks the haymakers for the hay they say they will give it if she fetches them a bucket of water from the stream; which she does. And then all of the others in turn get what they have asked for, and in return do what she has asked, and so she does get home that night with her pig.[47]

Always intrigued by this tale, Milner was particularly struck by the fact that it was the fetching of the bucket of water that had overcome all the refusals. For her, the whole affair 'became a kind of symbolic epitome for me of my struggle with Susan, since no talk about breasts and milk seemed to have achieved anything in the easing of her phobias'.[48] However, the bucket of water prompts Milner and her patient to think further about the themes of water in the analytic work; and when, in 1957, Susan again started to draw, water was, once more, central – this time, though, always 'as a supporting medium'. At this time, Milner had been attending to a careful reading of those papers (Kleinian, in the main) by clinicians such as Bion and Rosenfeld

114

on the analysis of schizophrenics – here she refers to Susan without comment as 'schizophrenic'.[49] However, such papers focused largely on defence mechanisms such as splitting and projective identification, approaches that did not speak to Susan at all, calling forth only a 'dismayed kind of hopelessness' as to how such splits could ever be healed.[50] The nursery rhyme, with its water theme, was a much more fruitful clue.

Part IV of the text, covering the years 1957–1958, looks at Susan's re-entry into the world, considers the symbol of water and the resumption of Susan's drawing (but only in the frame of the sessions themselves) and looks at certain moments of particular significance. To take just one image, Susan expresses a certain desire for a fresh start, and there is a drawing with a new theme: 'Right in the centre of the page is a big sailing yacht with two figures on board, very actively managing the sails (its seems to have no rudder), and a keel going right deep down into the water.' This, for Milner, showed some acceptance of the situation of analysis, with the ship representing 'both of us cooperating in it [. . .] while the lack of rudder can refer to her feeling that she has not, consciously, any idea where we are going'. This, surely, Milner thinks, is 'a move towards accepting the truth that her conscious mind cannot steer the process, nor can mine'.[51]

Holding true, as ever, to this principle, Milner abstains from interpreting the next image (of a Christ figure): 'Again I say very little about this, since there does seem to be a process at work which I do not dare risk interrupting.'[52] As this process continues, Susan's drawings focus on re-birth: a little duck getting ready to come out and a chrysalis. The images are combined with a new appreciation of Milner and doubts about, if she were to come out into the world, who would be there to receive her? Love is difficult for her to conceptualise at this point – a drawing of a spider connects with a maternal image of potential entrapment and devouring. And, says, Milner, 'is not this why she hates love: it is for her too mixed up with a spider's kind of loving, both in her mother and herself'.[53]

A dream of a Christmas card, revealing the issue of expressing feelings of appreciation, heralds Susan's struggle 'with the momentous task of making me real', a task hinted at in her comment, a session or two previously, as to how well her analyst looked after the break. An image of a duck, now supported by water, actually swimming, and even looking a little like a swan, prompted Milner also to reflect upon the role of her own body state:

> It served also to remind me of my own observation (which I was always forgetting): that it was when I was able to be calmly aware of my own body-weight, not impatiently seeking to bring about changes in her but finding nourishment in my own sense of being, it was then that there seemed to be some lessening of tensions and rigidities in her.[54]

Their interactive body awareness seems to lead to Milner suddenly finding herself able to see Susan as a woman. The sequence here is particularly striking: she sees her patient as a woman; Susan says there is a taste of lilies, of funerals in the room, and wonders if Milner will die. Milner says 'will I last long enough for you?' Susan says 'yes.' She then tells Milner that when standing by the bus, she suddenly had a feeling 'that here she was with a body'. After this, an image of a nailed-up cat brings the analyst to ask: 'Could she be saying that she intuitively perceived something in my own thinking that was holding up our progress?' One element in this hold-up was Susan's dread of being eaten, her primitive way of seeing her own sexuality – also an anxiety that came into the analysis as the fear that Milner would consume her.[55]

After the nailed-up cat come images of her developing sexuality and of the idea of losing herself to find herself; then, asking – or rather, listening – to the poets once more, as Freud had implied,[56] Milner finds a line from Blake resounding in her head: 'Holy Generation, image of Regeneration'.[57] It was, she tells us, through this kind of material that she was able to try and formulate Susan's deepest problem 'in terms of her denial of her own urge to become something; for I remembered her recurrent insistence that 'You can't have life without opposites'. Milner remembers concurrently, Blake's 'without contraries there is no progression'.[58]

Having found a body, and begun to think of her own sexuality, Susan now works on 'having a heart that can bear the pangs of grief', including the loss of separation, and draws her first 'landscapes'.[59] A key session on 28 May 1959 reveals the hidden content underlying all Susan's symptoms – that is, 'her dread of blushing, her dread that she will throw herself out of, or under a train, her inhibition over piano-playing, her compulsion to turn away her head'. All these can, perhaps, come down to intolerable rage and hate at witnessing the primal scene. Much primal scene material arises at this point, not only in the work around her head turning but also in her dreams and shows that she has now reached a much higher level of cognition and, importantly, was nearer to thinking of people as 'whole entities, not just as parts of bodies'.[60] The symptom of head turning now seems to Milner a re-living of the original (primal) situation with her parents, 'magically wiping out herself and me in the analysis'. Nina Farhi's comments on the analyst's survival with certain patients are apposite here: 'the primary quality that sustains us is our ability to endure. This endurance carries with it, in the midst of deeply adverse conditions, overtones of the inherent attribute of survival that forms a part of the Self at birth.'[61] By the close of this section on 'Her First Landscapes . . .' there are signs that things are starting to 'join up' – since she had had ECT one of Susan's most poignant complaints is that 'nothing has joined up'; now, the analytic couple are discovering that in 'the undifferentiated phase they can' join up.[62]

Joining up involved a new symbol for Susan – the use of a diagonal, a symbol of the problem of dividing a primary wholeness into two, which emerged in the context of her efforts to accept duality and on issues around the boundary, including that which is the skin.[63] In working with Susan on all these boundary issues and divisions, it is notable that Milner, in her notes, makes reference to R.D. Laing's *The Divided Self*, which she now finds 'contained vivid descriptions of some of Susan's main problems, particularly the statement that the basic doubt, in this state, is about one's own existence, including the feeling that one only exists if seen by others'. Laing also talks of what he calls 'a process of self-annihilation' and the relation of the schizophrenic state to other members of the family. Certainly, writes Milner, 'there were many hints that her mother had needed Susan's illness'.[64]

Susan moves away from the position, identified by Laing, of being able to feel real only in the eyes of others, and in the 'diagonal' section of the text produces further new kinds of image: a realistic drawing of a vase of anemones, for one – 'all too lively' as she sees it and yet full of new life – and a realistic portrait of Milner for another.[65] The end of the chapter brings a much more permeable image of the diagonal, with associations of laughter for the analyst, which caused Milner to think Susan

> was now nearer achieving an awareness of the inner surface or threshold between consciousness and unconsciousness, the idea of a permeable boundary which was also expressed in her use of the symbol of water; not only because of its undifferentiated quality, but also because of the quality of its surface which permits a two-way traffic across it, in that it can be emerged from or plunged into.[66]

The last section of this phase, 'The proudman dream and return to the world' finds Milner, for the first time, feeling 'in contact with [Susan] in a way that had never happened before' and feeling no need to smoke. Susan meanwhile is able to report: 'I am in the world for the first time in 16 years.'[67]

Part V, 'What Followed', opens with Milner's 'Crystallisation of Theory' and considers the new sense of communion and relationship in the analytic couple. Milner is preoccupied with a paper for the Athens Congress of 1960 on 'Painting and Internal Body Awareness', and she turns again to questions of the body and the impact on her work with Susan. Milner, over the years with Susan, had often been surprised, even dismayed, to note the poor attention paid in psychoanalytic literature to 'the ego function of learning deliberately to relax the whole body.'[68] Further, only in the writings of Wilhelm Reich, controversial psychiatrist and psychoanalyst, ultimately discredited for overstepping body boundaries in transferential work, had she found anything approaching what she had in her pre-analytic writings called the 'answering activity'.[69] This was 'the sensation of an inner warm outspreading flow, beginning in whatever part of one's body one was attending to and often then spreading to the rest of the body, something that might be described as an inner release or discharge.'[70]

117

Attentive as ever to her breathing, Milner looks at this in Susan, asking if her patient's image of an expanding, 'raying out' flower form might indicate, in symbolic form, an 'awareness of the expanding and contracting rhythm of the chest in breathing'. Milner parallels this with observations of her own breathing, noticing that when lying down, the relaxing of muscular tensions could result in a sensation of 'total melting', leaving self-awareness changed 'into a dark warm velvety puddle'.[71] This image segued into recollections of Susan's water imagery, and, especially, those pictures showing water as a supporting medium with the rhythm of lines like waves. Retrospectively, Milner sees how closely the paper on which she was engaged was linked to Susan's issues with background awareness. At the time, however, this was not in the forefront of her thinking – a paper by Adrian Stokes, given to the London Imago Society in 1959, was the immediate impetus. This paper was entitled 'Some connections and differences between visionary and aesthetic experiences', and Milner's response to it links her to a mystical tradition.[72] In his paper Stokes compares the experiences induced by the drug mescalin described by Aldous Huxley with one of Ruskin's when, as a young man, he was travelling in Italy for his health and stopping at an inn:

> he had felt so ill that he doubted his ability to continue his journey; feeling in despair he had staggered out of the inn along a cart-track and lain down on the bank, unable to go any farther. But then he had found himself staring at an aspen tree by the roadside and finally he had sat up and begun to draw it. He had drawn the whole tree and in doing so had had an intense imaginative emotional experience of understanding of all trees, as well as finding that his feeling of being close to death had vanished so that he was able to continue his journey to Italy.[73]

Stokes wrote in his paper of Ruskin's having 'gained a potency feeling' and, in psychoanalytic terms, having 'gained the measure of a good incorporated object'. Milner wished to elaborate this, adding the words 'good subject', intending to emphasise the 'external tree' as also, paradoxically:

> the symbol for this direct non-symbolic internal psycho-physical awareness of the body: in fact a symbol for the matrix of being, the on-going background which can yet become foreground if one learns the skill of directing attention inwards to one's own sense of being.[74]

Whatever the transcendental implications of Huxley's views, and Stokes's referencing of them, Milner felt there was more to be said about 'one's own ground of being', and she wanted to attend to 'what happens when consciousness does suffuse the whole inner background at the same time letting go all clinging to visual or auditory images'. It certainly appeared to her that

118

the meeting of opposites, or 'a dialectical reunion' can have an ecstatic or 'divine quality'. This view prompted her to question or at least re-think psychoanalytic views on auto-erotic and narcissistic states (she references Hoffer and Paula Heimann), positing the idea that there can be an effort 'to reach a beneficent kind of narcissism, a primary self-enjoyment which is in fact a psychic investment in the whole body'.[75]

These ideas made Milner re-visit Susan's use of the tree symbol, an image that she had employed in 1958 at the same time as she was experimenting with her 'new' diagonal line. Soon, Milner tells us, she drew a further tree, but this time it is a sign of Susan's 'growing sense of her own separate existence', standing upright with a body, with her feet on the ground.[76] As analyst Milner conceptualised the tree as 'a symbol for the ego's direct non-symbolic sense of its own being'; and here, she refers to the influence upon her of many papers of Bion's on the subject of 'schizophrenic ways of thinking' (interestingly, here, also, she does use the term schizophrenic). Particularly apposite to her work with Susan was Bion's 'view that the unwanted bits of the personality that may be expelled may be the inchoate elements of thought'. For Bion, it is this expulsion of the primary matrix from which thought derives that distinguishes the psychotic from the non-psychotic parts of the personality. Bion's 'inchoate state' was, for Milner, what Susan seemed to mean when she remarked that, after the ECT, she had lost her background. It was also what Milner had been attempting to describe when thinking her way through ideas about 'primary relatedness to one's own body, from inside'.[77]

The rest of Susan's analysis, that is, after January 1959, consisted of her struggles to realise her recent analytic achievements. The time leading up to her mother's death clarifies still further the lack of separation afforded her daughter by this mother who was unable to recognise her devotion or give any thanks for it. Brought a box of chocolates by Susan, her mother simply ate them all without offering her a single one.

On her mother's last day, however, Susan told Milner that there was a great change in her face, almost as if the mother was 'there' for the first time – as if she had only achieved birth at the time of her death. 'Of course,' writes Milner, 'I had no means of knowing whether this had actually happened or whether it was only something Susan had projected.' Whichever might have been the truth, the fact of Susan telling Milner about it was 'another expression of her intuition that she must lose herself to find herself, that only by accepting psychic "death" will she herself be completely "there"'.[78]

The last chapter, which I will discuss in some detail, is sub-titled 'The Place of Transformation' and deals with something of what is meant by this coming to be 'there'. The battle for independence, for Susan, continues. Married now, and with more security than ever before, she still suffers from a dread of harming herself or harming a child and is unable to travel on the Underground without her husband, for fear of throwing herself under a train. A previous dream image of a 'mad white horse' suggested to Milner that this continuing symptom might be an effort 'to by-pass the dread of being passively in the power of the inner mad-white-horse-me'; it was as if a self-chosen death 'was preferable to the continued dread of feeling destroyed from the inside'.[79] Milner's notes state that she was again reminded of Anna Freud's 1951 paper about how the surrender to the loved object is dreaded as a return to primary identification:[80] 'for I saw how Susan's dream of the mad white horse was partly her way of symbolizing her dread of merging with a mother who was really mad, as in the transference, she sometimes felt me to be'.[81]

Despite 'getting by' in the world and relating herself to common-sense reality, Susan had 'not yet learnt how to relate herself to her own creative urges', and she still struggled with the idea of her products as good or bad. What could her analyst do in this situation? Once more, Milner takes on the need to use herself in a new way:

> I came to feel sure she could not do it until I could, more fully than I had ever done before [. . .] I had to learn how to combat the urge to make interpretations out of my own need to help her, learn once more how to accept the apparent chaos, sink down into my own depths and simply wait.[82]

A dream of a pregnant woman and a birth reveals anxieties about the publication of Susan's case history in *Hands of the Living God*; and this is followed by a new symptom – difficulties in swallowing and, from there, the ability to drink only in very small sips. Symptomatic and dream details of this kind enabled Milner and Susan to reach 'a view of her illness as a truly mutual creation'.[83] The climax of her analysis of her life myth came when, one day, Susan arrived feeling terrible, and then ended the session saying, for the first time ever, 'I feel better'. Prior to this she had never felt 'the labourer is worthy of his hire'; and, indeed, 'she had devoted her life to trying to prove that she was not and never had been greedy'.[84]

Here Milner comments that she finds a particular formulation of the 'schizoid state' helpful – that is, one seeing it as a profound split between aggression and tenderness. In the relevant session Susan had made known that she could experience the analysis as breast feeding *and* allow for concern for her analyst's continued existence.[85] Once more, Milner follows Freud's dictum and 'asks the poets' to help develop and clarify her thought, There was one rhyme of Blake's that had always offered her 'a mnemonic through the intricacies of Freudian theory':

> The Angel that presided o'er my birth
> Said, 'Little creature, form'd of joy and mirth
> Go, love without the help of anything on earth.[86]

Blake's lines appealed to Milner because they focused on the idea that coming to maturity needs 'the capacity to set up inside one the fantasy of containing parents who love each other and can be conceived of as creating, in an act of joy and mirth'. With particular relevance to Susan's situation, Blake also, for Milner, seemed to be hinting in his words 'love without the help of anything on earth' that a person can create inside themselves a loving parental couple no matter how bad the real parents have been. Perhaps Blake's lines also hinted at a moment when a person could so believe in their own capacity for loving that they could stand alone, even tolerate real persecution, without losing belief in their own vision. Whether or not Susan would be able to find this capacity to be alone remained something of an open question – although Milner is cautiously optimistic that, having allowed herself to be 'fed' by a good analytic experience, Susan may now be able to let it go, to mourn the loss, and allow someone else to have it: 'that is, to let me go, which would be like giving a new mother and father, created out of the analytic experience, back to each other so that they can be happy together inside her'.[87]

In reviewing Susan's progress in analysis, Milner now returns to the use of the diagonal, a key image and, arguably, 'her way of illustrating the processes of projection and introjection between self and other, infant and mother, patient and analyst'. In the work, Milner had seen Susan 'come to try to lessen the rigidity of the dividing line so that there could be an easy two-way traffic across it, even an interpenetration'.[88]

Courageous as ever in acknowledging her 'mistakes', Milner now reviews her own negotiations and struggles with Susan's material of 'ecstatic experiences'; it had been an error to attempt to relate these to memory of feeding at the breast, as an orthodox Kleinian reading might well suggest; what Susan was concerned with was not the 'satisfaction of instinct but the establishing a sense of being'.[89] In her explorations in painting, Milner had found that the 'other' has to be created before it can be perceived; it had taken rather longer for this fact to be registered in her clinical work. She had been writing of the need to find a bridge to external reality in painting and the role of art in providing this, a place where the subjective and objective could become fused; but it had taken a long time for her to relate this to her analytic work with Susan. Eventually, the analysis of an image of spitting into a cup (the section on the 'Saliva in the Cup'), interpreted by Milner as 'projecting a bit of herself into me-mother-cup and then re-incorporating it',[90] led to the analysis having a different tone and a phase in which Susan was able to let her analyst know of the depth of her destructiveness. Milner was not 'fully real' for Susan, and at this point of being real, Susan was able to face the psychic reality of this. Milner had now seen the aggression of all the nursery rhyme animals and this could be freed.

Fascinatingly, this happened within the analysis in terms of the trees in Milner's garden – they had been in Susan's full view throughout the analysis but she had shown no sign of being aware of them. Suddenly, at the start of a session, she asks if the pear tree had blossomed (it had the week before): 'Now she thinks of a disease that kills pear trees, so that they have to be cut

121

down and destroyed.' Susan was thus now able to face the 'depths of her ambivalence towards me, instead of splitting off the love from the hate and projecting outwards either the one or the other'.[91]

During this last phase of Susan's analysis there was one final image that recurred in Milner's mind, an image from biology that linked back also the nursery rhyme and the bucket of water:

> I had read somewhere, and do not know whether it has been confirmed by other observers, that when the caterpillar turns into a crysalis [sic] all its internal organs dissolve into a fluid and that it is from this that the new organs and shape of the butterfly somehow emerge.[92]

Milner ends her account by questioning the future but feeling a sense of Susan's future: 'I do have some sort of belief that she may find that the process of transformation that has been initiated in analysis will continue [. . .] She has installed within herself the womb-like crucible of the analytic room enough to be able to go on growing.'[93]

Adam Phillips can have the last word here; he tells us, in his New Introduction to the text, of conversations he had with Milner towards the end of her life; once he had asked about Susan and whether the analysis had worked: '"Of course she never got better," she said briskly and there was a pause. And then she said, "but we got somewhere, she got somewhere", and there was another pause, and she said, "better".'[94]

Some critical views

Contemporary reviews in 1969–1970 of *Hands* stress the 'broadening influence' of Milner's work in this text, appreciating that she has not fallen 'into the hands of a theoretical framework'; Gorer, quoted at the opening of this chapter, praises the beautiful writing, and appreciates Milner's great awareness of her own 'body states'; 'I know', he writes, 'of no other study where the bodies of both the analyst and the patient are so solidly present.' The book for him provides also, as *A Life* did for Auden, many 'of the pleasures of a detective story'. He singles out the fact that Susan's drawings were a gift to her analyst, commenting on the 'unemphasized assumption about the equality of the patient. One accepts gifts from an equal.'[95]

Charles Kligerman, in a review from which Milner has extracted sections on a re-visit, welcomes the new book as:

> an extraordinary and often deeply moving account of a schizoid young woman that lasted over twenty years [. . .] she not only offers the unique opportunity to study the clinical course of such an extended treatment but has also detailed with remarkable candour her own inner probing and her ceaseless struggle to understand the patient.

Kligerman also points out (and Milner has extracted the comment for her own compilation of reviews) that the drawings 'appear to have functioned as vital intermediary agents, not only as transitional objects in Winnicott's sense but as forms of 'transitional self' that, when studied by the analyst and patient together, provided a 'prestage of a "mirror transference", a way station towards a stabilized self-cathexis and individuation'. He finds it a book 'bursting with ideas' and stresses how full of insight it is that it is 'both clinical and poetical'. He appreciates the fact that 'Mrs Milner grinds no theoretical axes and is quite eclectic in using any conceptualization that seems to fit, including the ideas of Jung and Zen'.[96]

Guntrip – in an extended piece in the same year (1970), again re-visited by Milner – was asked (presumably by the *International Journal of Psychoanalysis*) to comment on the methodology of case presentation on which clarification of theory depends. This is, of course, very much a current issue in the twenty-first century with a culture of hyper-confidentiality. Guntrip is arguably ahead of his time as he writes: 'The problem is that much of the case material is too confidential for publication. This patient, who agreed to the public revelation of her intimate personal life, is doing an outstanding service to mankind, and calls for our gratitude.' He recognises that Milner operates primarily not as a scientist, 'but as an artist, sensitively and so therapeutically experiencing, valuing, a human subject'. He praises her kind of 'reporting' of the process, for giving us 'as much of the sheer material as is possible' and then leaving us 'to learn from it ourselves, as she had to do'.

The book, exhorts Guntrip, 'requires not just reading but long pondering'; the aim, he states, of psychoanalysis is not 'the cure of illness' but 'the slow process of understanding and liberating a choked and distorted personality [. . .] This is not "curing an illness" but "growing a person".' Looking to the future, he remarks, 'Milner's book should give pause to the "scientific optimists", if they will read it, who tell the public that in 20 years GPs will cure all mental illness with pills.' Twenty years has long gone: and the function of analysis posited here by Guntrip still holds true, that is, 'to clear the ground and make the ultimate problem accessible, that of enabling a stunted and malformed mentality to grow into a spontaneous individual self'.[97]

Lore Schacht, Independent Group analyst (and one of Milner's supervisees), approves Milner's 'flexible approach,' which was 'far away from a rigid way of thinking and which made her also ask the writing of analysts of different schools apart from poets and philosophers for advice'; and she places *Hands* within the tradition of 'the great case histories as they were started by Freud'.[98] Later, Jean Kadmon, the artist, poet and painter, writing in 1992 in the *Jerusalem Post Magazine*, comments that Milner's understanding 'of the well-springs of creativity was more crystallised than in her earlier work' (she names *On Not Being Able to Paint*); while agreeing with Winnicott that *Hands* will 'become a source book', she says she has certainly 'found it one in any realm of thought dealing with the mind. This includes Child Development, of course, but also mysticism and philosophy.'[99]

Gustav Bychowski, writing in *American Imago* in 1971, approves of Milner's expanding of her insights in *On Not Being Able to Paint* 'in a most imaginative and productive way' and her handling of a 'fascinating process' in which was evident 'the constant self-awareness of the analyst'.[100] An essay of the early 1970s by Marian Strachan praises 'one of the exciting features of the case study is the variety of sources she draws upon to increase her own understanding'. Like Gorer, who wrote that the members of the analytic pair were well matched in their artistic sensibilities, Strachan draws attention to the communality of interests between analyst and patient: body-mind awareness; doodle drawing; and a love of the English language and of poetry.[101]

Amidst mostly positive responses, there are occasional, sometimes Kleinian, dissenting voices. One such is Peter Lomas writing in the *New Statesman* of 20 January 1970. Lomas thinks that the word 'illusion' is incorrect when describing 'the state of mind – common to infancy, artistic creativity, mental illness and regression'. He continues: 'It seems to me more a selection for attention, of a different area of experience – an awareness of a psychological union which really exists, using a mode of perception just as valid as that which enables us logically to separate the things around us.'[102]

Reviewing the book, as published in New York, one reviewer (AGW) praises Milner's 'sensitive' description of the treatment but comments upon the omission of the work done by Margaret Naumburg in the United States and Ainsley Meares in Australia.[103] A further American commentator, Aaron H. Esman, approves Milner's 'sensitive, empathic and untiring efforts' but has an important reservation:

> all this is couched in the language and constructs of the Kleinian school: distinctions between symbol and metaphor are lost and reconstructions of the earliest self and object representations are derived from dream interpretations without benefit of associative confirmation from the patient.[104]

Certain commentators in very recent years would agree with Esman's dismay about the apparent stranglehold of Kleinian thought. In her ground-breaking paper 'The Hands of the Living God: Finding the Familiar in the Unfamiliar' Nina Farhi, who saw the continuing of Milner's work as her 'destiny', recognises the background importance of the 'internecine battles of the 1940s and 50s', 'psychoanalysis' own world war' and the 'stifling of analytic creativity by insisting on strict adherence to Kleinian or Freudian models of the mind'.[105]

Farhi and Saketopoulou both stress Milner's misgivings about expressing ideas to do with the importance of pre-natal or intra-uterine life. Farhi writes:

Throughout her text, Milner turns to ideas that intra-uterine life may indeed hold the key to certain profoundly primitive identifications in later life [. . .] throughout her text, Milner refers both tentatively and fearfully to the idea that there may be sequelae to a mother's conscious and unconscious negative designs towards her foetus.[106]

Milner writes, 'I thought it was perhaps enough, and *safer theoretically* [italics added] [to note] her fantasy of being in the womb without having to make any guesses about what pre-natal life actually feels like.' Farhi sees this as Milner's acknowledging of her 'undoubted fearfulness in contradicting current psychoanalytical ideas'. Saketopoulou remarks 'Farhi knew that this would be a controversial position to take and a hard one to theorize, which is, perhaps, why she needed a decade after Milner's death to write about it.'[107]

Jean White's paper 'From Survival to Creative Destiny: The Psychoanalytic Journey of Nina Farhi' recognises the affinity between Milner and Farhi, both of whom displayed 'a radical approach to clinical work with people whose level of disturbance could not be treated or theorized within the psychoanalytic orthodoxy of the time'. For White, pluralist as she is, Milner, Winnicott and, arguably, Farhi 'prioritized the quality of subjective experience in whatever form it might take, intuition, passion, and cultural and aesthetic experience'.[108]

Farhi's seminal and original concept of an 'annealed identification', discussed by White, introduces 'an extremely serviceable clinical concept into psychoanalytic work with deeply disturbed people'. It offers 'a new way to think about the psychic interpenetration between patient and analyst and complements and supplements Ogden's "intersubjective analytic third"'. But, as White rightly says, 'this is one form of intersubjectivity only', and she then goes on to propose 'a supplementary' reading of the text, inflected by Lacan.[109]

Jeanne Wolff Bernstein's Commentary complements White's with a discussion of the *placental space* developed by Farhi 'to represent the psychotic's internal experience of living in fusion with the Other'. Interestingly, Bernstein, some fifty years after Susan's analysis, is quite critical of the analytic set-up whereby this very disturbed patient came into Milner's practice:

Susan had been handed over to Milner by her former analyst Winnicott, who had taken her in as a boarder for 7 years and paid for her analysis. Milner agreed to see Susan for one shilling a session due to Susan's lack of financial means. Extraordinarily difficult patients warrant extraordinary steps to contain their psychotic functioning. However, for Milner to have received such a disturbed patient from her former analyst who had housed and paid for her analysis must have created a tremendous transferential burden and a muddle of disturbing obligations for Milner.

Bernstein wonders if Winnicott was not 'enacting an omnipotent care-taking role which he eventually aborted when Susan became too taxing on his marriage'. She sees the referral not simply as an act of confidence in Milner but as 'a sadistic and demeaning act towards her, leaving Milner isolated in a confusing maze of analytic responsibilities'. This amounts to an 'egregious transferential blundering' unaddressed by both Milner and, indeed, Farhi. Bernstein argues for an inclusion of 'the Third whose presence is so powerfully lacking in the case discussion and in the patient's life'.[110]

Dodi Goldman, in 'Letting the Sea in: Commentary on paper by Nina Farhi', is mostly in agreement with Farhi in her view of Milner 'as an unacknowledged visionary'. Farhi sees Milner as one of the earliest analysts to recognise that intersubjective processes constitute the 'fulcrum' of analytic work. Some who knew her well claim that she also very much 'regretted that the counter-transference had to be kept in check in her days as a practising analyst'.[111]

Recent critical work on *Hands* includes Mary Jacobus's 'Milner and the Myth of Marsyas' in which she, too, engages with issues of subjectivity as she considers Susan's experiences through Ovid's account of the Flaying of Marsyas. The critic Harrison 'makes Apollonian aesthetics a mask for cruelty. Like Marsyas, Susan (a working-class woman) has been turned inside out by her electric flaying and lacks a protective skin [. . .] Hers is both a skin-problem and a space-problem.'[112]

Adam Phillips's Introduction to the newly published series of Milner's work situates *Hands* for further generations of reader as he points up her enduring pluralism in a 'book about art (and writing about art), about emptiness, breathing, ordinary language, mysticism, the body, the sexes, childhood, parenting, impersonality, God, theory, exchange, change, tact, forms of inattention, belief, scepticism'.[113]

Helen Taylor Robinson recognises the book's value which is:

> To be recommended to students across many disciplines but perhaps especially the discipline of psychoanalytic therapy, students beginning or well-experienced, for the honesty and integrity it maintains throughout. This is because Milner values experiencing both the pains and suffering, as well as the pleasures, of psychoanalysis, art, philosophy, literature and religion that inform her as she travails and travels.[114]

Milner's next book, *Eternity's Sunrise,* and its discussion move to her travels — actual, geographical explorations of worlds inner and outer — journeys, as one commentator had it, 'to the centre of the mind'.[115]

9

'THE FACTS OF ART'

Milner and art psychotherapy

In *On Not Being Able to Paint* Milner discovers the facts of art for her – the blocks in creativity that hold her up and disrupt those processes needed for full expression. She becomes in the text her own analyst and, in some senses (in that she de-codes her own marks), her own art therapist. In *Hands* the named patient 'Susan' is able to discover herself, and to convey feelings to her analyst, through her drawings. Susan had attended art therapy groups when in hospital, and her image-making is undoubtedly part of her recovery; and yet, Milner, her analyst, cannot be seen as her art therapist. The nature of her role and her attitude to her patient's images can be seen in her 1955 paper 'The Communication of Sensory Experience'.[1] Milner's standing in the world of professional art psychotherapy is more complex.

Commenting on the changed psychoanalytical attitude towards the artist, Peter Fuller writes: 'As Marion Milner once explained, this shift of understanding came about when psychoanalysis confronted *the facts of art*. Until such a shift has been made, art therapy remains either a diagnostic tool, or a contradiction in terms.'[2]

What is Milner's position in relation to art therapy? Susan Hogan in her book *Healing Arts* writes that MM told her categorically that she was not an art therapist but 'an analyst who uses images as an aid to analytic treatment.'[3] (And this is what she does in *Hands*.) Indeed it was Milner's view, as it is the art therapist Martina Thomson's, that images were often subject to over-interpretation in art therapy. 'Not an art therapist' and yet Milner was Honorary President of The British Association of Art Therapists (BAAT), succeeding Adrian Hill, the founder of art therapy, to the title. Milner said of BAAT, with a touch of her characteristic resistance towards anything institutional, 'I don't do anything for them but they use my name.'[4] Nevertheless she was and is something of a figurehead for BAAT.

Hogan states that Milner's work was definitely an influence on later art therapists, and she notes her importance for Rita Simon (whose response to *On Not Being Able to Paint* has already been noted), a 'pioneer art therapist'.[5] Milner's repudiation of the term 'art therapist' for herself needs some context;

by the 1980s when Milner was involved with BAAT, art therapy (the term having gained currency in the 1940s) was a recognised discipline with respected trainings and protocols. Milner was not trained in this discipline and although, as ever, interested in the image ('not the book'),[6] did not work along those lines. She was, however, deeply interested in the use of images to explore the unconscious and, in 1939, had been much influenced by the work of Grace Pailthorpe, seen at the Guggenheim Gallery in Cork Street in London – this it was that fuelled her enthusiasm for doodles. Milner also met Irene Champernowne, founder of Withymead, a Jungian centre for the healing arts; Champernowne tried to persuade Milner to train as a Jungian analyst, but Milner, intent on learning about child analysis, did not so wish and went the Freudian route.

As Hogan (and others) state, psychoanalysis was to have some influence on art therapy via the Object Relations school, and Milner's work had later influence; Hogan says that by the time she trained in the mid-1980s it was mandatory to read Milner,[7] and Rita Simon 'described a turning point in her thinking about art therapy' as occurring when she read *On Not Being Able to Paint* in 1950. She described the book as illustrating 'our capacity to create visible symbols of things we comprehend unconsciously'. Simon was at once struck by the similarity between Milner's descriptions of doodling as a means of liberating the imagination and her own experience of facilitating art therapy groups.[8] Hogan wrote that 'Milner was able to detect underlying emotions in her free scribbles'; these she interpreted psychoanalytically as a revival of 'infantile terror, rage and despair', while creative blocks derived from a fear of re-experiencing these primitive feelings.

Hogan remains firm that Milner never regarded herself as an art therapist although her work 'is often cited by art therapists'.[9]

One such who became a great admirer and a dear friend of Milner's is Martina Thomson, whose book *On Art and Therapy* (1989) pays affectionate tribute to her friend with the 'mischievous, wicked smile' who was 'beautiful, vibrant, humorous' to the end of her life.[10] (Beautiful and vibrant, elegant and colourful are the more frequent descriptions of Milner's mien; she has been compared with Katharine Hepburn, although Harry Karnac sees a rather different presence, finding her somewhat 'nannyish' and like Joyce Grenfell to look at.)[11] Milner and Thomson met in the late 1980s because of Thomson's book; at the Provost Road house, Milner took her:

> into a light, spacious room on the upper ground floor which was then still her consulting room with its analytic couch 'Would you like some tea?' She asked, 'Or some whiskey?' 'Whiskey, I think', I said. 'Good', she said smiling openly and we never looked back. At the many meetings that followed, the bottle of Teacher's, the jug of water and two tiny glasses were ritual.[12]

By the time Thomson came to know Milner in the late 1980s she had ceased to be involved with art therapy matters, but she always retained an affection for art therapists:

> Marion lived above all by images. Images were her sustenance – images she had made (or that had made themselves, as she might have said) in paint or clay, images from dreams, from memories, those thrown up by an 'interior vagabondage', from myths, from the Bible, from poetry.[13]

David Edwards in his paper 'On Re-Reading Marion Milner' comments that, although President of BAAT, there is little direct evidence of her influence – though Case and Dalley in their excellent handbook to art therapy, say she is 'a central figure in any enquiry into art and psychoanalysis. She embodies and links thinking about analysis, creativity and the artistic process.'[14]

Edwards says that *On Not Being Able to Paint* should be required reading for all art therapists; though it was written for teachers in the first instance, from a more contemporary standpoint it 'reads much more like a method for attaining the kind of personal insight required by art therapists'. As such, it has proved 'a source of solace or inspiration' to artists and art therapists.[15]

One such was Rita Simon, already mentioned; another, quoted by Edwards, was Tessa Rawcliffe, who writes of her experiences in an educational setting: for example, much in the tradition of Milnerite thought, she ponders the 'gaps' between the ideal and what can be achieved, between perfection and reality, and the feelings of disillusion that arise when the gap is 'unbridgeable'. Following Milner, Rawcliffe confronts the deleterious effect her art college education had on her own art, the pressure involved in 'rationalising the life of her paintings'. But for her, as for very many other artists, the pressure is also internal, not merely the pressure of the institution. Self-expression is pre-empted through an inability to accept chaos as but a 'temporary stage'[16] and Rawcliffe quotes Adam Phillips on the pressures to produce a 'consensual object'.[17]

Rawcliffe, Edwards shows, found a validation of her ideas in Milner's work; Simon also found such an affirmation. Impressed by Milner's use of doodling as a way of freeing the imagination and understanding 'blocks' within, Simon started to apply some of Milner's insights to her work with psychiatric patients; 'especially nourishing' for her was Milner's contention that 'there were two unconscious influences upon art, the creative and the reparative'.

Simon writes that she believes Milner's 'unique contribution lies in her appreciation of the value of our capacity to create visible symbols of things we comprehend unconsciously'.[18] Case and Dalley, having attested to her place as a figurehead in art therapy, contrast her thought on psychic creativity with previous analysts who had seen creativity as driven by the need to preserve the lost object, a reparative function. Milner, as we have seen, saw this as a subsidiary function of art – its primary function was to create something new on the basis of 'newly-created powers of insight into the inner world'.

They trace the genesis of her ideas, from her own experience of painting, her views of illusion and the (to her) unfortunate educational tradition 'which separates subject and object, fostering an intellectual knowing that is only half of our relation to the world'.[19]

Particularly interestingly, they give priority to Susan in *Hands of the Living God* and the role of drawing, which formed a Winnicottian 'transitional object' for her. Case and Dalley formulate this as follows:

> She [Susan] saw the paper as having a particular role, as it was substitute for the responsive ideal mother, receiving from her hands and giving back to her eyes [. . .] the drawings were reparative for all destructive intentions and actions. They were also a bridge between patient and analyst.[20]

The comparison with Winnicott is more extensive and Case and Dalley elaborate on this also: both Milner and Winnicott write on the importance of illusion in symbol formation; the transitional object is the child's 'first use of symbol and first experience of play'. At the 'stage of separation of mother and baby the transitional object becomes a symbol of union'. Like Milner, Winnicott valued a non-purposive state, 'a ticking over of the unintegrated personality', and the 'potential space' in the area between mother and child which evolves into the 'location of cultural experience'. (cf. Milner's valuing of her young son's space in his *Bothered by Alligators* drawings – see pp. 175–176).

Winnicott's influence on art therapy is summed up by Case and Dalley in this way:

> In summary, Winnicott explored and gave names to a series of concepts of importance to art therapy, from the child's first uses of symbol, transitional object, the necessity of illusion, the importance of play to the location of cultural experience.[21]

His positive view of these matters leads to these words he has on artists:

> They do something very valuable for us because they are constantly creating new forms and breaking through those forms only to create new ones. Artists enable us to keep alive, when the experiences of real life often threaten to destroy our sense of being alive and real in a living way. Artists best of all people remind us that the struggle between our impulses and a sense of security (both of which are vital to us) is an eternal struggle and one that goes on inside each of us as long as our life lasts.[22]

It is as an artist, one in search of the image, or 'beads' as she would have termed them, that Milner travels in mind and body in her next book *Eternity's Sunrise*; and it is fitting, with her stress on journeys, inner and outer, that she has left, through the generosity of her son John, the world of art therapy with a memorial to allow postgraduate students to travel – the Marion Milner Travelling Scholarship – 'enabling recent graduates of the MA in Art Psychotherapy to undertake a project outside the UK, related to the social, political and cultural context of Art Psychotherapy'.[23]

10

BEADS OF HER OWN

Travels inner and outer

The later stages of Susan's analysis with Milner coincide with her work on *Eternity's Sunrise*, the third book in her trilogy and an extension of her earlier *An Experiment in Leisure*, itself a development of *A Life of One's Own*. In an unpublished typescript Milner writes:

> Not only was it the surprise at having produced doodle drawings which seemed to make some sort of sense that had led me to write On Not Being Able to Paint it was also the surprise at my patient Susan's doodle drawings that led to writing the book about them and her analysis. In fact I had found myself having to write it in the middle of the time when struggling with the Greek beads.[1]

The 'beads' lie at the heart of *Eternity's Sunrise*, an essential part of its themes and structure, and Milner writes that it was not until 1958 that it occurred to her to repeat her earlier experiments 'to see what effects nearly twenty years of practising as a psychoanalyst in a rapidly changing world might have had on the nature of the memories selected and on the conclusions to be drawn from them.'[2]

These memories that form the core of the text are of a very particular kind; Milner uses the word 'beads' for those specially charged moments that have the certain glow of unconscious communications. 'Bead' in its original sense meant 'Prayer', and its later use for 'small perforated ball(s) threaded on a string' was, for a long time, the secondary sense (*Oxford English Dictionary*); Milner's introductory words take up the language and themes of meditative practice – it is an 'inner journey' and includes 'meditations on various experiences'. In the earlier *Experiment* Milner wrote of how she delighted in collecting certain objects – ancient iron ware, containers, objects from the natural world: *Eternity's Sunrise* is different. As John Fielding writes in his very appreciative notice of the book in 1988:

> At the centre of her new book is a series of visual images, drawn from the diaries she kept on journeys abroad, to Greece, Israel and the

Himalayas. As before, extracts from her diaries or notebooks are quoted and meditated on. Or rather, turned over, handled – one wants a word that conveys the physicality of the activity.[3]

The method and themes of this very distinctive book and its strengths are best seen with an account of the text; in this chapter I focus on its relationship to its predecessors in Milner's oeuvre and to the interchange of what she calls work (psychoanalysis) and play (travels, bead-gathering).

Milner, the consummate collector and re-visitor of images, begins her account of her first visit to Greece, letting go of words and simply sitting and staring in the 'cave of memory':

> I began to notice my thoughts coming back again and again to certain objects, those trophies and keepsakes that one brings back from holidays. As I watched what had seemed like a tangled mass of fragmented images, held it in the cooking-pot of my attention, some dimly sensed connecting links appeared to be forming themselves around the ideas of these objects.[4]

Her memories crystallise around certain objects – 'trophies' as she terms them: a model of a life-size duck; a reliquary; the skin of a snake; and an asphodel. This was, as Milner states, 'a promising beginning' but, like the analyst and patient, at this point the meanings are unknown and incomplete, and, as in an analysis, meaning and finding the truth of meaning will be a cumulative task of visiting and revisiting, accruing and refining. Milner the analyst will need to allow Milner the autobiographer to freely associate around her beads.

She finds that the official high spots, the famous sites of Greece, do not speak to her; Olympia, Mycenae, Epidaurus, the Corinth Canal are all silent. But something does often remain as a 'high point', for example:

> [this] was a kind of inner tapestry of shining gold mixed with grey, infinitely subtle variations of a grey pebble colour, a grey that seemed the perfect companion for gold; and against this background of gold and grey the intricate shapes of bracelets, cups, necklaces, daggers, masks, helmets, brooches – in fact, the treasure from Mycenae shown in the National Museum at Athens.[5]

Similarly, in the Kariye Mosque in Istanbul, home of some of the best known Byzantine mosaics, it is not the well-known mosaic that becomes the bead; rather Milner is struck, as so often and so characteristically, by something from the natural world: she had 'suddenly become aware of, perched amongst the bare black branches of a tree by the mosque door, a rose-coloured dove, round and fluffy and being itself so intensely and satisfactorily'. Then, looking in wonder at the dome of Hagia Sophia, all the space was 'made more intense, more real by the flight of a pigeon across it, a tiny moving speck'.[6]

From Istanbul and Hagia Sophia, Milner's trawl of her memory delivers Delphi; again, the image that she retains is not what one might most obviously expect – not the temple of Apollo or the steps of the Sacred Way:

> but the soaring eagles (or whatever they were) in the immense space
> of the valley below the shrine, a space contained by the brooding,
> enveloping, ever-silent presence of the mountains. And what I had
> brought away with me in my hand was the bit of asphodel picked
> in the sanctuary.[7]

In Venice Milner found it hard to believe she was not looking at a huge Hollywood set; looking back on her five-day visit she discovers that most of her memories are not of pictures and buildings but of water – and then there are two images from pictures that make their first appearance in this text, images that she will re-visit as the narrative progresses. These are the Torcello Madonna and Child and Giorgione's picture 'The Gipsy and the Soldier' (perhaps better known as 'The Tempest' – Milner is not, as ever, very troubled by the need for exact accuracy.)

A year later, in 1960, Milner has another chance to visit Greece, this time to give a paper on aesthetics in Athens; she planned to repeat her method, ascertaining the high points of each day and putting them into words. The guidebooks told her that Salonica was the second city of Byzantium and the guide directed his party's attention to a house where St Paul had lived. But Milner is not one to keep to the paths laid down by guidebook or travel brochure. As Hugh Haughton remarks in his New Introduction to the text, 'the book is less interested in the cultural icons she travels to [. . .] than the ways such culturally iconic sites are registered, resisted and translated into something else: a bead of her own.'[8] Milner, however, did not think she could see the place and slipped away into a courtyard and a little Byzantine church where in the shady place she saw 'a hen peacock, all soft shades of grey but with a gleaming patch of blue-green iridescence on the back of her neck: and with her, her half-grown chick'.[9] The peahen will recur.

On the Island of Thassos, Milner alights on a kouros, a shepherd god holding a ram in his arms with the ram's head supported by the god's' arm – the ram 'relaxed and submissive' and the god's face shaped like the ram's. An expert told Milner this could not be an important statue, but for her the fact that it was unfinished (the French caption had read *inachevé*) made it startling, and as she began to draw it, she wondered whether the ram was meant to be dead and was for sacrifice; but, in that case, surely it would have been killed first – so it was alive and carried in a 'queer way'.[10]

In 1961 there came a third opportunity to visit Greece, this time with just one other person (her sister Winifred seems to have been her companion) rather than with a group; and, again, Milner decides to 'collect the high points of the trip' with no clear idea of what she might find. She returns to Delphi and again is struck by one of the great 'soaring birds' (not yet knowing they were eagles), noting with her customary precision 'how its wing tips were spread like fingers to the air, the feathers surrendering themselves with the utmost of their spread to the enveloping element in which they have their being'.[11]

Milner then refines her remarks on her change in focus; deep in the flowers and wildness of the Cronion Hill (a place sacred to Cronus, father of Zeus) she suddenly becomes aware, on descending the slopes, of an orchid-like plant on a blackish stem. She elaborates:

> Instead of peering, scanning the wood for rare flowers, as I had been doing, narrowly, if not seeing a rare one then not seeing anything, suddenly I had found that the focus of my eyes had changed to wideness, so that I could now see that the dark earth of the wood was clothed in a whiteness, a lace-like garment of infinite delicacy, something I had missed on the way up because it was not a rare plant – probably just a kind of garlic.[12]

Similarly, she recalls a time at Epidaurus when, initially, the carpet of flowers had disappointed her, with no rare or new plants; but, with her change to a wide focus, she had 'escaped from the need to name; instead of scanning the ground for a rarity I had widely stared so that what was there made a pattern, a rich texture that was deeply satisfying, healing. I needed nothing else'.[13]

Chapter 4, 'Telling the Beads', engages with the meaning of Milner's beads and trophies; and yet she reports a disinclination to write about them. Why might this be? The phrase itself has religious overtones of counting prayer beads, and Milner 'hates creeds', consistently in her writings and letters regretting the savagery of religious dispute and the wars occasioned by religion. From his childhood, aged around nine, she was clear about not taking John to church because, she wrote, 'I think that Christianity has made a terrible muddle of a lot of the things that Jesus said'[14] – and yet she has a mystical bent and employs the lexicon of meditation and of prayer.

In this chapter she writes she 'could no longer evade the struggle to see where all this might be going' and decides to meditate on each of the bead memories to see what might happen. Thus, to take just one bead example, the wild duck:

> Of course, it's Ibsen's Wild Duck. Doesn't one of the characters say that when a wild duck is wounded it goes right down to the bottom and clings onto the weeds? This makes me think of how an inner gesture of going down into lowness, away from living according to a picture of what will please, away from the Jack Hornerism of 'what

a good boy am I', away from the striving after 'when all men speak
well of you' (I used to wonder why this was something to beware of)
how this inner gesture is a most potent way of dealing with wounds,
wounds to one's self-esteem, wounds to one's heart.

The process of association leads her to make a 'link with the reliquary' and
its showing of the Dying God; then the wild duck clinging on to the water
weeds reminds Milner of a section of the Bach *St Matthew Passion* music 'which
seems like a rhythmic swaying of primeval vegetation on the bottom of the
ocean. Which is also like that Sam Francis picture, as I remember it, the first
Action Painting that made any sense to me'.[15]

Her flow of associations moves now to the other side of the reliquary (one
of her 'trophies') – the Holy Mother and Child. In this image the halo seems
to have a slight divide, prompting Milner to notice two shapes that could be
the arms of the cross or, possibly, the wings of the Angel of Death. Lines in
the Virgin's cloak remind her of a tree symbol, and this, in turn, adds a
suggestion of Mother Nature, both giving and taking life away. The Virgin
is both protector of the infant but also the tree, the cross, on which the son
will die. Above is the dove sweeping down.

Then, following the sequence of her meditation or, we might say, her stream
of free association or consciousness, another image comes to Milner's mind –
the picture on a postcard of the line of lions at Delos. She allows her thoughts
to wander around her image – recalling again the day at Delos when she
found the snake skin, and saw wader birds take flight at the Temple of Apollo.
But there is something else, a kind of body memory: 'It was at Delos that I
kept finding I could not breathe properly – as also at Venice when I tried to
write up the trip chronologically. Why? What could there have been on the
peaceful island of Delos to rouse anxiety?'[16]

The answer comes in thinking of the eyes of the snake skin and of the
'inner bodily awareness that came with the times when I could achieve being
behind my eyes and how my breathing was deeper then'. But this memory
turns out not to be of a deepening breath but its opposite – a feeling 'that
something was trying to stop me breathing altogether'. What could this be?

She realises that she needs to 'turn inwards', to wait and guard the 'sacred
way', that is, the passage along which the air proceeds; so the breathlessness
could be a warning of the fears around 'learning how to turn inwards [. . .]
certainly it seems like taking a great risk'. She had to let the breaths carry
her, waiting 'while the wave of the breath spreads itself upwards into the
whole of one's body, then it's like an incoming tide that smoothes out the
scuffled surface of the sand and brings a great peace'. But, who, Milner asks,
would have thought 'that such a simple act of attention could do so much'?
Just as she learned she was lived by unconscious forces and it was needful to
give up a sense of control over them, so here Milner writes, 'I had to let
breaths take me.'[17]

There were dangers inherent in this vital turning inwards, not least from the family; here she invokes her brother, her 'early love, who railed at my books when we met after so many years' though it was he who, some forty years previously, had started her writing by making her read Montaigne. He, the eminent scientist, called her writing solipsism and wanted her to devote herself to 'objective research', scientific writing with 'graphs and all that'. Milner could not understand why he so raged – and yet it was Milner he sent for when he was dying, 'sitting up in bed and looking like Don Quixote'.[18]

Images follow of dark and light, from Venice and from Daphni, then from the Caryatids, the female sculpted figures forming the pillars at Delphi, and her growing awareness that 'it was that moment of inward turning attention that made the Parthenon, out there "speak" to me'. Another image of darkness follows, from a film of a volcano, showing how the black sand surface was suddenly broken by black bubbles, evoking 'my fear of going down to the bottom of the breath and waiting for the new one to come' – perhaps what would result from the depths was anger, 'black anger': that which can come with the shock of loss of a loved one. Perhaps, however, the anger can be a way of avoiding the pain of grief: 'But the loss can feel like a great, black, spiny sea urchin, filling one's middle – as I felt about all those dead young men in the war cemetery at Gallipoli.'[19]

Notably, this comment about the pain of loss comes shortly after the words about her brother's criticism of her solipsistic writings and his death, and shortly before her description of a grief-filled day, perhaps the day of Patrick's death, 'thinking [her] world had crashed' and wanting to remain apart from others' eyes, stumbling to the National Gallery and reaching the Masaccio Mother and Child, and then, in her self-psychoanalytic mode, over time coming to see that the feeling of the shattering of her world did not belong to her present reality 'but was a memory from infancy, of bitter grief, "forgotten", hidden away in the depths'.[20]

It is not long before the author realises more of the core meaning of her bead-seeking: 'my explorations', she writes 'had brought me to the very bread and butter of my daily psychoanalytic task'. We could say that the method of this text *shows us* the psychoanalytic free associative process while the commentary brings us in tune with some of the grounding concepts of analysis – the task of trying to help patients come to terms with 'agonies of disillusionment', agonies brilliantly portrayed in *On Not Being Able to Paint* although not fully reached in the previous two books in Milner's auto-biographical trio. This was certainly a key part of the picture but she felt there was more; the 'volcanic violence' of the dispossessed 'king-child' was, of course, a reality, and although the beads of reliquary and wild duck had resonated with themes of loss, anger and despair, this was not the whole story. The next image bore this out in its configuration of mother and child in the form of the peahen and her chick 'in the cube of space made by the vines and the church door'.[21]

Eventually it becomes clear that the image of the peahen and her chick in the space was taking Milner back to that 'sense of inner spaceless space' that she had once before described, in *Experiment in Leisure*: a discovery not simply about inner space but also about silence – those 'great gulps of silence' she had experienced on a visit to Chios. This leads to the idea of 'wiping one's eyes free of images so that one accepts darkness, emptiness', and she echoes a speaker heard in her childhood who had adjured her listeners 'to wipe themselves free of learning'. It echoes, too, the mantra of the earlier books, 'I am nothing, I want nothing, I know nothing.'[22]

Led through thoughts of silence, noise and Mount Athos, Milner recalls a significant way in which she had perceived the Christ Pantocrator at Daphni on her second visit; the expression on his face, on this occasion, suggested a certain doubt – perhaps this was to do with 'the wholesale rejection of the body which had become so embedded in the way Christianity had developed since the days of Christ really was what Christ had meant?'[23]

The closing paragraph of this de-construction of Milner's beads looks back to the dome of St Sophia with its 'wide hovering brooding quality' and offers once more the opportunity to clarify her discovery of some years previously of the marked change in consciousness that comes when there is a change of focus from narrow to wide. The dome was a symbol of this wide attention but it also evoked the idea that in this kind of attention there is something physical, that which Milner had called 'concentration of the body'. In conclusion, she writes of 'an essential link between the St Sophia empty dome and the Torcello one that is not empty but presided over by the mother goddess and her child'. She finds the St Sophia one ' in some ways the more powerful by the very fact of its emptiness'.[24]

Chapter 5, 'The Gipsy and the Solder', continues with Milner's investigations into what the beads might mean; and it suddenly becomes clear to her that they are about very similar ideas to those included in the paper she had given in Athens in 1960 on 'Painting and Internal Body Awareness'. Milner lets us know of her astonishment that she had managed so far to separate work and play; on reflection, she thinks this could be seen as an example of 'an excessive split between work and play'. This recognition, however, is complicated further by the tendency of conventional education to keep apart 'the logical and the non-logical'.[25] This situation had led Milner over the years, when writing an intellectual paper, always to take an image as her starting point. Thus, with her Athens 1960 paper, the core image comes from the account by Ruskin about a journey across Europe when he 'had felt so ill that he had lain down by the roadside and thought he would die, but then found himself staring at an aspen tree and felt impelled to draw it. Having done so he then found himself totally recovered and able to continue his journey'.[26]

Milner now re-visits her Athens paper, having found that its conclusion was an effort to show in psychoanalytic terms much of what she had found from her 'trophy' of the snake skin from Delos:

Thus it seems that, behind the states that are often rather loosely talked about by psychoanalysts as auto-erotic and narcissistic, there can be an attempt to reach a beneficent kind of narcissism, primary self-enjoyment which is in fact a cathexis of the whole body, as distinct from concentrating on the specifically sexual organs; and which, if properly understood, is not a rejection of the outer world but a step towards a renewed and revitalised cathexis of it.[27]

It shortly becomes clear to Milner that one thing the beads are about is the idea of making contact with an inner something by means of turning the attention inwards, maintaining an inner silence and letting go of purposive aims and actions, and it is at this point in her musings that she is 'called back' by a picture in Venice – Giorgione's 'The Gipsy and the Soldier' ('The Tempest'); this leads her to recall an image from Ravenna and thence the Daphni Pantocrator. These images were undoubtedly saying something to her, whatever they might have signified to others in other times – and this something was linked with her earlier phrase 'Answering Activity' described in *Experiment* as 'a knowing, yet a knowing that was nothing to do with me; it was a knowing that could see forwards and backward and in a flash give form to the confusions of everyday living and to the chaos of sensation'.[28] This was written more than fifty years before *Eternity's Sunrise*, and, with hindsight, Milner feels that it does not give the importance to the body and to attending to 'every cell in the body' that she had come, over the intervening years, to feel so crucial.

The next question emerging was why it was sometimes so difficult to tune into the Answering Activity; invoking Blake once again, Milner thinks this might well be to do with an ignoring of opposites – in Blake's words 'without contraries there is no progression'. Here, she realises that she had collected a rich store of good memories, trophies – very good beads; and yet were there not also bad moments? One such was from her second visit to Delphi. It had been 'A cold wet evening that I had so far avoided re-remembering'.[29]

The point of this association was that Milner's companion was ill, and Milner had been reading Murray's translation of *The Bacchae*. After this she was 'haunted by the mad Agave and her Bacchantes' and the narrative of how they had torn her son to pieces 'and she had come home in triumph with his bleeding torn-off head cradled in her arms, claiming that it was a lion that she had cleverly hunted and killed'.[30] Milner is now, in a way she could not do in her earlier book *Experiment*, confidently able to link the idea of a benign Mother Nature and a destructive Mother Nature with the psychoanalytic concept of splitting the image of one's real mother into extremes of good and bad, as later conceived as 'Madonna and Whore'.[31]

Concurrently, she realises that there was something else she had been ignoring – in Giorgione's picture, its other, better-known title 'The Tempest' evokes storms and threats from nature, 'sunlight and storm, opposites again'.

Milner now re-remembers her view in 1936–1937 of the Answering Activity and how she 'felt she was being lived by something not myself.' This was something that could be trusted and indeed was 'something that knew better than I did where I was going'.[32] Notably and characteristically Milner does not call this force 'God'.

The sixth chapter further explores the Answering Activity and its nature; her beads, she writes, brought her back again and again to the same thing – 'to this something that happens when one turns one's contemplative attention inwards'. Milner's work with Susan and her standing as 'a well-trained psychoanalyst' result in certain emphases here: commenting on the paradox of the Answering Activity, she remarks that this is 'something the schizophrenic can't tolerate'. As she ponders plugging into something positive, she remarks that she has, professionally, 'learned to use that clumsy name for it, "the good internalised object"'.[33]

The Answering Activity can take the form of an inner voice, but Milner still has questions – what about repetition, our habit of doing the same 'stupid things over and over again'? Psychoanalysis struggles with this all the time, Milner comments, but, for her, such a pattern needs to be brought into conscious 'relation to one's reason'. Two minds have to be taken into account – 'the deliberative and the spontaneous'. If this is not done, then 'there can be a Hitlerian certainty of a sleep-walker, so many terrible things done by people saying their God told them to, made people doing dastardly things, convinced it was a divine voice that prompted them'.[34]

Here another question arises in Milner's mind; is it, she wonders, possible that all she had been talking of could be construed as aspects of praying? She recalls a very painful memory of her brother's words in his last illness, words of one who had been agnostic since young manhood. At a time when he was failing and finding speech very hard, he asked Milner what she thought of prayer; taken aback she had replied:

> I don't know what it does for the outside world but I do know a bit
> of what it does for one's inside world. Blake said it. 'And the Lord
> turned the captivity of Job when he prayed for his friends.'

Milner and her brother were never able to return to the subject (his speech was declining too quickly) but she endorses her view of prayer thus: 'I have found again and again that what I call praying does free me from the captivity of egocentric preoccupations from that ego-island that I once drew a picture of.'[35]

By 'praying' Milner does not mean 'Church-praying'; she means a kind of holding the image of a person in mind, but also remembering to 'plug into the Answering Activity'; this she likens to 'suddenly remembering to open a kind of little trap-door inside and finding a great expansion of spirit'.[36] This is essentially a bodily experience and, as such, very different from the kind of praying Milner had been taught when young. The 'great expansion of spirit' reminds us also that Milner's beads echo in some senses Woolf's 'moments of being' or Joyce's 'epiphanies'.

Unfortunately there are times when there is no Answering Activity: thinking this over in some detail she comes to the view that one important thing that could be blocking the way in terms of contacting the Answering Activity was 'the feeling that one had, in imagination, killed it, like the Ancient Mariner and his albatross'.[37] Also, there could be an element of grief denied lying at the back of the anger at dispossession, 'denial of the need to accept the loss of all that glory of Torcello', denial of the need to turn away from the nourishing, loving mother to confront the world and its realities.[38]

When she looks further into aspects of inner body concentration, Milner turns her attention to dancing, always important in her life right up until her eighties when she won a competition for two free dancing lessons (which she attended.) A bead of a young girl dancing in Mykonos leads her to expatiate on dances she had been to in the 1920s – 'high moments of maximum joy' – and learning figure skating just before the war. Many moments are recorded in Milner's diaries, noting changes in the sense of self resulting from shifts of attention – and one very typical conclusion she draws is about the need to 'learn how to hold one's bones gently – as once one was held in one's mother's arms'.[39] As so often in her autobiographical works, Milner regrets that ideas such as these about careful attention to the body and its experience is generally omitted from traditional education – should these things be taught, 'there could be such a deep source of peace available to everyone that envy would become quite unimportant, irrelevant'.[40]

Thinking about the need for 'full incarnation', by which Milner means here the full meeting of body and soul, she engages with the idea of mysticism. Milner is disinclined to call herself a mystic – she loved 'the sensory things of the world too much' – the song of blackbirds, clowns, the smell of geraniums . . . She writes that the body as part of nature is as mysterious to her as it was when she was at school and 'expected to go to Holy Communion and partake of the bread and the wine'. Engagingly, she 'always took a leaf from the garden with [her] feeling [. . .] that it was as much the body of God as the bread and wine, only I could not then have said so'.[41]

The incarnation of the body is linked to her findings when lying on the ground, flat on the floor, a practice that I understand Milner continued until the very end of her life. When she did this she found 'An unbelievable transformation'. Asking herself what this was, she says the 'incarnation' happens 'if living properly' every morning on awakening:

> For then the imaginative body, which has been doing all kinds of things in its dreams, has now to descend to indwelling in its own flesh and bones. Sometimes this does seem to happen by itself (if one

has gone to sleep properly relaxed?) and one wakes to find body and soul already reunited, a miraculous meeting, one's body humming like contented bees in a summer garden.[42]

Milner's fourth visit to Greece, in 1967, took her back to Thassos for another visit to the unfinished shepherd god; this time, there were no diary beads, only issues to do with drawing and painting. She decides to think about these in case they were part of the trail to the kind of experience she had undergone in the 1940s leading up to *On Not Being Able to Paint*. It is in this chapter significantly that Milner begins to describe her methods of developing her collage work, her most important artistic endeavour of her later years. At Delphi she had made a tiny collage out of contemplating her harbour drawings; then, in the following years, a surprising thing happened. This became a full-sized picture. As in parts of *On Not Being Able to Paint* the agency is interesting:

> It took to itself bits torn from an old failed picture of mine which now seemed to be asking to have themselves used as background for the upright pink post. Again the whole was done as a cut-out and pasted on. But something else had to be added to balance it and I found another scrap cut from an old picture of mine, one kept from years ago for possible future use because I liked the texture of it. So I now stuck this on, as well, to the right of the post.[43]

While she was contemplating this picture, a Biblical title emerged: 'And she, supposing him to be the gardener', those words ascribed by John to Mary Magdalene returning to Jesus's empty tomb. Milner is 'astonished' by this; and then she realises that all she had been struggling to write about was to do with the resurrection of the body although in this life, 'not knowing at all whether it also happens after death'. The shape then came to suggest the frog they had seen on the road to Karalla. Why had her 'inner navigator' chosen this symbol? The answer came loud and clear: 'because it jumps', suggesting a leap into the unknown, a willingness to accept the condition of unknowing. The next chapter gathers beads from other occasions and other places with a different kind of not knowing as Milner comments that she did not, in fact, know just 'how all the beads in this chapter would eventually become strung together'.[44]

In 1971, Milner set off on a trip to Kashmir, made possible by a seventieth birthday gift from her colleagues. She wanted, she had told them, to see the Himalayas before she died. The plan was to go on a botanic tour of Kashmir, camping in the mountains but also to see Kulu in the Valley of the Gods, a place with many temples and not far from the Tibetan border. She had dreamed of it with bells and gongs like some monastery music she had once heard on the radio. But they never got there – the plane to Kulu had a fault and it would be a week until there was another flight. Their guide, however, whisked them off to Agra to see the Taj Mahal and thence to Srinagar in Kashmir to stay on houseboats until the time came to go to their mountain camp.

Milner had agreed to write something for a tour magazine about this trip, and later she returns to her piece in search of beads. There were none except possibly the haunting Kashmiri music but here were no presences forcing their way into the memory that Milner by now comes to think of as definite beads. Sadly, she remarks that she had only seen the snowy Himalayan mountains twice and these sightings were but fleeting, the mountains enveloped in heat haze. Then, though, she remembers one morning after a great storm, when she awoke and saw through her window the whole white range of them. She elaborates: 'I could not believe it, of course they had been there all the time and I had not known . . . But then the heat-haze had hidden them again.' This is what emerges as 'the real bead' – 'it was not seeing the snow mountains, although they had been there all the time', a negative hallucination.[45]

Part II, 'Diary keeping between holidays', offers Milner's series of jottings, conceived as possible 'signposts'. These include her noticing how many of them include sayings or ideas taken from the Gospels; indeed, she recalls how, in *Experiment,* she had come to see them as 'a kind of handbook describing the process by which psychic creativity is achieved'.[46] They also comprise thoughts as to whether or not she might use 'God-language' for her ideas of the Answering Activity (which, itself, as she remarks, sometimes comes to her with capital letters and sometimes does not.) Body concentration has a firm place in these jottings; and with it the telling question as to why there are so few beads with people in them. She suggests to herself that the bead carries something other than people: 'It is more a question of finding how contacting one's body's innerness affects one's relation to people outside.'[47]

In the 'Creeds' section Milner enlarges on her religious disquiet: concerned especially with how creeds can become but excuses for savagery, she is not happy with allying herself with a Christianity that destroyed the Incas or sacked the city of Constantinople – so many atrocities, she finds, 'done in the name of a God of love'. The real ill lay in 'the insistence that your statement is absolute – and then killing the people who don't agree, pretending it's to save their souls, but really to bolster up your own beliefs'. So what Milner is doing as she writes is searching for 'A method for finding one's own personal way, not for those who feel they have found their "salvation" through accepting a particular ideology, creed'. Certainly her method – her own beads if you will – 'is not for the orthodoxly religious nor for the orthodox atheist'.[48]

Psychoanalysis intervenes in the section on 'The devil, the goat and the chapel' as she recalls the belief of one of her patients (Susan in *Hands*) that she was possessed by a very particular kind of devil, one who is '"all will, he thinks he does it all himself and tramples underfoot what isn't his"'.[49] Psychoanalysis further informs the text as she writes about 'Failure and

Forgiveness', telling us of several patients who have told her they will never forgive, and she herself had felt the awful modern church by the Acropolis 'could only be forgiven if it was pulled down and rebuilt'. She links this with psychoanalysis, which 'means having to accept that one may have to go back and feel like an infant, temporarily, so as to have a fresh start'.[50] Milner is clear, too, that, as a psychoanalyst she does not heal her patients: 'I only try to clear away the blocks so that they can find the answering activities in themselves.' As a clinician, she is deeply grateful for the Oedipus myth. On her first Greek visit, on the way to see the church of Hosius Lukas, their guide had told them they were passing the crossroads where Oedipus is believed to have killed his father. This was not a bead for Milner, but she did think of:

> pouring out a little libation of gratitude for the Oedipus myth and Freud's use of it, considering how often it has provided a clue to what my patients are miserable about – both the direct one and the reverse one for the girl, the Elektra story.[51]

In the section on 'Holiness' Milner states that she 'gets restless when people talk about religion' and yet she continues to listen. She had bought William James's *Variations of Religious Experience* when she was in the United States in 1928: disarmingly she tells us that she has not yet managed to read it.[52] Although some of her meditative practices look very like those of a mystic, Milner assures her reader that she is 'no mystic' – and she reiterates how she loves the created world far too much to turn away from it for any sustained length of time.[53]

At times autobiographical elements from her childhood press into the narrative of this A–Z, Part Two of the text; one such comes with her use of the story of Persephone. She sees this as, above all, a myth of separation, of the time when the child has to take responsibility for themselves. Here she comments:

> And if one had a secretly depressed mother one intuitively knew that she could not stand very much rebellion, even that she might need compliance, need the feeling of at-one-ness with her child, too much, too much for the compliant child's good.[54]

(This was a matter with which Milner continued to negotiate throughout her life. Right up until its end she is mulling over her own mother's severe, but largely hidden distress, and this is a recurring theme in her last text, *Bothered by Alligators*.)

The Persephone story is particularly poignant here as Milner realises that Persephone, the daughter, had to pick the flowers (which would lead to her 'abduction') and had to be lost to her mother:

A bit of ruthlessness that has to be accepted, if one is to grow, accept the guilt for hurting the sorrowing mother Demeter. So, of course, Persephone had to leave. It's described as an abduction, really it was her own need. But she came back; although by then she was a different girl, no longer just a child.[55]

The sorrowing mother motif occurs once more in the A–Z section on 'Up and Down' when her body self with her hunched shoulders leads her to compare the 'burden' she carries with 'having to support one's mother, shore up her depressions by being the good child, the white lamb of God not the black one'.[56]

Aspects of the black one, however, do come into the section on violence in Milner's A–Z, one that well shows the interpenetration of her analytic and earlier self. Thus, she describes awaking one day and getting in touch with her anger, recalling the intensity of her emotion registered in her 1938 drawings of the heath fire, which came when, consciously, she had intended to draw a peaceful summer morning. (see pp. 63–64) just as stunted blasted beech trees arrived when she intended stately summer ones.[57]

These drawings pre-dated the bulk of Milner's psychoanalytic work and thus she comments that at that point in 1939 she 'had not fully recognised the possible extent and depth of infant anger at the fall from kingship, from being the Torcello infant in glory so had not had to live through with them the agonies of the fall'. She then experienced 'great muscle tensions' with fears about violence, either done by herself or done to herself; and this, for Milner, with her analytic intuition, means that a self-image of a loving person also has its opposite – 'a violent self-aggrandising ruthless gangster self' or even at its most extreme the wild Agave who tears her son to pieces, 'wild because so split off and denied'. Milner well knows that both these are true aspects of the self – and knows, too, that it is only when the two can 'meet and interpenetrate' that something truly human can grow. Milner locates the meeting place, so typically, in the body, in her middle, 'probably around the diaphragm area where breathing happens'. Similarly, feeling herself into her jaws, she is aware of a self-image of great power – power that is to crush, but also power to hold tight. Anecdotally, she remarks of her tight jaw that it is 'as if there's something I can't let go, that I'll die if I do let go. But when I make it relax by just attending to it, what I find there is laughter, laughing at myself.'[58]

Here Milner returns to a theme of reparation, the issue of making amends for hurtful things one has done: this is something, as she notes, that psychoanalytic (especially Kleinian) thought has much to say about – this impulse to restore and repair 'the damage through actions in the outer world, which then works to restore the inner image of what's been hurt and so restore one's self-respect'.[59]

145

Her A–Z concludes with a section, 'Waters of Comfort', and Milner's realisation that time and again the beads are taking her back to the same thing, that is, 'to the something that happens when one turns one's contemplative attention inwards' – and this is a kind of blessedness although, as she wrote in 1936, 'God is not your name.'[60]

In 1975 Milner knew she must go to Israel in order to add to what she had already experienced in Greece and Byzantium. In Jerusalem there is a first bead but then, in days seeing many of the famous holy places and the procession for Easter, no more beads, except one that was pre-Christian and indeed outside the city wall. Milner's diary elaborates this:

> They call it the tomb of Absalom but the guide book says it belongs to the time of the Hasmonean kings of Israel, about 200 BC. But why so important to me? I think it's not only the beauty of the curves, but perhaps the fact of their being the opposite of the swelling curves of the domes of the mosques so obviously breast-like, a breast that is full. Whereas this Absalom's Tomb is more like an empty breast after one has taken one's fill; as if one could be asking oneself – can one love the answering activity even when one gets no answer?[61]

(A parenthetic question here might be: can one love the process of psycho-analysis knowing that there will be no direct answer in terms of an individual's desires? There will be but an abstinent response.)

Milner's responses to this tomb and her commentary in the text are enlightening: Haughton in his New Introduction writes of her resisting history[62] and I would like to take this up. Milner at first feels the Tomb is a bead because here was something that was just the same as it was in the time of Jesus when, according to the Gospel stories (which she of course finds very inconsistent), Jesus would come up to the city with his disciples from Bethany and cross the Brook Kidron.

Thoughts around these matters led Milner to read many books by historians as she tried to test out the reliability of the Gospels. However, fascinating though this was, she eventually decided that this reading could lead her astray – away from her central endeavour:

> of discovering what the stories meant to me personally, rather than what the experts tried to maintain that they meant. In fact I realised afterwards that it was really seeing the Tomb of Absalom that was another landmark, just as the moment in Mycenae, *when I gave up the little map and resisted the lure of history*.[63]

She repeats a variant of this about the Dead Sea Scrolls and what the experts might be saying about them – 'a field I must not now be lured into at the cost of being distracted from my main task'.[64]

146

Here there may very well be an embedded influence of Milner's many years of psychoanalytic practice; the analyst in attending to the minute-to-minute changing text and texture of a fifty-minute hour often has to resist the 'lure' of an analysand's history, the beguiling narratives of the consulting room and focus on the charged (unconscious) energy of a particular image, a word or a gesture in the immediate context of the session.

Her analytic experience comes directly into the text as she recalls the Sermon on the Mount (Christian and secular concerns are interwoven throughout this book) and the words 'Blessed are they that mourn, for they shall be comforted', commenting that this is what psychoanalysis is about: 'helping [her] patients to accomplish the work of mourning'.[65]

The analyst Michael Parsons, writing one of the few serious papers on Milner's work on the Answering Activity, concerns himself with the 'organic' nature of the images in *Eternity's Sunrise*; and Milner's next bead is one such. Having been to the Hill of Beatitudes and returning by car to Tiberius, she sees a Bedouin tent on the hillside:

> It looked quite black in the bright sunlight against the dried-up grass and as if made of woven wool or skins blackened with age. I was most surprised that, out of all we had seen around the Sea of Galilee, it was this that stayed in my mind and had undoubtedly become the bead for the day, for I found that it had slowly collected to itself meanings from the Sermon on the Mount and the other sayings of Jesus; for instance, the idea of a woven tent somehow linked up both with 'Take no thought for the morrow' and my own struggles to weave the cocoon or bodily tent containing the dark inner states. Also with finding that when I did succeed in this, even if only a little, something did open up inside, like a 'lily of the field'; and once again I thought of all those Japanese flower shapes that expand in water.[66]

The organic nature of the tent lies also in the way it accrues meaning after the seeing of the image – Milner sees later how it also contains the beatitude about the kingdom of God belonging to the poor in spirit: 'I saw that the dark tent could stand for that turning inwards which is away from concern with outer possessions, not necessarily material ones but all the interesting things there are in the world to think about.'[67]

One experience on the third day of Milner's visit to Jerusalem was most startling, 'a kind of silent explosion from within'. It followed a visit, with a colleague, to the Holocaust Museum built to commemorate the destruction of the Jews by the Nazis. When she got there, the enormity of the figures of those killed from each country had frozen her responses – 'both feeling and thought were totally paralyzed'. In the end, all she could relate to was the metal door as they left the meeting: 'It looked like iron that had somehow been cast into forms of charred blackened bones and I thought again of the blackened cliff in the valley of Gehenna.'[68]

What follows is a fine example of Milner as one who thinks in images. On the evening of the next day Milner, having been provided by her hostess with some coloured boards and a pot of jesso, began to do some finger-painting, enjoying the sensation of dabbing and daubing with her finger-tips. At first the result seemed nothing but a mess; she could make no sense of it. But then:

> Finally, however, I added four linked squares, to try and hold it together. It was not until the next morning that it was pointed out to me that there was a face in the left-hand compartment and a very horrifying one. Then I knew that my picture was an unconscious response to visiting the Holocaust Museum so I set out to free-associate while contemplating it.[69]

This done, Milner realises that the only way she could try to make sense of the picture was by way of the (Jungian) idea that we each possess a shadow:

> a part of oneself which is the opposite of the good qualities one likes to think of oneself as having; also of what happens if we do not admit this to ourselves but just try to get rid of it by secretly projecting it into any convenient scapegoat and then setting out to destroy it, get rid of it altogether, seek a 'final solution'.[70]

Milner's next idea was about a Judas-Face in her picture, giving way to thoughts of human kind's capacity to destroy itself. However, what really concerned Milner at this point was not the symbol itself so much as the way in which, in but a few seconds, her fingers could get such ideas on to the paper while her deliberative mind lagged far behind. Her image-making also leads her once more to appreciate the 'intensely serious' nature of what is conventionally called play; and once more, at the close of the chapter, Milner reiterates her need to resist the lure of history and its potential enticement away from her main task.

Part IV is entitled 'Work and Play' and offers further meditations on her beads, starting with a childhood memory from the time before Milner went to school. It is very much a bead memory, of making beads out of yellow clay, baking them and painting them in bright colours. Then she had baked the clay overnight in the ashes of the nursery fire and, in the morning, with astonishment, had found the clay had turned into a 'lovely pinkish red' – 'out of the ashes comes transformation', the transformation of a bead.[71]

There are also re-visitings of previous beads and more thoughts on the Answering Activity, and to whether or not this can be seen in Christian terms. Milner adds thoughts on Funny Beads, 'a whole string of beads about clowns in general' and on beads residing in pictures – notably Seurat's 'Bathers'.[72]

On a darker note, pondering thoughts of death at the close of the section, Milner recalls how in 1977, after her return from Israel, she had shown her book *An Experiment in Leisure* to a friend who had survived torture. He was half-French and had been in the Resistance during the war. He wrote to her after reading her book:

> I had the good fortune to learn in a torture house that, if you 'wipe out yourself', the first result is to remove that on which pain relies to secure a hold and the second result, provided you submit and do not hanker after the expertise of the matador, is to give you all that comes with 'poverty of soul' in the moment of truth. Not until forty years later did I read your book and discover in Chapter XVI that the method should be applied to the blank page.[73]

Thoughts of the survival of torture lead to issues around bodily pain, and her mantra from Nietzsche, 'The body is a big sagacity', leading to thoughts on the capacity of the body to correct itself, even those distortions that have come about through misuse. Milner here writes of joining up her beads; the wild duck now 'joined up both with the Seurat picture and "the moment that Satan cannot find" and also the Bach *St Matthew Passion*'. It is here that Milner sees fit to remind herself, and her reader, that her bead-seeking had produced not only positive but also negative images – had delivered Madonnas but also the terrible Agave. Her response to this realisation is born of her years with psychoanalysis as the contrasting poles pinpoint 'the primary either-or tendency inherent in one's earliest forms of thinking, and liable to persist because it is so much easier than allowing the opposites to meet and interpenetrate'.[74] And in 'Living the paradox', thinking of her overlapping circles, Milner sees them as an image for a situation where a creative illusion can take place – and how, in the safety of the framed analytic space, the transference can develop.

Fittingly Milner's last bead comes in gratitude for inner gestures that foster this:

> it seemed to represent what the inner gesture of directing attention to the Answering Activity felt like. It was Michelangelo's picture of Adam's finger touching the finger of the Creator, though not up in the sky, but inside one's bones, which then can begin to sing. Also to reach out in feeling to other people and the world, so that in some sense this whole book is a saying 'thank you'.[75]

The tenor of gratitude also pervades responses to Milner's book: John Fielding's critique was already quoted earlier. He appreciates, too, the poetry inherent in this work; 'For us,' he writes, 'she has used words to create moments of poetry to help us find our imaginative body.'[76] The esteemed child analyst Frances Tustin, whom Milner had known since 1983, wrote in the same journal:

> In Joanna Field (Marion Milner) I felt I met a friend who would never 'put me down', who would be alongside me as, tremblingly, I met myself. I'm sure that I'm not alone in this, and that it has served this purpose for many other readers; some much more sophisticated than I was at that time.

An expert in autism, Tustin also finds Milner's texts of value in the field, and, as friend of Milner, she may have the last word:

> Autistic children, and the autistic parts of many of us which are disconnected from the mother and from relationships in the outside world, have become paralysed by primitive paroxysms of sensuous surges of rage, panic, agony and ecstasy, because there has not been adequate reception and transformation of them. Appropriate psycho-therapy can provide such reception and transformation. Marion Milner's diaries may also begin to break the autistic spell.[77]

11

FORTY-FOUR YEARS OF PSYCHOANALYSIS

The Suppressed Madness of Sane Men

Eternity's Sunrise brings together beads from Milner's inner and outer journeys over many years; *Suppressed Madness* is a retrospect of her professional life or as she puts it herself 'forty-four years of exploring psychoanalysis'. Asked by the British Psychoanalytical Society for a volume of papers to be included in the New Library of Psychoanalysis,[1] Milner at first sought to find a 'thread' to join the pieces together. This proved too hard and she alighted on the image of a tree with a number of branches as a more accurate description.

The book consists of twenty papers and a final section of 'afterthoughts'. In 1987 she re-introduces each paper and includes some comment upon it as well as including by way of contextualisation some responses in letter form from major members of the profession. The book was, in the main, warmly welcomed by critics. Masud Khan said it showed above all Milner's 'genius for energy'.[2] Michael Brearley, despite one or two reservations about Milner's Pickwickian habits about differentiation, found it 'vivid and exploratory' as well as 'a welcome bringing together of the main psychoanalytical contributions other than *The Hands of the Living God* of a particularly individual member of the Independent tradition in the British Psychoanalytical Society.'[3] Ellen Spitz, appreciating Milner's 'sensitive, deeply personal questing spirit' in her previous books, suggests that readers will now 'rejoice in her latest volume'.[4] Simon A. Grolnick in *The Journal of the American Psychoanalytic Association* warmly recommended the book, writing that, despite its uneven and at times repetitive nature, it is 'almost always interesting and not infrequently stimulating and inspiring'. Grolnick recognises that Milner is hard to 'pin down' but firmly insists that she is one of those of whom 'the psychoanalytic movement should be proud'. Further:

> She is reminiscent of the early Freudians who were honoured by being able to attend Freud's Wednesday night seminars [. . .] They brought with them the riches of world culture, as did Marion Milner to British psychoanalysis. This emerges throughout the entire book.

Helpfully, Grolnick's essay contextualises Milner's book in the 'kaleido-scope of knowledge' that Milner as a young woman brought with her to her psychoanalytic training; these influences included Bernard Berenson, Suzanne Langer, Jacques Maritain, Herbert Read, Christopher Caudwell and Elton Mayo as well as anthropologists, Eastern philosophers, and the major psychoanalysts of her day such as Ella Sharpe, Anna Freud, Melanie Klein, Michael Balint and Hanna Segal. Grolnick mentions the influences on Milner in some detail, not just to demonstrate what she brought with her to the training, but also to stress her efforts to 'correlate' this knowledge 'with the controversial area of ideas in the British Institute during the forties'. (Her impulse towards reconciliation is likely present here as in her earlier years.) Grolnick also perceptively pinpoints one of the reasons why Milner may have been marginalised by the psychoanalytic movement – both artist and scientist: 'Her artistic inclinations could not accept any rigidities within a fixed psychoanalytic movement.[5] That she rode out the next 44 years within psychoanalysis is a tribute both to Milner and to the psychoanalytic movement.' A more contemporary view of Milner's marginalisation comes from Donald Campbell, who suggests that Milner was more artist than analyst and thus difficult to fit in psychoanalytically. He considers that her main contribution to psychoanalysis was in the area of ways of thinking about art and the unconscious. He also comments that a number of Milner's elder colleagues tended to go to her for further analysis to deal with the 'unfinished business' of their previous analyses.[6]

Gilbert Rose from New York, despite a few caveats, again praises the book as one 'engaging as it is rewarding'. He finds it:

> unselfconsciously dedicated to the spirit of psychoanalysis [. . .] open minded yet questioning, down-to-earth yet *unafraid of mysticism* [. . .] One feels after reading it that one has not only learned a great deal but from a person one would wish to know.[7]

One who did indeed know Milner in person and through her books was Michael Brearley, already quoted; he highlights the importance of her work on symbol formation and her questioning and re-thinking of Kleinian concepts. He writes:

> The author argues – and this is central to her book, and to what she means by illusion, separateness and other key ideas – that the Kleinian concepts referred to above [i.e. splitting, projective identification and introjective identification] are not adequate to account for all the meanings of such play, for which the notion of a healthy return to a state of oceanic oneness is required.[8]

Brearley deals also with Klein's implicit criticism of Milner's work, and specifically her non-interpretation of the child's sadistic side, in her letter on the subject of this paper. Brearley is clear in thinking this criticism is largely beside the point:

> the analyst reports at length the aggression and sadism of the patient and suggests some improvement as a result of her interpretations of them. But she feels this is not sufficient. Also the author explicitly defends her idea that projection and projective identification do not fully meet the case since such mechanisms imply a clear boundary between self and other . . .

Klein believes, suggests Brearley, that all early states can be 'adequately described in terms of projection and introjection'; Milner would disagree because a patient in a very early state 'is not amenable to interpretations in terms of projection etc. because [they do] not have a clear enough vision of self and other, inner and outer, or because this is not the root problem'. Klein had castigated Milner for her idealisation of the 'baby self'; Brearley refutes this firmly – Milner's claim that too much paranoid anxiety in very early life and too limited an experience of that blissful early state lead to 'massive defences and a premature pseudo maturity' does not merit this characterisation.[9]

A further negative response from the Kleinian school comes from Susanna Isaacs Elmhirst who, while heralding the book 'as a biography of the British Society', is saddened by 'the circularity of Mrs Milner's explorations' – Elmhirst's sadness derives from her view of Milner's 'failure to comprehend that there is no such thing as totally benign, object-free, primary narcissism'. This results in a certain confusion that 'is not given the gentle, detailed, disentangling attention so movingly described by Rosenfeld'.[10] By contrast, a thoroughly approving and extensive treatment of *Suppressed Madness* is offered by the Independent Group analyst Andreas Giannacoulas who admires this 'wide and exhaustive view of the author's personal development' and these papers that 'prove that Marion Milner's contribution, beyond its literary quality, remains fundamental for the whole of British psychoanalysis'.[11]

Two papers, in particular, demonstrate Milner's personality in the field of psychoanalysis and her individual professional contributions: her work on Blake and her paper on mysticism. (Other papers have been drawn on in earlier chapters.)

Quite early on in his career, the psychoanalyst, Roger Kennedy tells how Milner, his supervisor, taught him to think not of his own view of a matter of belief but of what it meant to the patient (see p. 99). In the case of Blake, colleagues and friends became very much engaged with Milner's papers, and there were – Heinz Koppel, for one, suggests – very lively, even heated debates on the subject of Blake's view of Job. Here we have to heed Milner's recommendation to her supervisee – and think about what Blake's *Job* meant to *her* and avoid the distractions of Biblical/poetical exegesis or indeed of factional interests in the discussions.[12]

Psychoanalysts are known for their attachment to particular artists or works: Freud to Leonardo; Ella Sharpe to *King Lear*, Masud Khan also to *King Lear*; Winnicott to *Hamlet*; Bernard Barnett to George Eliot. Milner attached herself to William Blake. 'Unafraid of mysticism', as Rose states, it was possibly this that underpinned the connection between them; but I am not so sure. Milner quite often disavows the mystic label, and she always, when writing, thought first of an image.[13] Certain commentators on her books invoke Yeats's 'An image not a book'[14] when considering Milner and it is the drawings/etchings that catch Milner's gaze in her work on Blake – hers is a very visual take on the piece.

In re-visiting her paper, 'The Sense in Nonsense (Freud and Blake's *Job*)', Milner recalls that in 1956, Peggy Volkov, editor of the educational magazine

Figure 11.1 Engraving from Blake's *Job* – first illustration

154

The New Era had arranged a weekend event at which analysts of different persuasions were asked to give a paper on what they felt their orientation could best offer teachers. Milner chose Blake's *Illustrations to the Book of Job* as the text most germane to her purposes. She had come across this text very early on in her career when treating her first clinic patient, a young violinist who could no longer practise his instrument. Hitherto she had not been aware of the book, but when she found it, it seemed most relevant to her problems with the young musician as she discovered that the first picture 'showed Job and all his family sitting under a spreading tree surrounded by their flocks but on the tree are hanging musical instruments unused. However in the last picture, the twenty-first, they are all playing on them.'[15]

After this experience, Milner came to see Blake's *Job* as a 'kind of handbook for trying to understand blocks in psychic creativity',[16] and in 1956 she first

Figure 11.2 Engraving from Blake's *Job* – last illustration

155

wrote about Blake in this way when her thoughts turned to education, art and psychoanalysis. In the *Job* paper she homes in on that something that is omitted from the school system – and this is in the area of psychic creativity. For her, at this time, *Job* is a narrative of those processes in us when we become 'sterile and doubt our creative capacities', when we doubt our 'powers to love and work', those struggles with which Freud was so crucially concerned. In the 1956 paper and in her paper 'Psychoanalysis and Art', Milner gives her description of Blake's version of the Job story. This is from the second paper:

> the story of Job, the perfect and upright man; how Satan appears before God and says it's all very well for Job to be so good when he has everything he could possibly want, but what if he really suffered, would he be so good then? So God gives Satan permission to plague Job in every possible way short of killing him [. . .] Job at first bears all patiently, but finally succumbs and curses the day he was born. And then when Job has reached the depths of despair a new figure appears, Elihu; after this Job gradually goes back to his original state – but with a difference [. . .] In the first picture of Job with his wife and family, surrounded by his flocks, they are all shown grouped under a spreading tree upon which hang musical instruments, unused [. . .] The last Picture, showing Job with his family and flocks restored to him, has the same design but now they are all singing or playing upon their instruments.[17]

Milner reads the story though a Freudian prism – for her, Blake's *Job* is strongly inflected by psychoanalysis. She thus sees his belief in his own perfection as a denial of his human nature – he considers he is good because his conscious intention is benign. His inner world, however, seen in the form of Satan and his destructiveness, tells another story. What, asks Milner the psychoanalyst, is the cause of this destructiveness? She links the situation in the first *Job* pictures back to the earliest state of infancy when 'all goodness seems to be part of oneself . . . all heaven is ours and in our power'. But this condition does not maintain; its and our omnipotence have to be relinquished; and so hard is this for us that we project the memory of it on to a heavenly father – and, by obedience to this being, imagined though he be, we believe we can regain the paradise of our lost infancy; but we are also rebellious beings, angered at our loss – and, if this rage is split off, we come to believe it is Satan's rage and destructiveness and not our own. Thus, in the third picture Satan is seen filling the sky and towering over the bodies of Job's children. The news is then brought to Job, who has been quite unaware of it until now, so separated has he been from his own destructiveness. It is at this nadir of Job's experience of multiple losses that he gives his last crust to a beggar. Milner interprets this as Blake's way of showing that Job is 'desperately attempting to defend himself by philanthropy' and she suggests further that it is this unconscious hypocrisy that causes the disaster in his inner world and occasions him to sink deepest.[18]

Illustration 6, 'Descent to the Depths', has an image of Job prostrate on the earth with Satan pouring a fiery tempest upon his head. Job still maintains that he is a good man, a faithful servant of God, but he does now understand that, as an infant, he was helpless, not omnipotent. Here is Milner's psychoanalytic reading:

> A Freudian could say that this is the beginning of his becoming able to recognize a fundamental fact: the fact that his initial feeling of wholeness, unity with the universe, was only made possible because he had a mother there, separate from himself and therefore able to nourish and protect him [. . .] But he does not yet recognize his anger at eventually having to give up both that protection and also the illusion that he did not need it because he thought he did it all himself. He does not yet recognize his anger, but his body breaks out in boils.[19]

Job's bodily state bespeaks the anger that has been unexpressed, a graphic somatisation. The following picture further suggests that Job's inner war extends to his sexual powers – his lack of creativity is also sexual impotence; 'here Freudians would say that the denied rages of his infancy at the loss of the first feeling of total possession of his mother have now made him doubt the goodness of his own sexual love . . .',[20] while in the next picture Job comes closer to realising that the real trouble is within himself. Again, Freud is invoked: 'And what he sees through the vision of Eliphaz is what Freud would call the persecuting super-ego, a terrifying figure, not an indwelling spirit of love, life, action, but an angry sternly commanding God.' Job is not able to understand that this fearsome figure is his own creation; and soon he is at the mercy of the Devil, the victim of Satanic force. In the illustration, the tablets of stone, representing Mosaic law, preside over the whole while the text shows (a characteristic Milner reading) that Job's battles express themselves in symptoms of the body as he becomes confused with what is good and what is evil.

His adherence to the letter of the law had been but a denial of the inner unconscious realities of human nature. Seen through Milner's Freud, it looks like this:

> And Freud would say it is this very idea of omnipotence which explains why Job has had to set up such a wholesale defence against knowing the bad in himself, against knowing the difference between himself at his best and himself at his worst. For if one is omnipotent for good one can also be omnipotent for evil.[21]

The next section of the essay is on 'Recovery', heralded by the appearance of the figure of Elihu and the start of Job's awareness that the conscious life is not the only kind, not the only wisdom; and he realises, too, that his mind is not omnipotent, that he is not himself responsible for all that happens, good or ill. He also re-thinks his position in relation to those powers outside himself as he becomes able to accept his own ignorance, something that, Freud would suggest, 'begins with the first momentous questionings of childhood'.[22]

A Freudian, Milner considers, would read this in terms of a 'child's coming to believe in the real creative forces, both in himself and the universe; a problem which has at its centre his anger at having to face the fact of that union of his parents which created him'.[23] So far, so good; the next connections (with education) are more forced and at times suggest that the *Job* text, and its Freudian gloss, may have been co-opted to fit an educational agenda. (I return to this below.)

Milner, always attentive to the need for wide attention, comments on 'The Morning Stars' illustration as an image of what happens when the spirit 'is spread out to embrace and give itself to the whole of the external world'. When this happens, the world is transfigured, in a way comparable to Freud's notions of cosmic bliss and the oceanic state. Job's attention is directed inwards to the monsters Behemoth and Leviathan, male and female, 'the life power within himself in its most primitive form'.[24]

Controversially, given its Old Testament setting and source, Jesus now appears in the illustrations. Job sees him in what is an extremely powerful experience and now, contends Milner, no longs needs an omnipotent, paternal God outside himself for he has found a kind of inner control that is no longer separated and split off from himself. When all the loss and anger have been faced, something new emerges – through the imagination.[25]

Milner now confronts the popular, and misguided, view of the Freudian unconscious, the erroneous idea that it contains only bad things, those murkier matters that we dislike (and sometimes disown) in ourselves. (This is a notion about which she also expresses her disquiet to Donald Winnicott.) But, she insists, 'any practising analyst knows also how strong is the repression of love' and, once more, she invokes Blake's 'O Human Imagination! O Divine Body I have crucified!'[26] There is no doubt, Milner argues, that we do crucify our imagination, kill our 'capacity for understanding others' to avoid admitting responsibility. Our imagination also helps us avoid too rigid a holding on to logical thought, to those principles, based on the idea of duality, that 'require a split between subject and object'. Holding that Blake uses Jesus to stand for Imagination, Milner suggests that he makes important claims for unconscious thinking; Satan meanwhile is a symbol of the isolation resulting from an insistence 'on the complete self-sufficiency of the conscious individual ego'.[27] At the time of writing, 1956, Milner contends that this problem of an over-reliance on the conscious mind is coming to the fore in cultural life – and she quotes Winnicott: 'we are poor indeed if we are only sane.'[28]

As the process of Job's recovery develops, Milner continues to read the illustrations through her Freudian lens; she sees the story as one where Job

158

comes to accept the 'primitive within himself', his need for dependence on others, and also the 'destruction he has done in his secret thoughts'; and moreover, his learning 'to realize how, in his early belief in the omnipotence of thought, he felt he had really destroyed those he loved and so had had to build up the wrought image of his own perfection to compensate'.[29] In the pictures of restoration, Milner again reprises 'a Freudian would say' – namely, how the drawings show how Job's relation to the internal mother has been restored – the mother who initially causes the infant's disillusion and thus becomes the object of the child's rage. In the final picture, creativity is restored, and all the characters are seen with their musical instruments.

Milner now steps back and asks what Blake is actually saying; and this she considers from the perspective of what a Freudian might 'corroborate from clinical experience.'[30] In brief, he is, for her, saying that societal constraints have produced extreme rage that, if unacknowledged, can lead to disaster; the primitive in ourselves can be dealt with in a non-punitive way; traditional ideas about the management of our primitive selves are deeply flawed; and when we aim to know the truth about ourselves, then a new force enters the picture – 'the caveman within us becomes tameable'.[31] For Milner, these ideas were and are 'revolutionary'. She thought the single most important Freudian sentence was 'A man who doubts his own love, may, or rather must, doubt every lesser thing.' It follows that 'learning how to love means learning how to mourn', to accept separation and loss; in Freud's view, 'we must allow ourselves our griefs, otherwise our joys will be stunted'. The ability to mourn is a vital part of psychic growth. Leaping to Blake, Milner states that he is saying, as psychoanalytic experience finds, 'that change of heart, growth of spirit does not come about in the same way as that by which we alter our material surroundings, it does not comes from purposeful activity.'[32] Situating her ideas at the time, she points out that psychoanalysis began as a way of curing neurotic symptoms, but it has become more and more involved with problems of character and personality, with change and growth.

Turning now to the implications for education, Milner has already stated that the child can be seen to protest against an education that disavows the idea that growth and change can come from 'the interplay and integration of opposites' and wrongly privileges that 'narrow focused attention of expediency' and 'purpose-driven life of adulthood'. She now reiterates Freud's discovery that over-reliance on the logical could be released in the analytic session. The emphasis on non-interference and freedom could lead to some misguided ideas: the view, for instance, that no authority in schools would rule out neuroses – not, of course, the case. The teacher, for better or worse, must be the one to disillusion the child. Thus: 'the teacher represents that society which refuses to accept the primary instinctive ways of showing love and demands that substitute ways be found however painfully.' Importantly, Milner elaborates, for the child to be able to learn '[he] has to climb down from the original heights of omnipotence, to discover how little he knows, where once he felt he knew everything, how little he can do, where once he felt he could do everything'.[33]

Moving on to consider the 'Use of Hard Work' in the next section, Milner suggests that the public examination is not so much a test of what a child might know as 'an initiation ceremony intended to give public recognition to our power to take pains, to undergo pain for the sake of something we value'. The Freudian viewpoint, for Milner, sees work well done as part of the struggle to come to a belief in one's power to love. Clinical experience shows 'that the inner structure of the unconscious art of our psyche is essentially animistic' – what does she mean by this? 'That is,' she explains, 'we build up our inner world on the basis of our relationships to people we have loved and hated, we carry these people about with us and what we do, we do for them – or in conflict with them.' Moreover it is through these 'inner people', as Milner was later to call them, that we conduct our relationships even when the original people have long gone and 'we find external representatives of them both in new people who enter our lives, and in all the interests and the causes that we seek to serve'.[34] Teachers, Milner suggests, might find it helpful to be aware that however neutral and impersonal their activities seem to be they are basically about people: for example, 'the extent to which the staff of any school are used by the children as the dramatis personae of their own inner dramas can, at times, be a source of irritation or mystification, if the teachers have not understood the inevitability of the process'.[35] Indeed, they may be destabilised to find themselves cast in the role of Satan or demons or even in the role of Elihu or Christ.

Milner does not feel it is stretching the point to suggest that Blake in *Job* might also be saying that Job's one-sided approach to life involves an 'underestimation of the importance of the image-making capacity of the mind', and she points out that in another picture – one not, in fact, included in the final series – Blake shows Job surrounded by the figures of Painting, Poetry and Music.[36]

Freud discovered that it was not by conscious reasoning that his patients were helped but by attending to what they 'freely imagined'; Milner links this with the idea that teachers could be offered vacation courses in the arts that would enable them to realise their own, possibly untapped, creative powers; and in the last section of the paper on 'Absentmindedness' she wonders if Blake is perhaps saying something about those occasions 'when the free imagination interacts with perception and produces moments of vision', moments when for the Freudian (*her* Freudian) 'there is a temporary fusion of inner and outer' – moments most likely to occur in the free (but framed) setting of the analytic hour. The paper concludes with Milner's vision of the future based on her interpretation of Blake's *Job*: further psychological discoveries will become of use to education, and 'they will be to do with a deeper understanding of the creative relation to internal spontaneous forces, making for wholeness'.[37] Whether or not this has been or is the case is for the reader to consider.

The dialogue between Milner and Blake, or Milner, Blake and Freud, in which Milner originally had the approval of Winnicott, called forth a rich vein of correspondence: from the V&A (writing paper headed 'Ministry of Education') George Digby writes, on 9 December 1957, that Milner's is 'one of the most illuminating essays I have yet read on Blake' and wishes only that some of the Blake scholars would attend to what she says.[38] Some did; one such being the poet and Blake scholar Kathleen Raine. In the main, she writes, Milner has 'rightly interpreted Blake', and she was impressed by Milner's view of Elihu: 'the feminine principle as representing the arts and non-conceptual thought, the crust of bread as a piece of self-righteousness, and Behemoth and Leviathan as the life and death instincts of the male and female or both . . .'

Raine takes issue with Milner, however, in a major way over the interpretation of Satan as a figure born of that which Job has repressed; in Raine's view the arrival of Satan is 'the advent of selfhood [. . .] the sense of an identity apart from God'. For her, Satan is 'the self, or the self-conscious ego, who once he exists is the tormentor. He is the rule of a kingdom apart from God's kingdom.' Milner, who has re-visited the text of this letter a number of times, has inserted a marginal comment 'work out re Piaget' – we do not know if she did this, but the remark is typical of her ever-continuing quest for further insights.

Raine recognises that Milner may well feel that she, Raine, has given insufficient attention to Milner's words about 'Satan as rage'. However, she resumes that she cannot see how it is possible 'to interpret the Satan figure in any other way than as the selfhood, whose laws of righteousness and punishment are a perpetual scourge to the innocence of the figure of divine humanity'.[39]

Raine had her misgivings; not so Anton Ehrenzweig, a firm supporter of Milner. On 1 January 1956 he writes, 'I often found it difficult to distinguish between your ideas and mine and sometime [this] felt like a fear of "losing identity".' After hearing her *Job* lecture he comments that she has altered *his* status with the British psychoanalytic movement. He had always felt he was writing 'for the artists rather than the psa-sts [psychoanalysts]. May be that this will change now.' He hopes that Milner will write a study of Blake to show 'how an analysis of formal structure ought to accompany the analysis of symbolism.' He praises her analysis of the Christ picture and, increasingly, admires her as an artist: 'your chiaroscuro drawing was very beautiful, incidentally, and at once established you as an artist for the audience.'[40]

Adrian Stokes is similarly positive; he has read the piece avidly and much admires Milner's 'achievement of expressing so many different things in a simple, ardent way.' With his 'Italianate prejudice' Stokes is, unsurprisingly, no devotee of Blake. Nevertheless, Milner can be lauded for managing 'to convey on the peg of Blake [. . .] bountiful wisdom, the new wisdom and the only one relevant in our age'.[41] Roger Money-Kyrle thanks Milner for sending a reprint of her lecture as he is always 'very interested in any study of the factors' that impede creativity, while Dr Gordon Levinson remarks that the *Job* piece is 'an excellent approach to educationalists'; and Victor Goddard congratulates Milner, agreeing with her that the approach she advances is indeed 'revolutionary'.[42] Heinz Koppel regards Milner's reading of *Job* as important. It seems from his letter to Milner that at the public lecture there had been heated debate about Blake's reading of the Book of Job and related, possibly religious matters. Koppel sensibly writes that what matters is what she, Milner, found in Blake's *Job* 'and the only thing under discussion is wether [*sic*] your reading of creative processes (and not Blake's reading of the bible or yours of Blake's work) is to the point'.[43] From the same archive of letters about *Job* comes this from a psychiatrist from Rotterdam, R. Fentener Von Vlissingen for whom 'It is simply astonishing [. . .] that someone is able to show others these central themes of life not only, but the most perplexing fact to me was the metaphysical aspect you showed in psychoanalysis.'[44]

Von Vlissingen singles out Milner's metaphysical bias as do earlier and other commentators on her books and life; in a paper of 1973 she brings together some ideas on the subject. This paper, she tells us in *Suppressed Madness*, was originally written in honour of Paula Heimann on her seventy-fifth birthday, and was prompted by Milner's need to enquire into the subject because of, on occasion, having patients who practised some form of meditation. It is an account of her own ideas before and after becoming a psycho-analyst and also a comment on what has been written by other analysts. In the process, she became aware of another process described restrospectively as similar to Bion's 'an idea in search of a thinker'.[45]

The archive of Milner's material on 'Mysticism and Spirituality' shows her investigating Freud's *Civilisation and its Discontents*, quoting Freud's writing of a friend who claimed that the practise of yoga in fixing attention on a bodily function, especially breathing, brings new sensations of coanaesthesia: 'Freud sees in this a physiological basis for much of the wisdom of mysticism.' In 'Moses and Monotheism' Freud writes of how Jewish monotheism, borrowed from Egypt, involved the rejection of magic and mysticism; and Milner included in her forays into the subject remarks from Freud's post-humously published 'Findings, Ideas, Problems': 'Mysticism is the obscure self-perception of the realm outside the ego, of the id.'

As she feels her way through Freudian ideas on the subject, the archive shows Milner also consulting Fenichel, Brierley, and, again a last reference to Freud in 'A case of homosexuality in a woman' where he states, 'I know indeed that the craving of mankind for mysticism is ineradicable.'[46]

Is Milner a mystic? She herself resisted the label as has been seen in *Eternity's Sunrise* (p. 141); and yet, others have claimed her; Michael Eigen, for one, in *The Psychoanalytic Mystic* recruits her:

It is difficult to overestimate the role played by Marion Milner who, in her quiet, unassuming way, helped develop the climate for spontaneous interpenetration of psychoanalytic and mystical life. She naturally uses mystical language to portray and amplify psychoanalytic processes, and the latter to probe, cleanse and open mystical experiencing. In her work, the pregnant void, emptiness, creative chaos, the deep unconscious, and the I-yet-not-I experience are central.[47]

Similarly, the writer Kelley Raab has taken Milner into the fold of 'Transcendence', saying Milner has 'yet to be discovered by scholars of religious studies'. She references Dragstedt and states that, for Milner, Blake's *Job* 'served as a template for her explorations of blocks in creativity in her patients and herself'.[48] Milner also, as Raab correctly remarks, refers to Blake in her work with 'Susan' and then comments on the need to sort out the 'layers' of interpretation involved: 'The plots of the biblical story, Blake's spin on this ancient Hebrew tale, and Milner's own perspective on Blake's *Job*.'[49] Both Dragstedt and Sayers point out that Milner is one of those rather unusual analysts who sought to combine mysticism and psychoanalysis.[50]

The essay in honour of Heimann elaborates this. The first part of the paper traverses Milner's views from about 1916 and a comment by a friend, a mathematician, who said that a thought 'thinks you'. Some of the responses she received to *A Life* and *An Experiment* led her to think she might be termed 'mystical' and, like the title of the volume of papers, Milner's piece begs the question 'what is the relation of mysticism to madness'?[51]

In the early 1930s Milner tells us she had read Suzuki on Zen, then Lao Tze, Patanjali and a summary of Western mystical tradition whose title and author have escaped her – though from it one sentiment remained: 'it said that a beginning of mystical experience could be learning to attend to one's own body awareness, from inside, even beginning with one's big toe.' A little later she read Silberer of whose work she remembered little though it backed up her 'interest in those sudden moments of intensified perception of the outer world that I had already been studying in my first book and that I was about to continue to study in my second'.[52]

From the early stages of her psychoanalytic training Milner rather put ideas on mystical subjects to one side – they returned in 1947 with a boy patient and his 'lovely black' images and with the views of 'Susan' on her own mysticism (for example, Susan's concerns about the relation of mysticism to madness). Milner then found Wilhelm Reich and his 'insistence that all mystical experience is due to the misinterpretation of sexual feelings'. In 1950 Susan's images further contributed to Milner's thoughts and she became preoccupied with the idea of blankness as, indeed, she had previously with 'positive aspects of not-knowing'.[53] In 1952 Milner was to return to mystical ideas with a discussion with Harold Walsby, who had spoken of the problems of 'equating intellect with logic' and claimed that the other (non-logical) kind of thinking could 'be called mystical just because of its capacity for letting go the distinction between subject and object'. (Thus, for Milner, non-differentiation is inherent in her use of the term 'mystic'.) After hearing Walsby speak, Milner was able to think about bringing the psychoanalytic and the mystical closer together as, so characteristically, she seeks to make a bridge between disparate ideas (this was the case right from the start, from her early paper of 1945 on 'Some aspects of phantasy in relation to general psychology').

Walsby had drawn attention to the *Tao Te Ching* and Milner found an edition with his annotations particularly useful, especially the paradox of being able to feel 'oneself in touch with non-existence'. Then there was the very powerful statement 'Attain to the *good* of absolute vacuity'; this was linked for Milner with a speaker at a 1930s school prize-giving insisting on the importance of knowing 'how to wipe your minds free of learning'.[54] She has, then and typically, privileged the aphorism, 'He who knows the masculine and yet keeps to the feminine will become a channel drawing all the world towards it.' This was a concept that led back to some of her struggles in *A Life of One's Own* (this essay brings together ideas that have preoccupied Milner throughout her professional and pre-analytic life), also leading her to the saying 'He who knows the white yet keeps to the black'; for Milner an 'active' connecting with the dark is not a passive losing oneself in it; thence, once more, to Blake, and the Leviathan and the Morning Stars Image.[55]

Milner here reminds herself of her 1956 *Job* lecture and her referencing of Ehrenzweig who, in his first book, 'maintains that mystic feeling is explained by our rational surface mind's incapacity to visualize the inarticulate feelings of the depth mind'. A further step in her thinking comes from her recollection of writing her Athens paper of 1963 on 'The Concentration of the Body' and the importance she placed on the internal awareness of one's own body.[56] (This body concentration is very much part of Milner's particular idiom of mysticism and links here once more with Winnicott and his stress on the body and body-self.) A last landmark in this section had been in the 1960s when, after writing her account of Susan, she had chosen the book's title: Susan herself had said that before she had been given ECT she had known what St Paul meant by 'the length and breadth and depth and height of the love of God'. Milner thought that this notion of god 'being so spatial, containing, holding, sounded very much more like a mother god than a father god'.[57] The present title, *Hands of the Living God*, from D.H. Lawrence's poem, encapsulates all these ideas.

Milner now embarks on the second part of her investigation into mysticism and moves on to see what other analysts had to say. Her trawl through her bookshelves – not exactly a strict scientific method – yields: two references in Winnicott; three in Silberer; and none in Ella Sharpe, Hanna Segal, Herbert Rosenfeld, Money-Kyrle, Bertram Lewis, R.D. Laing and Melanie Klein. Reich, she discovered, wrote at some length about mysticism as 'distorted sexuality', and he gives examples of what Silberer would, she suggests, class as 'the diabolic kind of mysticism'. She finds one reference in the work of Joan Riviere and only two in all the Ernest Jones books she owns, and these references are both in volume 3 of his life of Freud: 'These are to do with Freud's admitting that his study of religious belief was limited to that of the common man, and that he regretted having ignored "the rarer and more profound type of religious emotion as experienced by mystics and saints".'[58]

There are three references, for Milner, in Freud's work: in *Civilisation and its Discontents*, as he deliberates on whether the oceanic feeling can be thought of as the source of religious need. In the work of Anna Freud, Milner found no references, while there was one in Fenichel's *The Psycho-analytic Study of the Neuroses*. His view was that psychoanalysis did include certain basic principles of mysticism but he compares these with the 'activities of the police dog in police investigations' – those seen by Reik as the survival of the 'animal oracle.'[59]

Most significantly, Milner now comes upon Brierley and Bion, and in preparing her Mysticism essay, she discovers both were quite vocal on the subject. Brierley 'tries translating the Christian mystics' accounts of their experiences into psychoanalytic terms', while Bion, states Milner, does the opposite; 'he tries using religious terminology to denote what happens in psychoanalysis' – he can do this because of his decision to use the terms 'mystic' and 'genius' as interchangeable. He also uses the term 'O' to convey the 'ultimate reality' or god; this he calls 'O' and, for him, the mystic is the one 'who claims direct contact with it'. Bion deploys the 'O' sign also to denote that which happens in a psychoanalytic session. Then there is Bion's concept of working with neither memory nor desire – ideas that, for Milner, omit that 'sensory awareness of breathing' so important in Eastern mystic traditions.[60]

Milner's habitual focus on the body and bodily experience, her attention to the bones (to be held gently) and the breath, so essential to her thought, do not enter into Bion's formulations.

Bion concerns himself with those who come into direct contact with the 'O', and Milner's concept of the 'Answering Activity' has some relation to this. Michael Parsons in his essay in honour of her ninetieth birthday traces the development in Milner's three autobiographical books of this idea, 'the experience of an inner being, being part of Oneself and greater than oneself, with which one can make contact through a particular kind of meditative awareness'. Parsons contends that in psychoanalysis, technique and creativity must be kept in equilibrium and that Milner's account of the Answering Activity 'can help us towards the theory of psychoanalytic creativity which this requires'.[61] I would suggest that the Answering Activity comes within the linguistic registers of the spiritual and the mystical as well as the psychoanalytic and outside the realm of the scientific.

Recent formulations building on Bion's work and resonating with Milner's include that of Mark Epstein who writes on 'Psychotherapy from a Buddhist Perspective' and brings Milner into his commentary on 'Right Mindfulness: exploring the Temporary Metaphor'. Writing of 'Body' he reads Milner's attention to breathing, and her discovery of attending to her big toe, as examples of the practice of mindfulness and quotes her art school experience of 1950 when she came to find the world 'exceedingly paintable.'[62]

Milner has always been difficult to place; where does she belong? The psychoanalytic establishment does not really know what to make of her, what to do with her. Perhaps tellingly, Michael Parsons engaged with her more mystical side in his ninetieth birthday honours for her; meanwhile Michael Podro, art historian and critic, gave her as his birthday gift his paper on Cézanne 'The Landscape Thinks Itself in Me', the comments and procedures of Cézanne.[63] Both papers stress her standing as 'mystic' and 'artist' rather than psychoanalyst; but this is too simple. Perhaps her mysticism essay in *Suppressed Madness* can help us further here. Milner is clearly anti-professional. Her *method* as indicated is decidedly unscientific, her approach a long way from any aspirations towards seeing psychoanalysis as science. She confines her search to hardbacks in her own personal library by known analysts – no paperbacks because they have no indexes. It is an idiosyncratic and anti-authoritarian take on the subject and typical of one who wears her knowledge very lightly.

Her focus in the Mysticism essay, as in the majority of her collected papers, is personal; she inserts herself as subject into the text (the painting school and the big toe are examples) – not for her the model of the neutral, anonymous analyst; and yet, there is here a true paradox. Very subjective in her writing, she is also very hidden. Her lifelong wish was *not* to be 'legible'; and yet she is one of the strongest, most visible of subjective presences in her analytic writings – conventionally the bastion of the invisible author.

Her next, and last, posthumously published book (in 2012), *Bothered by Alligators*, casts further light on the paradoxes and puzzles of this most independent of personalities.

12

BOTHERED BY ...
THE 1990s

The Suppressed Madness of Sane Men charted the course of Milner's professional life in the world of psychoanalysis. Her final and valedictory text, first published only in 2012, covers her central psychological preoccupations not only during her nineties (and the twentieth century's nineties) but also throughout her life.

The book came about when, on sorting though her piles of papers, 'so as to be ready for being dead whenever that might be',[1] she came upon her son John's story book, made when he was a schoolboy of around seven years old, unfound until then, and her diary she had kept of his babyhood. The book occupied a central part of her last years, arguably the activity most significant for her. The artist Mathew Hale tells how he came to be involved: he had known Milner from 1990 until her death, had read *On Not Being Able to Paint* when at art school, had loved the book but had thought, mistakenly, that it must have been written by an American (its open tone and consideration of the reality of failure suggested this) whom he presumed was dead. He takes up the story:

> In 1990 an old friend of mind who lives in Bristol phoned me and
> said: 'You don't fancy working for a fascinating old lady one morning
> a week do you – she's a famous art therapist, or something?' I quizzed
> him about who she could be (he couldn't remember the name) and
> on a whim said, 'it's not Marion Milner, is it?!'
> 'Yes.'
> 'She must be really old . . .'
> 'She is.'
> 'Ceri [MM's great-niece] brought her down for tea and Marion saw
> the collages you made with the kids and asked who'd done them.
> Ceri's trying to find someone to do odd jobs for Marion, up in London
> – so she thought of you.'[2]

This was the start of an important and productive friendship between Milner and the young artist. At the outset he was her odd job man and 'cleaner' –

167

never, he says, his strongest suit – and he also helped her in her much-loved garden. Delighted that she was in London and very much alive, Mathew soon acquired another role: his job description changed to 'typist' when Milner told him she was working on a new book and needed someone to come in and type up each week's work. She had very poor eyesight in her old age and could not do it herself, although she did sometimes use her electric typewriter until her son brought a word processor for Mathew to type up and store the manuscript on. And that is how they worked for years.

Milner's handwriting was very shaky, and, as we have seen, she did not always *wish* to be legible. Mathew was thought by his friends to be something of a genius for being able to decipher it, but, he writes, 'once you got the hang of it wasn't' as difficult as it looked. It was 'a curious mixture of the spidery and the emphatic, often in red or black felt pen. Her sentences would meander across a page and then frequently explode into capital letters as she reached her point.' He could see 'her thinking happening across the page'.

As Milner worked, Mathew witnessed the process unfolding; he comments that the signs of the work were

> everywhere in her house. As the manuscript proliferated so did her corrections and variations. Each week she would have prepared a list of material she wanted me to type up or change and I would do so on her electric typewriter and save the new definitive version to a floppy-disk. Before I left I would print out all the fresh material and incorporate it into the appropriate chapter files. She would then make handwritten notes in those files – or add new material, and the process would repeat itself as the weeks and years went by.

Mathew suggests cogently that the text represented Milner's chance to come to terms with various unresolved questions: others who she knew have pointed to the ambivalence she understandably had about it – Mary Reid (Pears), for one, remarks that, on occasion, Milner had called it, in writerly exasperation, 'that bloody book', a text driven by guilt and the need to make reparation.[3] Let us look at the book.

First, Milner recounts how, having had it typed by Mathew, she showed it to colleagues and friends who encouraged publication. The impetus to publish was her idea that the book 'could show parents some of the ways in which a child can struggle with the interplay of his own and his parents' problems, and how he can do this by using his poetic intuition long before he can express the problems in direct, logical speech'.[4]

She set out intent on avoiding technical Freudian language, but despite this aim 'quite deep psychoanalytic ideas [kept] cropping up' and there was a change of emphasis. What looked at the outset as if she was trying to analyse her own child turned out rather differently as she 'slowly came to realise that it was not a question of me analysing him, but rather of his images analysing me'. *Alligators* is the most autobiographical of all Milner's books and, fittingly, it follows the method of its predecessors: the journey is uncharted, as was Crusoe's in *A Life of One's Own*, and she 'had to go on with no idea where this undertaking was going to lead [her].'[5]

After a brief account of her time in America, her seminal use of doodles, and the war leading to her psychoanalytic training – with all of which the reader of this book is now familiar – Milner tells us of a change of aim: now, it seemed that:

> the writing of this book was an attempt to see if I could use J's images to make up for what had gone wrong in my own experience of being a patient in psychoanalysis, and to see how far this could be done without the help of the analyst and the psychoanalytic couch.[6]

Her investigation of her son's play and conversations (sadly, the original manuscript of the diary an unfound document at the time of writing) now follows, with its encounter with her son, now in his sixties, after more than fifty years. As Milner does this, it becomes clearer to her that from certain unexpected things happening to her, the material of the diary is acting upon her. For instance in February 1934 when John was two years old we learn that his father, because of his acute asthma, was advised to go to Spain for the winter. Thus, after Milner's school term was over, she went to join Dennis in Spain for two weeks, leaving Star, his nanny, in charge of John. When they returned her son seemed to be flourishing and unaffected by the absence. However, the diary gives another version: entitled 'Reaction to our absence' Milner writes of how, when visiting his Grannie, and not finding her in the sitting room as he had expected, he 'went dead white'; and then the absence of Star, who left the family after an accident, occasions the young boy's fear of flies in the garden.

Milner comments on her diary in her ninety-year old present in a series of headings and parenthetic comments; for example, of an occasion when John was tearfully upset and insisting that his grief was not about a physical matter, she wonders if it derives from 'his inner battle over the pain of having an ailing father'.[7] His disquiet over separation triggers a fear of birds after he has tried to prevent his mother going to Oxford for her schools work.

Most poignantly, in a section for January 1936, Milner looks back on how at this time she needed to go abroad, not only because there were tensions in the marriage but also for her creative self, 'deep internal reasons for this urgent need to write once more'. Her writing had taken her on the most profound of journeys leading to that surrender of self underpinning many of her aesthetic and psychological discoveries. But the cost had been high – it was that 'J got no picture letters'.[8] Ruefully, she comments that it had not even occurred to her that she could make them or that correspondence was a possibility with a four year old. In any event, among her journeys in her papers in 1990,

Milner found part of a letter sent to her in Spain by her husband enclosing J's drawings. First, he had asked for a drawing of a volcano, then he drew a dragon with two rows of very large teeth,* followed by a wrecked train; then a ship, a picture of Mummy, a seagull and a flood. As she re-reads the letter, Milner is assailed by guilt:

> the awful thing was that I had not the slightest memory of sending J back a picture letter [. . .] I certainly had no understanding of the message of anger in the letter; and the drawings were just scribbles, totally unrecognisable as being what J said they were.[9]

In 1936 when the letter was received, Milner was innocent of the psychoanalytic 'notion of an inner world in which there were psychic representations of the outer world, one in which loved people could be blown up, devoured, drowned, etc.' Of these matters, at the time, she knew nothing, and her diary 'continues as if nothing special had happened'. A further fantasy of flooding, in March 1937, reminds Milner of the unnoticed picture letter and 'the potentially disastrous effect of [her] failure to talk to him about the drawings and messages in his picture letter'.[10]

Milner's book *An Experiment in Leisure* is then inter-penetrated by the diary, especially her connection with Anton Ehrenzweig, which she now sees in a rather different light (a connection augmented by J's storybook and described later), linking his 'creative surrender' with a diary section with her son in delight telling everyone 'I let the sea do just what it liked with me.'[11]

Milner, later in the diary, deploys ideas clearly underpinned by her analytic experience: 'The man on the railway line' entry for 12 January 1937 is a telling example. She records her son's frequent playing with trains, making lines for them and building a farm:

> Put a little knight on the railway line, said he would not get hurt because of the armour. Another day he set the farmer on the railway line and made the train run into him. Yesterday he was making the fireman climb up the signal and sit on top, and then jump off onto the line. Said the train would not hurt him because he would lie down under it. Said this with a sly important look, not answering my questions about it.[12]

Milner comments that as, by now, she knows more of psychoanalysis, she 'could not help seeing in all this something of J's inevitable anxieties over his imaginings about adult sexual relationships as well as his worries about his father's intermittent illnesses'.[13]

---

* Cf. the dragon picture MM herself drew as a girl; see Plate 2 and ALO, pp.112–115. I am indebted to Michael Parsons for drawing my attention to this image.

In March 1939, Milner realises in retrospect that this would have been the time when the story book was being written, but they had no knowledge of it; it was a secret book – and there is no mention of it in the diary, 'for we knew nothing about it'.[14] Thus, in a sense, John's story book is hidden, the narrative of a self sequestered from his parents. Shortly after this, in May 1939, Dennis Milner has a bad attack: 'It was here that his father, now himself in psychoanalysis, had his most severe asthma attack, having morphine injections, with his doctor visiting him thirteen times during the weekend.' J would, Milner writes, 'have been downstairs or out in the garden so would have been unlikely to have seen his father's struggling for breath'. The diary, however, tells another story, as J asks his nanny to smack him, being sure that he had been naughty, returning from school very truculent and saying that were he to have a baby sister, he would bully her to death, and grumbling that he could not see more of his father.[15]

After this, due to the change in J's mood and behaviour, the diary records his parents' decision to get him some treatment from a Child Guidance Clinic. At the time, Milner emphasises that the clinician's comments could not be seen through the lens of the story book because they did not know of its existence. Its stories of retaliation and killing were yet to be seen by J's parents. Once more, as so often in autobiography, memory itself is on trial: 'I have no memory of the book being brought from the school, or of reading it. Perhaps with so many anxieties about the looming war, it remained unnoticed.'[16] When it did turn up much later, it was to throw light on certain aspects of the diary – May 1940, for example, deals with anxiety over compliance, and Milner's note that her son seems to feel that if he helps his parents, in matters of chores or housework, this becomes total annihilation. (The helpful porter in the story book elaborates this idea – see pp. 172, 175.)

This section of the text is, inevitably, informed by Milner's own experience as a child; in the entry for May 1941 she notes J's slowness in going to bed, followed by her threat to cuff him if he did not hurry up. She then pretended to cuff him, he to avoid her good night kiss; she to cry:

> (Here I well understood why I had made a note of this; it was a kind of play aggression that I could never imagine having happened between myself and my own parents. It also occurred to me that my ability to do it now could be a by-product of the intermittent psychoanalysis that I had been experiencing during these last few years.)[17]

In 1941 there follows material about J's time at boarding school; 15 October is 'the only visit we were allowed to make to see J at School'. They had a picnic on the Downs and J had shown extreme anger at the headmaster, Mr L, who was not only mad and a liar but had reneged on his rule that parents could see their child twice a term (it was only once). Milner had never known her son to be so verbally angry. She comments (and once again it is separation that is the key issue):

> now it was Mr L who was the cause of the too-long separation from us, only one visit in the term. So I realised more and more, with horrified shock, how totally blind I had been to the intensity of his anger over separation, something that I had then never read anything about.[18]

Not only does Milner realise, albeit retrospectively, that anxiety over separation is at the heart of her son's disquiet, she also faces the likelihood that his sadness around this time was occasioned by the breakdown of his parents' marriage about which she had told him at this time.[19]

Part 2 comprises the story book itself, another 'found object' in Milner's papers. A short summary indicates the kind of material from which Milner, the ninety-year old psychoanalyst, elaborates her interpretations. The first story is of 'The Farmer' and includes a cock killed by a fox who is in turn killed by the farmer. The farmer sets fire to the traps and eight foxes are killed as are eight rabbits.

Next comes 'The Woman', a tale of a cross, grumpy woman who throws stones at lots of people; then there are 'The Kittens', whose mother is dead but they are living in a very comfortable house. 'The Fox', in the next section, meanwhile, moves home from an uncomfortable house to a comfortable one.

'The Train' tells of a puffing train and a man sitting on a safety valve that went off and blew off the man. More transport follows with 'The Two Boats': there is a boat with three people in it and there is a boy who tried to jump into a passing lifeboat. A lighthouse keeper is seen putting new wicks in lamps and new candles in lanterns; a game of dominoes is 'great fun'. Then, there is a goods train that travels 104 miles each day carrying coal and oil.

Lastly, there is a bus that goes over Westminster Bridge three times a day and Battersea Bridge four times a day; and a porter who lived at the Station Hotel and was engaged in cleaning out the boilers of all the engines. It was his job to turn on the gas lamps and to make up the waiting room fire; when the train came in he helped the passengers off because the step was rather high; one day an express train came and he did not need to do this as it had a lower step than the regular trains.[20]

In Part 3, Milner proceeds to see how the story book might relate to her diary; although, as she reminds her reader, she had set out intending to avoid Freudian language, she could not help seeing the story of the farmer and the fox in terms of the Oedipus myth; and many of her 'first thoughts' are inflected with and informed by psychoanalysis. To start with, she assumes, as do many observers of children's drawings, that 'J's houses represent his self' and the black smoke issuing forth from their chimneys 'must surely depict a fiery anger within his house self.'[21] Thus, the first story can be looked on as illustrating Freud's observations of what he named the Oedipus Complex, the idea that the boy child secretly wishes to kill his father (or his potency) in order to take sexual possession of his mother. Seen in these terms, the farmer-father's cock is destroyed so that the son-fox can have chick babies with the chicken-mother.[22]

Milner, however, also notes that in the house picture here one quarter of the structure is a rosy red (not the black of the other three quarters), suggesting, perhaps, a doubleness of feeling for his father, and an 'appreciation of him' and of his efforts 'to teach him the use of tools in carpentry, and being a comfort to him when I was away'.[23]

Turning to the stone-throwing woman, Milner considers that this is part of her son and his anger with her, but that it might also be 'a bit of me that he was aware of and I was not'. At first this idea seemed very difficult to take, but then she recalled that when J had written his stories she was herself at the start 'of intermittent psychoanalysis, and so really having to face the fact that there could be such a secret part of myself, one that I was totally unaware of, since it did not fit in at all with my idea of myself'. Indeed, Milner was very 'rarely openly cross', and one of her main problems, indeed, as she saw it herself, was with expressing her anger. She then allows her free associated flow of thought to elaborate on the matter until she can conclude that the images richly suggest that her son 'must not let himself know about all this [anger and hidden anger] in either of us'.[24]

She offers us an incremental investigation of her son's narratives and of her understanding of them, structuring the whole with a psychoanalytic method moving from discursive to free associative thought and letting us walk with her as she comes to further and deeper insights and understanding. It is as if she is sharing her memory of the *method* of her earlier autobiographical books from *A Life of One's Own* onwards.

Milner is faced now with the implications of the dead mother in the kittens' tale. She considers this as a move towards her young son's realisation of his separate identity but also found herself needing to think about what had actually taken place in J's inner world 'as a result of his having sent me, while I was in Spain, the chaotic picture letter with its "wrecked train", "terrible dragon,", etc. (all quite unrecognisable as such)'.[25] More painful still was the thought that she had taken no notice of the images once she had returned home.

Nor does Milner's ninety-year-old self flinch from the pain of memory as she confronts the story of the boat that rocked, moving from the idea of the risks of being a separate person to the memory that she had, very early in the son's life, let him 'rock himself down'; it was when Star, the young woman Dennis Milner had engaged to help look after his newborn son, was on holiday and they were staying with cousins in the country:

> On the first evening I had tucked him up in the Moses basket we
> had brought him in, and put it on a very low sofa while I went out
> of the room for a little while. What I did not realise was how
> energetically he could bounce himself around before sleeping. So when
> I came back I found he had bounced himself, cocooned in the basket
> and blankets, onto the floor. He did not seem upset, after I had put
> him and the basket somewhere else, he went off to sleep quite easily.[26]

Only now, in the present of her late life, did Milner ask herself if this
memory could have surfaced in the story of the rocking boat; and, when she
looks at some photos of that time, taken the day after his fall from the sofa,
she sees on his face 'a rather affronted look, even suppressed indignation'.[27]

Quite often in this text, Milner interleaves her son's experiences and her
own situation, seeing events and images with a double focus; thus her remarks
on 'living in a hollow tree' suggest J's images are not only about his experiences
of coming to live in his own body but also, conjecturally, 'an attempt to
depict his awareness of my own problem of still being deeply immersed in
my school research job, thus living too much in my head, and liable to make
things a bit cock-eyed for both of us.'[28] Then she refers to his ability to find
a 'good emptiness' and to her time in Spain, and the 'unanswered picture
letter', and her discoveries there of that internal gesture of nothingness so
central to *An Experiment in Leisure*.[29]

A reading of *Bothered by Alligators* reminds and shows us just what kind of
literary personality Milner is as she tracks her thoughts during re-visiting the
diary and the story book – a re-visiting that we have seen in her papers, in
her essays and in her autobiographical works. As she mulls over J's lighthouse
images, she tells us that she had been thinking 'what an apt symbol a house,
or a lighthouse, is for one's body-mind self-awareness, since it allows for
different meanings on different levels or storeys'.[30] Thus with the story book
itself and its different storeys – its meaning(s) for J, for Milner as psychoanalyst,
and for Milner's ninety-year-old self. 'Aspects of Nest Building' demonstrates
some of the storeys (and stories) both for him and for herself. Concluding the
section, she writes: 'I felt that the real culmination of all the nest building
was the story book itself, a self-created container for his growing awareness
of his separate and unique identity.'[31]

A rather different kind of story, with a different interplay of levels or storeys,
comes in the story of 'The Caravan' (and considered in 'Having His Own
Tent') and Milner's reflects on it here: she recalls that, in reality, she had
bought a caravan in that year 'in order to have a little foothold in the country',
although she doubts that J had actually seen it when he wrote the story. The
drawings suggest to Milner that certain items were 'expressing his joy in the
idea of freedom to mark out and take possession of his own living space –
now set wherever he pleased, even, as the story says, in a ditch – and that it
would be fun'.[32]

Quite an extended analysis of the images is included around the story of the devoted porter felt by Milner to be 'especially interesting in the light of some of the diary entries'. The porter is found cleaning out and putting water in the engines; Milner links this with the idea that perhaps J 'was making amends for the idea, described in the diary, of dirtying his father with faeces and laughing triumphantly'. Thus, she conjectures, the little man at the foot of the page, with one black and one white hand, 'seemed to be marking the possibility of being able to bridge the gap between loving and hating his father, accepting that both feelings are part of himself'.[33]

The Station Hotel itself seems to be to do with travel and moving on; while the very helpful porter suggests 'one of J's ideals for himself, what some part of him feels he ought to be like'. And the mention of an express train that meant the porter did not have to help the passengers down might bespeak a wish for 'parents who did not need too much help from him' through his being the so-good child (i.e. the very helpful porter). There is another level: the story could be a metaphor for J's increasing awareness of two kinds of thought – 'the slow process of the logical discursive kind and the quick flashes of intuitive thinking',[34] the former the kind, for Milner, so much over-emphasised in traditional education.

In 'The End House and the Semi-detached One' Milner summarises her thoughts on the story book as she finds a 'thread developing through all the stories to do with the idea of survival' – a way of getting beyond or coming through the first story of anger, violence, killing and retaliation. She considers his image of a 'see-through house' where he seems to reach a new kind of awareness, in spite of one figure showing a crossed-out eye. Certainly, there is an apprehension of the complexity of being human 'all shown by the different levels linked by staircases': 'Even the little man with one eye crossed out did produce for me, an echo of my own experience in Spain, something that I had taken so long to know how to begin to understand for ordinary living.' Again, one can note the cross-over of the mother's thoughts and experiences and the son's images.

Acquiring his own house in a wood indicated to Milner an idea of comfort in just being, 'being in his own body' and also being able to move about. Then boats, trains and buses lead on to matters of speech, 'regularity, predictability'; and then came the whole theme of bridges 'the bridging of opposites of all kinds, contraries', comfort as well as danger. In the end he has his own tent. So, suggests Milner, J could now for a time afford to be the helpful porter while the 'smashed windows in the see-through house could also be seen as stars, as givers of light'.

Here, in her last years, Milner looks back to 'the kind of tree or chart of levels of experience I had made use of in the schools research'. It is an image Milner draws on to think out the use she could make of J's stories on different levels: for example, there is one aspect of the picture of the Station Hotel that she finds especially important – 'the use J has made of the space on top of the chimneys, which he has for inventions of his own'.[35]

Part 4, 'Towards a Change of Aim', opens with a particularly strong example of Milner's fearless re-encounter with herself, as she shows her reader how her purpose evolves and her aim changes from a broadly philanthropic one to help other parents to a form of self-discovery. Thus:

> I now had to ask myself, again, whether his story of the kitten whose mother was dead, might be not only an idea growing from his anger at the ways I had failed him, by going to Spain; it could also be something he felt about me, something that I did not then know in myself.

Despite this Milner continues to try to find what J's book might have been trying to tell her and only 'now and then could I glimpse the ways in which I would have to use his images for my own needs for more self awareness'. Her misgivings grew as the attempt to analyse her son became wide of the mark as she was assailed by the sudden thought that it was a case of *his* images analysing her, helping her discover 'what had been left out of [her] own couch analysis'.[36]

She comes now to have to deal with images on a number of different levels, and first is the cross; she traverses Christian ideas here, leading to J's putative use of the symbol as carrying his ideas about pain and fears of dying; following this, she thinks of the red cross with its conventional associations but also its relevance to her son's thoughts on 'those he had hurt himself in imagination and also the hurt he himself had suffered'. But then Milner doubles back, asking whether this could apply to herself; and here she recalls the different use of the word 'cross' in relation to the angry, stone-throwing woman in the story book: bravely she asks: 'could it even be that neither he nor I had then really faced the stone-thrower in ourselves?' Though it was possible that he had done so more than she 'since he had at least drawn a house with what could partly be seen as having smashed windows'. The cross, too, is linked with the fact that many of the pictures have a house and a tree, and for Milner this image (one she has already deployed in *Suppressed Madness of Sane Men*) 'seemed an apt symbol for a way in which one can experience one's body-mind existence, once having learnt to stand upright'.[37]

The section following – 'Having no arms' – again re-combines Milner's own experiences, recollections and associations with her son's drawings and their likely meanings. Here is how her discursive method operates: first she poses the question – why is it that nearly all the little men in J's pictures have no arms? Searching for an answer, Milner remembers how when she and the newborn J had first come home from hospital he was 'neatly pinned up in a shawl' and how she had continued with this practice because he seemed to like it. But she now says, 'I had gone on doing it too long, as a friend later pointed out.' Now she asks whether some kind of memory of 'an over-long constriction of his arms' might be featuring in the drawings; or, again, could there be some masturbatory anxiety; or possibly there were some covert ideas about attaching his father as a rival; might this, together with his (phallic) enjoyment of his own body have driven the 'obliteration of the arms of the little men'[38] – apart, that is, from the lighthouse man and one small figure underneath the story of the porter who cleans the engines.

Continuing to follow her habitual incremental method – now familiar to the reader of this book – from *On Not Being Able to Paint* and *Hands of the Living God*, Milner is taken back to the first story to the image of the house with much black smoke. She continues to interpret as follows: if the house is himself, and the black smoke indicates his own angry fires, 'then perhaps the blackness of three-quarters of the house could have a further meaning, in terms of the darkness of sorrow for what his fox self had done'. The rosy red on this formulation could then suggest hope for a 'happier solution' for rivalrous feelings towards his father. Ultimately, Milner suggests that J's 'pictorial ability was leading him to the truth that there is no healthy escape from the agonising experience of both loving, longing to preserve, and at times wanting to hurt or even get rid of the same person'.[39]

The next section 'My Father's Dream' (in which, incidentally, he dreamt that, were he to move, his arms would fall off) interleaves thoughts on J's pictures, Milner's discoveries and her situation and problems – namely that her own psychoanalysis had not remedied her hunched left shoulder, a condition that had troubled her very much in her schooldays.

Intriguingly, when working on the text of *Bothered by Alligators*, Milner found another of J's drawings, one entitled 'Those splendid feet' – it had, she comments, been made when he was aged three and a half, that is, six months before the angry picture letter sent to his mother (but not remembered by her) when she was away in Spain. The loss of such splendid feet in the intervening period engages his mother until she recalls that he had had quite severe whooping cough, his first serious illness, the summer before the story book. The dates are uncertain but 'it was almost certainly after he had made the drawing of the little man with such splendid feet'.[40]

Milner now pulls together the various images involving steam, of which there are a number of metaphors all to do with 'the fires of feeling', for instance, in his 'not-blown-off-safety-valve picture'. The mother's cumulative insights lead her to this: could these images 'be to do with his 4-year old inner explosion of rage at my being away in Spain, the one that had produced the wrecked-train drawing three years before, including what he had called "such a terrible dragon"'? It was possible that his mother's coming home safely had shown him that this steam-dragon was not quite so powerful 'after all, as no one gets blown off.[41] This said, however, there was still the matter of the dead mothers in the kittens story; and it could be, could it not, that this dead mother was still around in her son's inner world? (The complex of the 'dead mother' had been described by André Green, colleague and friend of Milner's, in 1980, and possibly there are resonances of his ideas here.)[42]

Subsequent to the ideas of the dead mother in her text, Milner moves on to 'J's God', feeling that she has to face up to his use of the word 'God' (notably a word that she preferred to avoid, quoting herself to Alexander Newman, for instance, 'The less said about God the better, don't you think?')[43] Milner herself, as she writes here, had been brought up in an Anglican Church-going family but around the age of six had been upset by the Athanasian Creed and its distressing view of damnation for all those who did not believe in its tenets. She has been anxious about this until Blake's words rescued her: 'All religions are different manifestations of each nation's poetic genius.'[44] His words, however, did not resolve the matter of the many people who insisted that their own was *the* right and only religion; nor did it negate the many people killed in the name of religious right. But, in the 1930s at the time of keeping the J diary, she had not wholly clarified these issues for herself so had not talked directly with her son on the subject but had left him to develop his own ideas, and to make such statements as 'It's God that makes him grow'.[45]

Although the story book contains much about God, there is, as Milner points out, plenty also about his wolf, a symbol carrying notions of 'various capacities in himself', illustrating a growing insight into 'the many aspects of his own self'.[46] Perhaps most crucially here, Milner links her son's (unconscious?) longing for motherhood, his 'preoccupation with what will hatch out of him' with his own story book – it was this that had actually 'hatched out of him', an object that would eventually 'feed its readers' and, even more significantly, one indicating his 'gradual discovery that he could learn to make meaningful marks on paper which in the end had become the story book, something live enough to make a bridge of communication both with other people and with hidden parts of himself'.[47]

The disillusion with what one produces is a theme that has haunted Milner from very early on in her creative explorations (the idea that the beautiful stuff that gives a person such pleasure in production is not in itself art) and it comes to the fore again here: She reports J's having had a 'nasty' dream in which there were some 'bird faeces in his room', speaking once more for that 'shock there could be on first discovering that what drops out of one's body is not alive, but just dead stuff to be thrown away'.[48]

Such thoughts of dead matter take Milner back to J's story of the kitten with the dead mother, a theme she 'seemed to have been constantly avoiding'; facing it head on here, Milner allows herself to wonder (and to publish her thoughts or, more accurately, to prepare her thoughts for future publication; we know she wanted the book published) 'whether the story could have been due not only to my many absences and the angry ideas expressed in [. . .] his picture letter when surely he could have felt he had killed me in his imagination'. There was a further possibility: perhaps he was 'trying to convey a feeling of something intermittently not sufficiently alive in me.'[49]

178

Disquieting as it was to confront this, and to hear the thoughts from herself, Milner faces the possibility that her son had realised that she was 'managing to keep dead' her own misgivings and doubts about her marriage and its viability. Possibly her own sensitivity to his needs had been in some way diminished.

Nevertheless there was a more hopeful view: his story book not only showed all the work that had been done by himself and his teachers; it also indicated his ability to make and play with images of his own experiences, and to express a range of emotions and feeling, 'the story-telling in fact a loving gift of himself', a gift that had lain unfound for more than fifty years.[50] If the story book can be seen, and I think it can, as a loving gift of *himself* to his mother, then perhaps we may also see *Bothered by Alligators* as an equally loving gift from mother to son, a love letter from Moll to J as he always called her.

Part 5, 'Water, Tears and a Use of Gravity',[51] finds Milner much clearer about her changed aim; she has now seen what J's images might be saying for him but she 'did not really know how to use this for myself'. Her previous ideas on her images and the 'beads' (of freely associated thought) she had discovered must be looked at once more. First, her dreams had led her to ponder her thoughts on water and its associated images, then to fragments of folk song and poetry, the gathering of flowers and the images of caravans.

In the case of the caravan images, Milner had been asking herself why J had done two drawings of the caravan; in the second picture she was particularly struck by very carefully drawn strong hooks looking like wooden buckets, which she sees as some kind of container. At this stage, J, now aged sixty-two, arrives in real time: 'He said (although he had before told me he had no memory at all of writing the book) that he felt sure they were buckets for water.'[52] She mulls over the meaning of the placing of the buckets and then returns to thinking how the 'hooks could apply to' herself. In the process of thinking about his, she recalls J's picture of the lighthouse keeper and becomes aware that he *does*, unlike many of J's other figures, have arms.

After writing this, Milner reports a surprising bodily event; she had, during the time of writing *Bothered by Alligators*, been having what were called 'play times' with an Alexander teacher she names K; and K had suggested to Milner the importance of walking, letting her arms swing freely and experiencing 'the full flow of the experience of their weight'. This changed her perception of herself in a radical way: 'It felt almost as if what had happened was that my hidden stone-throwing bit, and my usually so well-behaved everyday self had somehow come together, interpenetrated.'[53] It was even possible that J's men acquired arms at a point when he realised on some level that his mother would need to accept her 'stone-throwing self'; he would then be able to ingrate his own stone-thrower.

In this section bodily meanings also accrue to ideas of having no hands (thus no sex), to the compromised position of J's father who has no work, to Milner's habitual too fast speed of moving and to her own beginnings – of a mother (arguably depressed) who, 'after she had fed me, she would have had the nanny put me straight back in the cot, no time being allowed for playing with her breast after feeding from it'.[54]

Inevitably, at the age of ninety-three, thoughts of her beginnings lead (here through another 'bead') to thoughts of her own ending via the phrase 'shuffle off this mortal coil', which, in turn, evokes the bead of the snake skin in Delos. The re-visiting of this bead from *Eternity's Sunrise* now brings a different kind of change both in Milner's image of herself and in the quality of what she is observing: 'it brings a kind of doubleness of space, the dark inner one held simultaneously with the lighted outer one of the surrounding world, an interpenetration which is, I suppose, what a good drawing is a record of'.[55]

The next section, 'Using My Own Pictures', moves on to a reprise of key Milner themes and then to examples of Milner's late-life images found in her collages of the period. First, in 'Always protecting your mother', she has to face a strange physical, or visual, event in her life – when reading she was apt to read the 'opposite of what was printed'; this had to be looked into.[56]

The first recollection that arrives is of an osteopath's wondering aloud whether his patient realised she was 'always protecting [her] mother'. Initially Milner feels she knows all about his, and the need to care for her mother in the face of her father's irritable disposition. But then, she recalls her mother's contributions to her six-year old nightly prayers and the addition to these of 'Keep the door of my lips that I offend not with my tongue.' It was bewildering that these prayers still had an effect after so many years: 'I still had great difficulty about expressing anger, combined with anxiety about having given offence by my tongue, even on occasions when it might have been right to do so.'[57]

Insecurities about anger now come to mind in connection with the Mrs Punch drawing featured earlier in *On Not Being Able to Paint*. Surprised by her need to re-visit this drawing after more than fifty years, Milner starts to think about the kind of opposites it portrays (the link is with reading the opposite of the printed word). Now, she is able to build on her experience of J's story book and the stone-throwing woman and to see how Mrs Punch is the very opposite of how she likes to consider herself, a hidden part revealed through the physical practice of arm swinging recommended by K., her Alexander teacher. As a result of reading J's story book and thinking here on her drawings, Milner is able to confront her anger with her own mother and the themes of rivalry with her, seen in her nature diary drawing of the ducks.[58] In fact, a revisit to another drawing from *On Not Being Able to Paint*, 'The two beech trees' allows her to accept her 'great anger with both [her] parents as separate people'. The drawing had been made around 1939 when they were living in Sussex, and this would have been around six months after J made his story book, then 'remaining unfound' in the family's London home.[59] Milner had set out to draw 'two huge splendid beech trees that I had delighted in' but what arrived on her paper 'were two little stunted bushes struggling against a raging blizzard'. When she first wrote about these drawings, she had understood the 'themes of opposites' but had not investigated further. She is now, with benefit of the experience of J's story book, able to ask 'more bravely' what might have been going on unconsciously in these images. Thus perhaps the trees stood for parental power of which, in some 'remote part' of herself, she had achieved 'an imaginative castration'. This 'cold blizzard of scorn of authority' might conceal a very early, infantile terror about the 'precariousness of one's own existence'.[60]

The drawing of the two beeches evokes a last image from J's book – its cover with the two trees 'dancing', as she puts it, beside one another. His trees have allowed a renewed and deeper reflection on her two stunted bushes. J's book, too, drives another experiment – left-handed drawing. (Milner was naturally right-handed.) His picture of a little man with a dark left hand in one of the images prompts the thought that the left hand is 'most likely to have access to ideas of the darkly hidden powers'.[61] After a time, an image appeared that 'called itself' 'Alligator': a head, with open jaw and one tooth, and, arguably, a lead on the alligator(s) bothering *Milner* at this point. Picture prompts memory, as Milner finds herself again with the J diary, and prior to that in his babyhood and her memory of the 'pain I had felt at his one and only moment of biting me'.[62] J's babyhood segues into Milner's present with a pain in the heart at the sight of an empty plate after a good meal, and then to a memory of the fact that her own mother had to wean her prematurely at four months due to the occurrence of a breast abscess. This, Milner believes, would have meant that there was little chance of her gradually learning that her 'devouring intentions' were fantasy not reality; 'So, was there really, still hidden away in my secret inner world, a belief that I had had the power to destroy, with the "door of my lips" and of my jaws, just what I most needed and valued?'[63]

In considering the jaws drawing, Milner remembers that quite recently in her early nineties she had developed a bad jaw pain (angina); this again reverts to thoughts of her own mother's pain in suckling her infant daughter, and thence to the nature of the mother's response to her baby's 'gaze': 'Could it then be that I had seen in her eyes the pain I was causing?' Again, the words of William Blake clarify and contain *her* pain:

> The caterpillar on the leaf
> Repeats to thee thy mother's grief[64]

Section 8 moves on to Milner's last artistic endeavour, her 'Play of making collages from my old failed paintings'. She describes her approach to this activity, how she has enjoyed

> tearing or cutting up what I considered to have been my own failed
> paintings and then picking out the bits of colour or shapes that I

particularly liked, putting them in a heap on a tray, and letting my
wandering eye, often only out of its corner, select any of them that
caught my attention.

These pieces would then be arranged on a sheet of paper and pasted on to it.
In time, each 'would tell me what it was about'.[65] (In an unpublished document
on 'Painting as Playing' she says at this time she 'was tired of pure abstraction
and wanted to experiment with combining the figurative with an abstract
non-realistic background'.)[66] Milner adhered to only one rule – the end result
must not be abstract but must figure some kind of human or animal encounter.

These collages, interpreted here by Milner, focus on many of her central
preoccupations at the time – thus 'The Temperamental Hen' calls forth her
ideas about control of her tongue, and of the harsh God of the Athanasian
Creed she had resisted from her early years. Another – which 'called itself'
'The Listeners', interestingly constructed from Milner's having cut out the
form of two figures from an old painting and backed the shapes with black
– reminds her of J's house – indeed, she sees this collage strongly through
the lens of J's story book, his see-through house and his little cock-eyed house
on the hillside.[67] His book thus helps her interpret her own collages. Milner's
practice was to leave around twenty of the collages hanging in her studio for
friends and visitors to comment upon; and this is just what happened in the
case of 'The Listeners': a friend said that it was, of course, from the Bible, the
story of the walk to Emmaus. The biblical reference drives Milner on to
consider J's Station Hotel and the chalice shape he had incorporated into one
of its pictures. Thence she ponders the ritual (Communion) whereby Christ
wished his disciples to remember him and its essential nature as a 'cannibalistic
act' – an act that it had taken almost another two thousand years for Freud
to notice, from attention to the dreams of himself and his patients: the fact
that we are all 'cannibalistic in our infant loving desires'.[68]

Her experience of infancy is once more revived when considering the collage
that called itself 'The Green Baby': here Milner had cut out of another old
painting the shapes of two figures, a 'double hole': this, she conjectures, had
come to suggest those empty feelings of loss, both at the time she was left
without her parents after her father's breakdown and the occasion in infancy
(implicitly) when she had endured the loss of the mother's breast.

The poem that had 'written itself' well before the years of compiling
Alligators draws together some of Milner's central preoccupations here, with
her collage 'Woebegone' imaging, among other matters, 'trust in emptiness,
trust in the gap in knowing':[69]

('What is mind, no matter?'
'What is matter, never mind'.) Who said this?
'Mind the Gap!' shouts the mechanical voice at the
Embankment Tube station.

'Mind the gap!'
I do, I did, I have never fallen between the platform and
the train
I don't mind, it doesn't matter.
Or does it?
I do mind the gap between what I can dream of and what
I can do.
And I do mind the gap between what I can dream of the
Earth
And what we are doing to it.
Destroying the living matter on which we depend for life –
Like the Amazon forests.

Milner is now almost ninety-six years old, and is worrying that the book will never be finished; she needs to accelerate her narrative, and decides to revert to diary form as she mulls over such topics as her own funeral (and how to think about this in the light of the problem of her 'love-hate feelings about the Christian Church'). She moves from diary writing as such to inventing for herself 'a particular mind-body incantation', an exercise in 'words made flesh': 'It is an act of simply naming a part of my body, while attending to the sensation of that bit of body's weight held by the floor. And this has had the effect of at once relieving its tension, and adding an increased sense of truly being.'[70]

The incantation in turn takes her back to thoughts of her book *An Experiment in Leisure*, 'the book I had made in Spain', its links with her connection with Anton Ehrenzweig, and her other (silent) incantation: 'I know nothing, I want nothing, I am nothing.'[71]

As well as being deeply preoccupied with body-mind matters, Milner was much engaged with her own 'alligators' at this time, and in Part 7, 'The Family Setting', she confronts her mother's depression, the happiest time in her mother's life, her youthful hatred of her sister Winifred and *her* death in 1969, the death of her brother Patrick in 1974, and, once more, her intense inhibition about speaking in public.[72] Much of this material has been covered in the preceding chapters; here I will concentrate on Chapter 13, 'Me being physically ill and the Undine story'.

Milner looks back to the time when on reaching puberty she was really ill, with influenza, abscesses and whooping cough – the only time in her life so far that she had been seriously ill. At that time she had read the German fairy tale 'Undine', and it is this tale to which she returns now in her nineties. Martina Thomson says 'Marion lived in that story towards the end of her writing of The Alligators.' *Undine* is a novella by Friedrich de la Motte Fouqué about the water-sprite Undine who marries a knight Huldebrand to gain a soul. He abandons her for another, more respectable bride, and she, Undine, is banished underground but visits him on the wedding night, kisses him and, weeping, speaks the words that, Martina says, were [were to have been?] the last of one of Milner's chapters, even of the book: 'I have killed you with my tears.'[73]

Milner asks after a gap of very many years why it was that the Undine story had so gripped her – her associations lead her to wonder if the wild girl of the lake, Undine, was a shut-off bit of herself, a split-off part. Possibly her acceptance of her mother's prayer (that inhibiting speech) had meant that she was unable to accept her Undine self and allow it to join up with the 'more civilised' part of the self? In addition, she also feels generally she was too good because of a fear of the anger of the vengeful Mrs Punch/Red Queen figure who had featured in her earlier drawings.

A more rebellious side of the self is revealed, however, in another aspect of the Undine tale as recounted by Milner aged ninety-six: the wandering knight tells the story of how when he has 'been sent to the forest by a grand lady called Bertalda as a test of his love for her, Undine suddenly bites his hand'. Despite this, the couple become close and are wed. After the wedding ceremony Undine is described as still wild and 'full of pranks'; however, after the wedding night, to Milner's irritation, she becomes 'so gentle'[74] On re-reading the tale again when writing *Alligators,* Milner finds herself asking what had happened to the part of Undine's personality that had bitten the knight's hand when he spoke of Bertalda; where had this infantile jealousy gone? And, given the end of the story, perhaps what is achieved for Undine is not a soul but a split personality: the biting, un-gentle part of the self finding expression in the uncle Kulibore – he who had decreed that Undine's last embrace with her lover will kill him with her tears.

The eighth part of *Alligators,* 'D.W. Winnicott and me' highlights elements unresolved in Milner's last years – namely, the nature and effects of her analysis with Winnicott and central, unanswered questions that 'bothered' her up until the end of her life. These issues are covered in Chapter 5; what is interesting here is that they still and centrally trouble her, and her realisation that, in writing *Bothered by Alligators,* her son's images were analysing her, in a kind of role reversal. Winnicott's 'secretly depressed' mother, seen in 'The Tree' poem quoted earlier (see pp. 56–58), chimed with her own. It is perhaps not surprising that Milner in *Alligators* ponders in some detail the iconic Winnicottian squiggle of mother and baby in its different guises. She thinks of the three versions known to her. The 1997 version evokes this comment:

> The one shown here, a reproduction of the original, has this black central column, making it impossible to see the contact of the mother and baby's bodies, though the baby's beautifully drawn left arm is shown as if holding on to the mother's neck. Whether it is actually supporting her, or hanging on to her for dear life, is not clear – perhaps both. The baby's feet are also beautifully drawn and tucked under its bottom, but the mother's right forearm and hand, which should

be supporting the baby's feet, are shown as having lost all solidity, and a gap is left between her arm and the baby's feet.[75]

Shortly after writing about her analysis with Winnicott, Milner experiences an eye burst. Interpreting herself, in the manner of a dream, she thinks of what had been happening the day before – she had attended a lecture that had included one of the original engravings for Blake's *Job*, the one of Job's nightmare in which Job and Satan have the same face, just as in the first picture in the series God and Job have the same face.[76] Recognising that conventional medicine might well dismiss her views as nonsensical, Milner considers whether the eye burst might not have been occasioned by an intense fear that a 'split off and angrily rebellious bit' of herself might reveal itself with terrible results. Perhaps it was safer to have a burst eye vessel than to injure with speech? Once more she recalls the Undine story and that split in the personality; and here, she embellishes the ideas further, making a link with 'a new aspect' of her rebellious self, an extreme inhibition about reading her own handwriting – this idea has turned a full circle from its presence in her thirties as her wish to be illegible until her nineties.

The eye burst meant that Milner could no longer read the titles of her books on their shelves, so picking a book became something of a random matter – thus she alights on a volume including 'Catholic Faith and Easter Stories: Reflections on Hubert Richards': here, a Jesuit, Fergus Kerr, draws on Richards' comments on the fictional nature of the Gospel stories: '"the stories were never intended as literal descriptions of a sequence of events and should not be treated as such."'[77] The stories are organic, growing over time and, as Richards says, '"stories that grow like this in the telling need to be taken as stories, not as history."'[78] There is thus a necessarily fictional element to a reading of the Gospels, an idea that takes Milner back once more to J's story book, the nodal point of the *Alligators* text, and 'his inventions in the space on top of the chimneys.'

Before alighting on the Kerr piece Milner had been writing about J's use of this space, an in-between space of the kind Winnicott considered in his work on Transitional Objects. She finds herself at this time searching for these ideas in the DWW canon and finding in his 1951 work comments on that 'intermediate area of experiencing to which inner reality and external life both contribute.'[79] This connects with J's chimney-top space and his apparent intuitive decision 'that here was a place where there would be room for the play of invention.'[80] As has been seen there was much invention in the family environment for the young John Milner, his father 'an inventor by temperament' engaged on designing a boat around the time his son was creating the story book and drawings.

The area of an intermediate or 'half-way' space takes Milner back to Jan Gordon's words about outline that had so influenced her young artist self in the 1920s, about 'outline being the most unnatural thing in nature'. It also leads her to think about the religions symbolism in J's pictures and his use of the chalice, as if 'part of him already knew that his particular kind of in-between space is where religious creeds and rituals belong'.[81]

Creeds and symbols of this kind did not belong to Milner's plans for her own end; there was in the plans for her funeral to be no mention of God although the Order of Service does not entirely bear this out.

Milner was working on *Bothered by Alligators* right up until the end of her life: Mathew tells of how work on the book was 'quite dramatic towards the end. Marion seemed to speed up – she seemed to sense the climax in the work (and her own mortality?), and she was more agitated than she usually was'; 'the past' as he says 'did not lie peacefully'.[82] There was the re-emergence of Susan, the named subject of *Hands of the Living God*, who, full of recriminations, had telephoned and written. Martina Thomson's 'Marion' is the best valedictory – to this book, and to Marion Milner:

> You'd moved your bed down and now slept among
> the spades and buckets – beanpoles, trowels, baskets –
> there the new commode and, yes, the glass door to the garden.
>
> You sat bolt upright on the crumpled sheets
> and when I greeted you I found your cheek
> was wet with tears: 'Forgive me if I don't get up',
>
> your eyes without your specs so intimate, so bare,
> A letter had arrived. 'The second drawer
> up in the tallboy, you'll see it, bring it down' –
>
> a letter spun of accusations. 'So what d'you make of it?'
> 'I want to put my arms around you, that's all.'
> 'Well then –', and now your tears were hot.
>
> Your heart-beat stayed with me when you drew back;
> there was a stillness in the room and dusk;
> the gardening tools lost contour, substance –
>
> shadows of a chorus closed around us
> and you now with the wicked lightening of your smile,
> the tilted head: 'I think that's drowned that letter.'
>
> Ready for the whiskey, we raised the tumblers eye to eye,
> You told me you'd found words, end words, for your chapter
> which made the book complete. We toasted it
>
> on this last night. O Marion you wanted me to stay
> But then said: 'No, come see me when it's day.'[83]

Marion Milner died the next day: on 29 May 1998.

NOTES

1 EDWARDIAN HOME

1 Marion Milner, *Bothered by Alligators* [BBA], Hove, Routledge, 2012, p. 224
2 Letter from MM to D.W. Winnicott, no date, 'About the Doctor's meeting', archives of the Wellcome Library, PP/DWW/B/A/21
3 Patrick Blackett quoted in Mary Jo Nye, *Blackett: Physics, War and Politics in the Twentieth Century*, Cambridge MA and London, Harvard University Press, 2004, p. 16
4 Anthony Highmore King, *Blacketts, Maynards, Hillyards & Kings*, unpublished document, 1962, p. 14
5 Ibid., p. 28
6 Nye, op. cit., p. 86f.
7 See, for example, Naome Rader Dragstedt, 'Creative Illusions: The Theoretical and Clinical Work of Marion Milner (1900–1998)', *Journal of Melanie Klein and Object Relations*, 16, 3, September 1998, p. 434
8 Nick Vine Hall, 'My Name is Blackett'. Marion Milner Collection, Archives of the British Psychoanalytical Society [MMC], PO1/G/01
9 King, op. cit., p. 31
10 Dragstedt, op. cit., p. 434
11 BBA, p. 219
12 Ibid., p. 173
13 Ibid., p. 174
14 Ibid., p. 226
15 Ibid., p. 220
16 King, op. cit., p. 10
17 BBA, p. 213
18 Ibid., p. 222. Patrick Blackett married Constanza (Pat) Bayon in 1924
19 BBA, p. 214
20 Martina Thomson, personal communication
21 King, op. cit., p. 11
22 BBA, pp. 214–215
23 Notes, 'Giovanna while staying with Mol', John Milner Papers.
24 King, op. cit., p. 11
25 BBA, p. 216
26 MMC, PO1/4/49
27 *Mollie Blackett's Nature Diary*, John Milner Papers
28 MMC, PO1/G/02
29 Marion Milner, *An Experiment in Leisure* [EIL], London, Routledge, 2010, p. 7
30 MM, 'The Golden Cockle-Shell', MMC, PO1/E/D/01
31 See p. 135

32 Marion Milner, *The Suppressed Madness of Sane Men* [SMSM], London, Routledge, 1987, p. 1
33 Ibid., p. 2
34 Ibid.
35 Marion Milner, *The Hands of the Living God* [HOLG], London, Routledge, 2010, p. xli
36 Ibid.; 'The body is a big sagacity' from F. Nietzsche, 'The Despisers of the Body', *Thus Spake Zarathustra; A Book for All and None* (1883–1885)
37 Marion Milner, *A Life of One's Own* [ALO], London, Routledge, 2010, p. 173
38 MM Personal Notebooks, no date (?1943), PO1/E/B/46

2 A LIFE OF ONE'S OWN

1 MM Personal Notebooks, 8 June 1926, MMC, PO1/E/B/08
2 ALO, p. 16
3 BBA, p. 260
4 MM Personal Notebooks, 14 July 1926; 20 July 1926; 21 September 1926; 27 September 1926, MMC, PO1/E/B/08
5 Letter to Mrs Stuart Blackett, 11 December 1927, MMC, PO1/C/01
6 ALO, p. 29
7 Letter to Mrs Stuart Blackett, op. cit.
8 SMSM, p. 3
9 Letter to Mrs Stuart Blackett, 20 February, 1928, PO1/C/01
10 Janet Sayers, 'Marion Milner; Psychologist to Psychoanalyst' *Psychology of Women Section, Newsletter* 3, Spring 1989
11 BBA, pp. 5–6
12 Ibid.
13 Ibid.
14 ALO, pp. 31–32
15 For further information on the Gordons, see 'Vagabonds Abroad', www.duncan jdsmith.com
16 BBA, p. 6
17 ALO, p. 30
18 Letter to Mrs Stuart Blackett, November 1928, MMC, PO1/C/01
19 ALO, p. 32
20 BBA, p. 7
21 EIL, pp. 17–18
22 BBA, p. 7
23 Personal Notebooks, 30 January 1932(?), MMC, PO1/E/B/19
24 Personal Notebooks, February 1931, MMC, PO1/E/B/18
25 Personal Notebooks, March and July 1932, MMC, PO1/E/B/18
26 BBA, p. 8
27 SMSM, p. 3
28 Ibid.
29 'The Human Problem in Schools', Supplement to *Bulletin, International Bureau of Education Geneva*, 52, 3rd quarter, 1939, MMC, PO1/A/C/10
30 BBA, p. 26
31 Personal Notebooks, 25 July 1929, MMC, PO1/E/B/12
32 Personal Notebooks, August 1929, MMC, PO1/E/B/12
33 Ibid.
34 Personal Notebooks, 20 October 1929, MMC, PO1/E/B/12
35 Personal Notebooks, 11 January 1932, MMC, PO1/E/B/19
36 BBA, p. 29

37 Ibid.
38 ALO, p. xxxiii
39 Ibid., p. 173
40 Ibid., p. 174
41 Ibid., p. 15
42 Ibid., p. 38
43 See also Margaret Walters, 'On Robinson Crusoe's Island' in Lesley Caldwell (ed.) *Art, Creativity, Living,* London, Karnac, 2000, pp. 121–133.
44 ALO, p. 40
45 Ibid., p. 48
46 Ibid., p. 53
47 Ibid., p. 79
48 Ibid.
49 Ibid., p. 174
50 Ibid.
51 Ibid., pp. 174–175
52 Ibid., p. 175, 55
53 Ibid., p. 176
54 Ibid., pp. 177, 178, 179–180; William Blake, *Auguries of Innocence* (1803)
55 Interview with Alexander Newman, The Squiggle Foundation, 1986
56 Fan letters, John Milner Papers
57 EIL, p. xliv
58 BBA, pp. 24–25

3 AN EXPERIMENT IN LEISURE

1 Personal Notebooks, 22 December 1936, MMC, PO1/E/B/37
2 Personal Notebooks, 13 April 1935, 25 April 1935, MMC, PO1/E/B/35
3 Personal Notebooks, 17 April 1935, MMC, PO1/E/B/35
4 Personal Notebooks, April 1934, MMC, PO1/E/B/35
5 Personal Notebooks, May 1935, MMC, PO1/E/B/35
6 EIL, pp. xlliv–xlv
7 SMSM, p. 5
8 Ibid. p. 4
9 Ibid., pp. 5–6
10 *New English Weekly*, 18 November 1937, MMC, PO1/A/B/01
11 Ibid.
12 From John Milner Papers
13 ES, p. 194
14 EIL, p. xxxvii
15 Ibid., pp. 166, 167f.
16 SMSM, p. 6
17 'Anton Ehrenzweig', 'Read at Memorial Meeting', ICA, 21 June 1967, MMC, PO1/D/A/31
18 A. Ehrenzweig 'The Creative Surrender', *The American Imago*, 1957, 144, 3, 193, MMC, PO1/D/A/31
19 Ibid., p. 194
20 Ibid.; EIL, p. 28
21 EIL, pp. 38–39; Ehrenzweig, op. cit., p. 194
22 Ehrenzweig, op. cit., p. 196
23 Ibid., p. 196
24 Ibid., pp. 203, 204
25 Ibid., p. 204
26 Ibid., p. 206

27 EIL, p. 85f.; Ehrenzweig, op. cit., p. 207
28 Ehrenzweig, op. cit. See, in particular, Janet Sayers in Stephen Bann (ed.), *The Coral Mind: Adrian Stokes's Engagement with Art History, Criticism and Psychoanalysis*, Philadelphia PA, Pennsylvania University Press, 2007, pp. 123–138
29 See pp. 169–170
30 Personal Notebooks, September 1939, MMC, PO1/E/B/42
31 Letter from John Milner to Letley, 10 March 2010
32 BBA, p. 65
33 Letter from John Milner to Dennis Milner, 'Blitz', MMC, PO1/G/08

4 THE ROAD TO PSYCHOANALYSIS

1 Paul Watsky 'Marion Milner's Pre-Freudian Writings, 1926–1938', *Journal of Analytical Psychology*, 37, 4, 1992, 455–473
2 BBA, p. 234
3 SMSM, pp. 6–7
4 Recorded interview with MM by Pearl King and Riccardo Steiner, 14 April 1996; also 'A Recorded Interview with Pearl King', typescript, no date, John Milner Papers.
5 Recorded interview with King and Steiner, 14 April 1996
6 Ibid.
7 'Recorded Interview with Pearl King', op. cit.
8 See www.enotes.com/controversial-discussions-anna-freud-melanie-klein-reference/ (accessed 8 August 2012)
9 Recorded interview with King and Steiner, op. cit.
10 SMSM, pp. 83–113
11 'Recorded Interview with Pearl King', op. cit.
12 Ken Robinson, 'A Brief History of the British Psychoanalytical Society', in Peter Loewenberg and Nellie Thompson (eds), *100 Years of the IPA 1910–2010, Evolution and Change*, London, IPA and Karnac, 2012, pp. 196–227, 215
13 Ibid., p. 216; see also F. Baudry, 'Revisiting the Freud-Klein Controversies Fifty Years Later', *International Journal of Psychoanalysis*, 1992, 1992, 367–374
14 SMSM, p. 6
15 Janet Sayers, *Mothering Psychoanalysis*, London, Penguin, 1992, p. 242
16 SMSM, p. 292
17 Sayers, op. cit., p. 242
18 Pearl King and Riccardo Steiner (eds), *The Freud-Klein Controversies 1941–45*, London, Routledge, 1991, p. 866
19 Robinson, p. 219
20 King and Steiner, *Freud-Klein Controversies*, op. cit., p. 54
21 SMSM, p. 88f.; Phyllis Grosskurth, *Melanie Klein: Her World and Her Work*, Cambridge MA, Harvard University Press, 1987, p. 396
22 Recorded interview with King and Steiner, op. cit.
23 SMSM, p. 91
24 Grosskurth, op. cit., p. 396
25 SMSM, p. 39f.
26 Ibid., p. 42
27 Ibid., p. 58
28 Personal Notebooks, 20 August 1940, 'John', MMC, PO1/E/B/43
29 Personal Notebooks, 20 October 1940, MMC, PO1/E/B/43
30 Personal Notebooks, March 1942, MMC, PO1/E/B/46
31 Ibid., 5(?) July 1946
32 Ken Robinson, personal communication, July 2011

5 'A HUGE CATHERINE WHEEL'

1 HOLG, p. xlvi
2 SMSM, p. 248
3 Recorded interview with Alexander Newman, The Squiggle Foundation, 1986
4 Robert F. Rodman, *Winnicott: Life and Work,* Cambridge MA, Da Capo, 2003, p. 136
5 Ibid., p. 59
6 Ibid., p. 132
7 Recorded interview with Alexander Newman, op. cit.
8 Letter from MM to DWW, 15 July 1940, Wellcome Collection, PP/DWW/B/A
9 BBA, p. 232
10 Ibid.
11 Ibid., p. 234
12 Recorded interview with Alexander Newman, op. cit.
13 BBA, p. 235
14 Ibid., p. 237
15 Letter to MM from Margaret Little, August, 1991(?), MMC, PO1/D/C/06
16 BBA, p. 234
17 Letter from MM to DWW, no date, Papers of Roger Willoughby; also mentioned in Rodman, op. cit., p. 137
18 'Notes from a Talk with DW', 20 July 1950, MMC, PO1/D/D/33
19 Nina Farhi, personal communication, December 2006
20 Rodman, op. cit., p. 140
21 Letter to MM from DWW, 22 March 1943, MMC, PO1/D/D/33
22 MM to DWW. 'Part II. About the Doctor's Meeting'; Wellcome Collection, PP/DWW/B/A
23 Letters to MM from Alexander Newman, 5 May 1992 and 25 May 1992, MMC, PO1/D/C/26
24 Christopher Bollas Email Communications, July 2011, July and August 2012
25 See pp. 184–185
26 Recorded interview with Alexander Newman, op. cit.; BBA, p. 237
27 Ibid., p. 237
28 Recorded interview Alexander Newman, op. cit.
29 BBA, p. 238. Margaret Little writes to MM on this subject saying: 'I have been mulling over your struggle to separate yourself from your mother's depression – having to change or adjust. It seems that something in today's life represents that, probably to do with your own body [. . .] She let you down, not meeting your needs bodily or emotional.' Letter to MM from Margaret Little, 29 June 1988, PO1/D/C/06
30 BBA, p. 238
31 BBA, p. 236
32 Ibid.
33 'Marion Milner's Personal Response to Winnicott's Drawings', interview by Angela Baum, (?)November 1976, MMC, PO1/D/D/33; BBA, p. 236
34 Milner quite often refers to this in different forms, referring apparently to Freud's discussions on the translation of ideas into visual images in *The Interpretation of Dreams.* King and Steiner comment on a 'slightly incorrect' quotation about Freud's words on 'visual images'. Thus 'Freud even in this translation is referring to 'Thinking in pictures' and not to 'visual memories': 'Thinking in pictures is therefore, only a very incomplete form of becoming conscious – in some way it approximates more closely to unconscious processes [Freud, S. 1923b:23].' King and Steiner, *Freud-Klein Controversies,* op. cit., p. 473
35 BBA, p. 242
36 SMSM, p. 246

37 Ibid. p. 249. Lesley Caldwell and Angela Joyce, *Reading Winnicott*, London, Routledge, 2011, p. 10
38 From recorded interview of MM by Pearl King, typescript, no date, John Milner Papers
39 SMSM, p. 247
40 Ibid., p. 91
41 Ibid., p. 92
42 Ibid., p. 99
43 Ibid., p. 103
44 John Milner Papers
45 Review of Melanie Klein, *Envy and Gratitude*, reprinted from 'Case Conference', 5, 7 January 1959
46 John Milner Papers; and see Robert F. Rodman, *The Spontaneous Gesture*, London, Karnac, 1999, pp. 79–80
47 John Milner Papers
48 Letter from D.W. Winnicott to Charles Rycroft, 25 June 1953, typescript, John Milner Papers.
49 Ibid.
50 Letter from MM to DWW, 8 November 1955, Wellcome Collection, PP/DWW/B/A
51 Letter from MM to DWW, Wellcome Collection, PP/DWW/B/A
52 D.W. Winnicott, *Playing and Reality*, London, Penguin, 1971, p. 44
53 Letter from MM to DWW, no date, Wellcome Collection, PP/DWW/B/A
54 'Critical Notice of *On Not Being Able to Paint*' by D.W. Winnicott in L.Caldwell (ed.), *Art, Creativity, Living*, London, Karnac, 2000, p. 117f. (This is as published in the *British Journal of Medical Psychology*: it also appeared in *The New Era*, September–October 1950.)

6 ON NOT BEING ABLE TO . . .

1 Michael Eigen, 'Dual Union or Undifferentiation? A Critique of Marion Milner's View of Psychic Creativeness', *International Review of Psycho-Analysis*, 10, 1983, 415–428, 415
2 ONBAP, pp. 5, 7, 8, 13
3 Ibid., pp. 18, 19
4 SMSM, p. 81
5 ONBAP, p. 27
6 Ibid., p. 28
7 Ibid., p. 29
8 Ibid.
9 Ibid., p. 30
10 Ibid., pp. 33, 34. MM says: 'I think somebody once suggested that one could make a map of one's life in terms of images that stand for important things.' One of these from her childhood was in Guildford, 'part of the Pilgrim's Way, St Catherine's Chapel and the great steep bank and the River Wey.' Interview with Chris Crickmay (Open University) and Marion Milner in Mrs Milner's home, 28 October 1975, John Milner Papers.
11 ONBAP, p. 35
12 Ibid., p. 37
13 Ibid., p. 93
14 William Blake; 'O Human Imagination O Divine Body I have Crucified' from *Jerusalem* (1804)
15 ONBAP, p. 43
16 Ibid., p. 44

17 Ibid., p. 45
18 Ibid., p. 47
19 Ibid., p. 48
20 Ibid., p. 49
21 Ibid.
22 Ibid., pp. 50, 51
23 Personal Notebooks, 'Saturday', no date, MMC, PO1/E/B/63
24 ONBAP, p. 52
25 Ibid., p. 53
26 Ibid., p. 55
27 Ibid., p. 57
28 Ibid., p. 59
29 Ibid.
30 Ibid., p. 62
31 Ibid., p. 66
32 Ibid., p. 67
33 Freud alludes to this in relation to Groddeck's *Book of the IT* (1923) in *The Ego and the Id*, Standard Edition, XIX, p. 23. MM makes frequent use of this phrase
34 William Blake, *Auguries of Innocence*, 1803(?)
35 ONBAP, p. 73
36 Ibid., p. 74
37 Ibid., pp. 78–79
38 D.W. Winnicott, 'Critical Notice of *On Not Being Able to Paint*' in Lesley Caldwell (ed.), *Art, Creativity, Living*, London, Karnac, 2000, pp. 117–119
39 ONBAP, p. 80
40 Ibid., p. 83
41 Ibid., p. 84
42 William Blake,'The Marriage of Heaven and Hell' (1790–1793)
43 ONBAP, p. 99
44 Ibid., p. 101
45 Ibid., p. 104
46 Ibid.
47 Ibid. p. 107. MM alludes to being like Alice in a recorded interview with King and Steiner, 1996, and speaks of her realisation that one had to go backwards in order to go forwards. She also mentions this idea in her Personal Notebooks, e.g. she writes, 12 November, 1948(?), 'By *changing* myself, getting fat or learning French cooking course etc. etc. Is it possible that I was right about having to go in the opposite direction like Alice. e.g. instead of concentrating on loving arms and breasts and throat and thinking that will do it [. . .] this a.m. I thought of "realising" the opposite, the greedy relentless spider insect arms.' MMC, PO1/E/B/63
48 ONBAP, p. 115
49 Ibid., p. 116
50 Ibid., p. 117
51 Ibid., p. 118
52 Ibid., pp. 118–119
53 Ibid., p. 119 'In the destructive element immerse'. Joseph Conrad, *Lord Jim*, London 1899–1900, Chapter 20
54 ONBAP, pp. 120, 122
55 Ibid., p. 124
56 Ibid., p. 125
57 Ibid., p. 128
58 Ibid., p. 129
59 Ibid., p. 234

60 Ibid., p. 135
61 Ibid., p. 136
62 Ibid., p. 138
63 From John Donne, 'The Dream' (1635)
64 ONBAP, p. 139
65 Ibid., p. 144
66 Ibid., p. 150
67 The phrase 'pathetic fallacy' is generally attributed to John Ruskin 'Modern Painters' (1856); ONBAP, p. 150
68 Ibid., pp. 151, 152
69 'The Prolific and The Devourer' from William Blake, 'The Marriage of Heaven and Hell' (1790–1793)
70 Personal Notebooks, 1 September, no year, PO1/E/B/63
71 ONBAP, p. 154
72 Ibid., pp. 156–157
73 Ibid., p. 158
74 Ibid., p. 161
75 Ibid., pp. 161, 162 (italics mine)
76 Ibid., p. 164
77 Ibid.
78 Ibid., p. 165
79 Personal Notebooks, (?1948), MMC, PO1/E/B/65
80 ONBAP, p. 165
81 Ibid., p. 166
82 Ibid., p. 167
83 Ibid., p. 168
84 Ibid., p. 170
85 Interview with King and Steiner, op. cit.
86 Masud Khan, '*On Not Being Able to Paint* by Joanna Field', *International Journal of Psychoanalysis* , 34, 1953, 333–336, MMC, PO1/A/D/03
87 Rita Simon, 'Marion Milner and the Psychotherapy of Art', *Winnicott Studies*, 3, 'A Celebration of the Life and Work of Marion Milner', 1988
88 *BMJ*, 26 August, 1950; *Manchester Guardian,* 7 July 1950; *The Listener*, 15 June 1950. MMC, PO1/A/D/02
89 *The New Era*, April 1958. MMC,PO1/A/D/02
90 Letter to MM from Eric Newton, 14 May 1950, MMC, PO1/A/D/07
91 Letter to MM from Professor W.R. Niblett, no date, MMC, PO1/A/D/07
92 Letter to MM from Dorothy Burlingham, 6 November 1950, MMC, PO1/A/D/07
93 W.R.D. Fairbairn, 'Critical Notices', *British Journal of Medical Psychology*, 24, 1, March 1951
94 Michael Fordham, 'A Reaction', *British Journal of Medical Psychology*, 24, 1, March 1951, MMC, PO1/A/D/04
95 Letter to MM from Jacques Schnier, 30 May 1995, MMC, PO1/A/D/07; 'in house note', Jeremy Tarcher, 1983. John Milner Papers.
96 Janet Sayers, New Introduction, ONBAP, p. xliii; and see also Stephen Bann (ed.), *The Coral Mind: Adrian Stokes's Engagement with Art History, Criticism, Architecture and Psychoanalysis*, Philadelphia PA, Pennsylvania University Press, 2007
97 Sayers, New Introduction, p. xliii
98 Sayers in Bann, op. cit., 11, 12 note 1
99 Interview of MM by Pearl King typescript, no date. John Milner Papers.
100 'Note' MMC, PO1/D/A/32
101 ONBAP, pp. 173, 174
102 Ibid., pp. 176, 177

103 Michael Eigen, 'On Not Being Able to Paint', *The Psychoanalytic Review*, 64, 1977, 312–315; 'Dual Union or Undifferentiation?', op. cit., 1983, p. 417
104 ONBAP, p. 178
105 Ibid., p. 179
106 Ibid.
107 Ibid., p. 180
108 Ibid., p. 181
109 Ibid., p. 182
110 Ibid., p. 183
111 Michael Eigen, 'On Not Being Able to Paint', op. cit., p. 419
112 Ibid.
113 Letter to MM from John Padel, no date, MMC, PO1/D/A/32
114 Letter to MM from Michael Eigen, 30 November 1983, MMC, PO1/D/A/32
115 Letter to MM from Michael Eigen, 3 December 1983, MMC, PO1/D/A/32
116 Interview with Michael Eigen in Anthony Molino (ed.), *Freely Associated: Encounters in Psychoanalysis,* London and New York, 1977, p. 115
117 ONBAP, p. 184
118 Ibid., p. 185
119 Ibid., pp. 184–185
120 Ibid., p. 187
121 Ibid., pp. 187–188
122 Ibid., p. 190
123 Ibid., pp. 191–192

7 INFLUENCES, FAMILY AND FRIENDS

1 Janet Sayers, New Introduction, ONBAP, p. xxxviii
2 ONBAP, p. xxii
3 *Marian Bohusz*, Max Wyke-Jones (intro), London, Drian, 1977
4 Roger Willoughby, *Masud Khan: The Myth and the Reality*, London, Free Association, 2005, p. 44; MM 'A School for Painters', typescript, no date, John Milner Papers
5 Sayers, New Introduction, op. cit., p. xliii
6 Letter to MM from Marian Bohusz, 1 June 1961; letter to MM from Marian Bohusz, 1967, MMC, PO1/D/D/20
7 Cicely Saunders, Preface, *Marian Bohusz,* p. 27; 'Appreciation by The Rt Rev. Dr John Taylor, The Lord Bishop of Winchester', *Marian Bohusz*, p. 33
8 www.stchristophers.org.uk
9 Richard Walker, 'Marion Milner at the Drian Gallery', *Art Review*, 1971, XXIII, 2, MMC, PO1/H/A/06. Milner's work was also included in 'An Exhibition of Work by Eight British Artists (1919–1992)' at Shinjo in Northern Japan, organised at the invitation of the Japanese authorities by the British artist Nigel Capel. In addition to MM and Capel, the artists were David Bomberg, Harry Thubron, Miles Richmond, John Rodrigues, Ann Kiernan and David Seaton, MMC, PO1/H/A/07
10 'Dance', MMC, PO1/J/03
11 'Opera and Other Theatrical Productions', MMC, PO1/J/04
12 'Meditation, Relaxation and Posture', MMC, PO1/J/05
13 Mary Reid, personal communications, 2011, 2012
14 www.braziers.org.uk
15 J. Norman Glaister, 'The Braziers Approach', no date, MMC, PO1/J/09
16 Letter to MM from Dr R. Glynn Faithfull, 30 January 1953, MMC, PO1/J/09
17 Glaister, op. cit.
18 Pearl King, Foreword, in Willoughby, op. cit., pp. xiii–xiv

19 Interview with Charles Rycroft in Peter L. Rudnytsky, *Psychoanalytic Conversation; Interviews with Clinicians, Commentators and Critics*, Hillsdale NJ, The Analytic Press, 2002, pp. 67–81

20 Sayers, New Introduction, op. cit., p. xliii

21 Nicky Glover, *Psychoanalytic Aesthetics: An Introduction to the British School*, London, Karnac, 2009, p. 86

22 Phyllis Grosskurth, *Melanie Klein: Her World and Her Work*, Cambridge MA, Harvard University Press, 1987, p. 444

23 Letter from MM to DWW, 9 September 1960, Roger Willoughby papers

24 John Milner, personal communication

25 Quentin Milner, personal communication, October 2007

26 John Milner, personal communication

27 John Clay, *R.D. Laing: A Divided Self*, London, Hodder & Stoughton, 1996, pp. 68–69

28 Ibid.

29 Adrian Laing, *R.D. Laing: A Life*, London, Harper Collins, 1997, pp. 65–66

30 R.D. Laing, 'What is Schizophrenia?', paper given at the First International Congress of Social Psychiatry, MMC, PO1/D/C/01

31 Pearl King, *Time Present and Time Past; Selected Papers of Pearl King*, London, Karnac, 2005; Pearl King, personal communication, July 2006

32 'Charles Rycroft, In Conversation with Jeremy Holmes' *The Psychiatrist, Psychiatric Bulletin*, 1996, 20, 726–732; Jenny Pearson, 'Glimpses of a Life', Jenny Pearson (ed.), *Analyst of the Imagination: The Life and Work of Charles Rycroft*, London, Karnac, 2004, pp. 204, 195

33 Interview Roger Kennedy, 2006

34 Christopher Bollas, email communications, 2011, 2012

35 Masud Khan, 'Marion Milner: *The Suppressed Madness of Sane Men*', MMC, PO1/A/G/01

36 Willoughby, op. cit., p. 126

37 Ibid., p. 128

38 Ibid., p. 129

39 Linda Hopkins, *False Self: The Life of Masud Khan*, New York, Other Press, 2006, pp. 203, 207

40 Willoughby, op. cit., p. 139

41 Ibid., p. 140

42 Hopkins, op. cit., pp. 137–138

8 SERVANT OF A PROCESS

1 G. Gorer, 'The Hands of the Living God: by Marion Milner', *The International Journal of Psychoanalysis*, 51, 1970, 531

2 HOLG, p. 1. Reviews of HOLG are in MMC, PO1/A/E/03

3 HOLG, p. xxxv

4 Ibid., p. xxxviii, p. xlvii

5 Ibid.

6 Lucas, Richard, 'The Relationship between Psychoanalysis and Schizophrenia', *The International Journal of Psychoanalysis*, 84, 2003, 3–15

7 HOLG, p. 26. A letter to MM, 1940s, from D.W. Winnicott comments that she may have to 'fail' with Susan who may have to 'to go into a "bin", or she may do herself in as the saying is: you just don't have to mind if you are pioneering in psychoanalysis of psychosis.' MMC, PO1/D/D/33

8 HOLG, p. 30

9 Ibid., p. 32

10 Ibid., p. 35

11 Ibid., p. 41

12 Ibid., p. 44
13 Ibid., pp. 45, 46
14 Ibid., p. 48
15 Ibid., p. 76f.
16 Ibid., p. 56
17 Ibid., p. 95
18 Ibid., p. 117
19 Ibid., p. 218
20 Ibid., p. 266
21 Ibid., p. 267
22 Ibid., p. 269
23 Ibid., p. 284 note 3. Harold Searles, 'The Effort to Drive the Other Person Crazy: An Element in the Aetiology and Psychotherapy of Schizophrenia', *British Journal of Medical Psychology*, xxxii, 29, 1959, 443–444
24 HOLG, p. 275
25 Ibid., p. 276
26 Ibid.
27 Letter from MM to Adrian Stokes, 28 March, 1954, Stokes' Archive [this has now moved to the Tate Gallery London]
28 HOLG, p. 286, note 15. Janet Sayers comments on this, 'Stokes approved of Milner's distinctly different approach in emphasising twoness growing out of oneness.' 'Healing Art – Healing Stokes' in Stephen Bann (ed.), *The Coral Mind*, Philadelphia PA, Pennsylvania University Press, 2007, p. 132
29 Correspondence in MMC, PO1/D/C/06. Little's work on the illusion of unity links with MM's work in HOLG e.g. 'On Basic Unity', *International Journal of Psycho-Analysis*, 1960, 41, 377–384. See also HOLG, p. 286 note 15
30 HOLG, p. 286
31 Ibid., p. 277
32 See Figure 8.1
33 HOLG, p. 279
34 Ibid., p. 280
35 Ibid., p. 281
36 See Joe Berke and Mary Barnes, *Mary Barnes*, London, Free Association, 1972. Milner's papers show that she retained an article about the Arbours Crisis Centre (established 1970) perhaps as a possible resource for 'Susan' when she (Milner) needed to be away (John Milner Papers). Berke, Masoliver and Ryan comment: 'It was easier in the early days to be a 'purist'. Many of the people who sought us out had read *Mary Barnes*, the book Joe Berke and Mary Barnes wrote just after Kingsley Hall had closed, and were wide-eyed with enthusiasm.' J. Berke, C. Masoliver and T. Ryan (eds), *Sanctuary: The Arbours Experience of Alternative Community Care*, London, Process Press, 1995, p. 173
37 HOLG, p. 282
38 Ibid.
39 Ibid., pp. 282, 283
40 Ibid., pp. 283–284
41 Ibid., p. 290
42 Ibid. p. 292
43 Ibid., p. 300
44 J. Sayers, 'Marion Milner, Mysticism and Psychoanalysis', *The International Journal of Psychoanalysis*, 83, 1, 2002, 105–120; Kelley A. Raab, 'Creativity and Transcendence in the Work of Marion Milner', *American Imago*, 57, 2, 2002, 185–214
45 HOLG, p. 301
46 Ibid. William Blake, 'To annihilate the Selfhood of Deceit' from 'A Poem by Milton', 1804–1808

47 HOLG, pp. 305–306
48 Ibid., p. 306
49 See pp. 105–106 and footnote
50 HOLG, p. 308, note 5
51 Ibid., pp. 316–317
52 HOLG, p. 318
53 Ibid., pp. 326–327
54 Ibid., pp. 329, 332
55 Ibid., p. 335
56 One source of this idea from Freud, which MM mentions or adapts on occasion in different forms, is his alleged comment 'The poets and philosophers before me discovered the unconscious. What I discovered was the scientific method by which the unconscious can be studied.' First quoted by Philip R. Lehrman in 'Freud's Contribution to Science' in the journal *Harofe Haivri*, Vol. 1 (1940) and then cited by Lionel Trilling in 'Freud and Literature' (1940) ; see www.freud.org.uk/about/faq
57 William Blake, 'Jerusalem', 1820
58 HOLG, p. 338. William Blake, 'The Marriage of Heaven and Hell', *c*.1793
59 HOLG, pp. 342, 346
60 Ibid., pp. 353, 354
61 Ibid., p. 355. Nina Farhi, 'The Hands of the Living God: "Finding the Familiar in the Unfamiliar"', *Psychoanalytic Dialogues,* 2010, 20, 478–503, 483
62 HOLG, pp. 360–361
63 Ibid., p. 374
64 Ibid., p. 398, note 2
65 Ibid., pp. 383, 387
66 Ibid., p. 396
67 Ibid., pp. 418, 420
68 Ibid., p. 426
69 Ibid., p. 257, note 1. Reich was ultimately discredited for his use of touch and his espousal of 'vegetotherapy'. Milner however makes an interesting link with mysticism in his statement that 'the schizophrenic and the mystic are structurally very close together'.
70 Ibid., pp. 426–427
71 Ibid., p. 427
72 See Kelley A. Raab, 'Mysticism, Creativity and Psychoanalysis: Learning from Marion Milner', *The International Journal for the Psychology of Religion*', 13, 2, 2003, 79–96
73 HOLG, p. 428
74 Ibid., p. 429
75 Ibid.
76 Ibid., p. 430
77 Ibid., pp. 431–432, note 5
78 Ibid., p. 435
79 Ibid., p. 444
80 MM alludes here to Anna Freud's paper of 1951 read in Amsterdam on 'Negativism and Emotional Surrender'
81 HOLG, pp. 459–460 note 1
82 Ibid., p. 445
83 Ibid., p. 447
84 Ibid., p. 448
85 Ibid.
86 Ibid., p. 449. William Blake 'Gnomic Verses', 1793
87 Ibid., p. 450
88 Ibid., p. 452

89   Ibid.
90   Ibid., p. 453
91   Ibid., p. 454
92   Ibid., p. 457
93   Ibid., p. 458
94   Adam Phillips, New Introduction, HOLG, p. xxxiii
95   Gorer, op. cit. (note 1 of this chapter)
96   Charles Kligerman, 'The Hands of the Living God by Marion Milner', *The International Journal of Psychoanalysis*, 51, 1970, 531–540, MMC, PO1/A/E/03
97   H. Guntrip, 'The Hands of the Living God by Marion Milner', *The International Journal of Psychoanalysis*, 51, 1970, 531–540, MMC, PO1/A/E/03
98   Lore Schacht, 'Hands of the Living God', *Psyche*, 1972, 7/8, MMC, PO1/A/E/03
99   Jean Kadmon, 'Hands of the Living God', *Jerusalem Post Magazine*, 1992, MMC, PO1/A/E/03
100 G. Bychowski, 'Hands of the Living God', *American Imago*, 28, 1971, 91–93
101 Marian Strachan, 'Hands of the Living God', 1970s (?), MMC, PO1/A/E/08
102 Peter Lomas, 'Hands of the Living God', *New Statesman*, 30 January 1970
103 AGW, 'Hands of the Living God', *The Psychoanalytic Review*, 59, 1971, 157–158
104 Aaron H. Esman, 'The Hands of the Living God by Marion Milner', *The Psychoanalytic Quarterly*, 40, 1971, 165–166
105 Avgi Saketopoulou, 'Identifications Annealed, Adhesive and Political: Commentary on Paper by Nina Farhi', *Psychoanalytic Dialogues*, 20, 5, 2010, 510–515
106 Farhi, 'The Hands of the Living God', op. cit.
107 Saketopoulou, op. cit., p. 512
108 Jean White, 'From Survival to Creative Destiny: The Psychoanalytic Journey of Nina Farhi', *Psychoanalytic Dialogues*, 20, 5, 2010, 533–539
109 Ibid.
110 Jeanne Wolff Bernstein, 'Nina Farhi: Leaning on an Annealed Identification: Commentary on Paper by Nina Farhi', *Psychoanalytic Dialogues*, 20, 5, 2010, 516–520
111 Dodi Goldman, 'Letting the Sea in: Commentary on Paper by Nina Farhi', *Psychoanalytic Dialogues*, 20, 5, 2010, 504–509. Goldman quotes L. Caldwell, *Art Creativity, Living*, London, Karnac, p. 145
112 Mary Jacobus, *The Poetics of Psychoanalysis in the Wake of Klein*, Oxford, Oxford University Press, 2005, pp. 122–123
113 Adam Phillips, New Introduction, HOLG, p. xix
114 Helen Taylor Robinson, 'Marion Milner: On Not Being Able to Paint' and 'The Hands of the Living God', *British Journal of Psychotherapy*, 27, 3, 2011, 321
115 Anne Karpf, 'Journey to the Centre of the Mind', *The Guardian*, 3 June 1998

9 'THE FACTS OF ART'

1   MM, '1955:The Communication of Primary Sensual Experience', SMSM, pp. 114–167
2   Peter Fuller, Foreword, in Tessa Dalley, *Art as Therapy: An Introduction to the Use of Art as a Therapeutic Tool*, London, Routledge, 1984/2009
3   Susan Hogan, *Healing Arts; The History of Art Therapy*, London and Philadelphia, Jessica Kingsley, 2001, p. 83
4   Ibid., p. 84
5   Ibid., p. 83
6   See p. 154
7   Hogan, op. cit., p. 88
8   Rita Simon, 'Marion Milner and the Psychotherapy of Art', *Winnicott Studies*, 1988, 3, pp. 48–52
9   Hogan, op. cit., p. 306

NOTES

10 Martina Thomson, *On Art and Therapy: An Exploration*, London and New York, Free Association, 1989/1997; Martina Thomson, personal communications, 2011
11 Harry Karnac, personal communication, February 2012
12 Martina Thomson, 'Marion Milner Remembered', *International Journal of Art Therapy*, 3, 2, 2001, 83
13 Ibid.
14 David Edwards, 'On Re-Reading Marion Milner', *International Journal of Art Therapy*, 6, 1, 2001
15 Ibid., p. 7
16 Tessa Rawcliffe, quoted in Edwards, op. cit., p. 21
17 Ibid., p. 22. Adam Phillips, interview with Sameer Padania, June 2010; see http://bombsite.com
18 Simon, op. cit., p. 51
19 Caroline Case and Tessa Dalley, *The Handbook of Art Therapy*, 2nd edition, London and New York, Routledge, 2006, p. 124
20 Ibid., p. 125
21 Ibid., p. 129
22 Ibid., p. 130 (quoting M. Davis and D. Wallbridge, *Boundary and Space*, London, Karnac, 1981)
23 Information from the Department of Art Psychotherapy, Goldsmith's College, University of London.

10 BEADS OF HER OWN

1 *'Eternity's Sunrise'*, MMC, PO1/A/F/103
2 ES, p. xxxv
3 John Fielding, 'Telling the Beads', *Winnicott Studies,* 3, 'A Celebration of the Life and Work of Marion Milner', 1988, 64–68
4 ES, p. 3
5 Ibid., p. 9
6 Ibid., pp. 11, 12
7 Ibid., p. 12
8 Ibid., p. xxii
9 Ibid., p. 17
10 Ibid., p. 19
11 Ibid., p. 27
12 Ibid., p. 29
13 Ibid., pp. 31–32
14 Ibid., p. 35; 'To John', 11 November 1939, Personal Notebooks, MMC, PO1/G/08
15 ES, pp. 37–38
16 Ibid., p. 38
17 Ibid., pp. 38–40
18 Ibid., p. 40. Patrick Blackett died in hospital on 13 July 1974
19 ES, p. 41
20 Ibid., p. 42
21 Ibid., p. 43
22 Ibid., p. 45
23 Ibid., p. 47
24 Ibid., p. 47
25 Ibid., p. 48
26 Ibid., p. 49. Milner's repetition of this story from Ruskin is an interesting example of her tendency, like an analysand, to repeat examples that accrue meaning in their repetition.

27 Ibid.

28 EIL, p. 138; ES, p. 51

29 ES, p. 52

30 Ibid., p. 53

31 Estela Welldon deals with this in *Mother, Madonna, Whore*, London, Karnac, 1992

32 ES, pp. 53–54

33 Ibid., p. 57

34 Ibid., p. 58. Concerning this 'Hitlerian certainty', see Christopher Bollas, 'The Fascist State of Mind', *Being a Character: Psychoanalysis and Self Experience*, London and New York, Routledge, 1993, p. 193f.

35 ES, p. 59

36 Ibid.

37 Ibid., p. 65

38 Ibid., p. 66

39 Ibid., p. 72

40 Ibid., p. 74

41 Ibid.

42 Ibid., p. 75

43 Ibid., p. 81. In an unpublished typescript, 'Painting as Playing', MM comments on the titles of her collages: 'I never knew beforehand what the picture was going to be about. In fact the titles appeared just as a first free association to a dream.' John Milner Papers.

44 ES, p. 90

45 Ibid., pp. 93–94

46 Ibid., p. 96

47 Ibid., p. 99

48 Ibid., pp. 103–104

49 Ibid., p. 106

50 Ibid., p. 110

51 Ibid., p. 114

52 Ibid., p. 119

53 Ibid., p. 125

54 Ibid., pp. 130–131

55 Ibid., p. 131

56 Ibid., p. 140

57 Ibid., p. 141

58 Ibid., pp. 141–142

59 Ibid., p. 142

60 Ibid., p. 144

61 Ibid., p. 148

62 Hugh Haughton, New Introduction, ES, p. xxxix

63 ES, p. 149. Italics mine.

64 Ibid., p. 156

65 Ibid., p. 150

66 Ibid., pp. 150–151

67 Ibid., p. 151

68 Ibid., p. 152

69 Ibid., p. 153

70 Ibid., p. 154

71 Ibid., pp. 171–172

72 Ibid., p. 173

73 Ibid., p. 183

74 Ibid., p. 187

75 Ibid., p. 195
76 Fielding, op. cit., p. 68
77 Frances Tustin, 'A Personal Reminiscence', *Winnicott Studies*, 1988, 3, 57, 59

11 FORTY-FOUR YEARS OF PSYCHOANALYSIS

1 Letter to MM from Gill Davies, 4 March 1968, MMC, PO1/A/J/9
2 Masud Khan, '*Suppressed Madness of Sane Men*', MMC, PO1/A/G/01
3 Michael Brearley, 'Marion Milner: *The Suppressed Madness of Sane Men*', *Journal of Child Psychotherapy*, 15A(?), 1989, 133–139, John Milner Papers.
4 Ellen Handler Spitz, 'The Suppressed Madness of Sane Men', *The Psychoanalytic Quarterly*, 59, 1990, 137–142
5 Samuel A. Grolnick, 'The Suppressed Madness of Sane Men', *Journal of the American Psychoanalytical Association*, 39, 1991, 292–296
6 Donald Campbell, interview, July 2008
7 Gilbert J. Rose, '*The Suppressed Madness of Sane {Men}*', 1989, typescript, John Milner Papers. This was re-visited by MM, 6 September 1993.
8 Brearley, op. cit.
9 Ibid.
10 Susanna Isaacs Elmhirst, 'Marion Milner; *The Suppressed Madness of Sane Men*', *The New Library of Psychoanalysis*, Leaflet, 1987(?), John Milner Papers
11 Andreas Giannacoulas, '*The Suppressed Madness of Sane Men*', 1988, MMC, PO1/D/B/04
12 Letter to MM from Heinz Koppel, no date, MMC, PO1/A/I/09. Winnicott was one who was most enthusiastic about MM's Blake work and education; he was 'tremendously impressed' about her planned work, letter to MM from D.W. Winnicott, 9 September 1955, Archives of the British Psychoanalytical Society, PO1/D/D/33
13 See p. 154
14 Spitz, op. cit. included Yeats's 'Because I seek an image not a book' as the epigraph to her review of SMSM. The line comes from 'Ego Dominus Tuus', *Wild Swans at Coole*, 1919.
15 SMSM, p. 9
16 Ibid.
17 Ibid., p. 199
18 Ibid., pp. 173–174
19 Ibid., p. 174
20 Ibid.
21 Ibid., p. 176
22 Ibid., p. 178
23 Ibid.
24 Ibid., p. 179
25 Ibid., p. 181
26 Ibid. William Blake, *Jerusalem*, 1804
27 Ibid., p. 182
28 D.W. Winnicott, 'Primitive Emotional Development' (1945), *Collected Papers: Through Paediatrics to Psychoanalysis*, London, Tavistock, 1958, p. 150
29 SMSM, p. 183
30 Ibid., p. 184
31 Ibid., p. 185
32 Ibid., p. 186
33 Ibid., p. 188
34 Ibid., pp. 188–189
35 Ibid., p. 189

36 Ibid., pp. 189, 190
37 Ibid., p. 191
38 Letter to MM from D.W. Winnicott, 9 September 1955, MMC,PO1//D/D/33; letter to MM from George Digby, 9 December 1957; letter to MM from Kathleen Raine, no date, MMC, PO1/A/I/09
39 Letter to MM from Kathleen Raine, no date, MMC, PO1/A/I/09
40 Letters to MM from A. Ehrenzweig, 16 January 1956, 15 April 1956, MMC, PO1/A/I/09
41 Letter to MM from Adrian Stokes, 29 March 1956, MMC, PO1/A/I/09
42 Letter to MM from Roger Money-Kyrle, 3 May 1956; letter to MM from Dr Gordon Levinson, 23 July 1956; letter to MM from Victor Goddard, 15 December 1957, MMC PO1/A/1/09
43 Letter to MM from Heinz Koppel, no date, MMC PO1/A/1/09
44 Letter to MM from R. Fentener Von Vlissingen, 30 December 1959, MMC PO1/A/1/09
45 SMSM, p. 258
46 MM, 'Mysticism and Spirituality', MMC, PO1/1/12
47 Michael Eigen, *The Psychoanalytic Mystic,* London and New York, Free Association, 1988, p. 13
48 N.R. Dragstedt, 'Creative Illusions', *Journal of Melanie Klein and Object Relations*, 16, 1988, 425–536, 457
49 Kelley A. Raab, 'Creativity and Transcendence in the Work of Marion Milner', *American Imago*, 57, 2, 2000, 185–214, 187
50 Janet Sayers, 'Marion Milner, Mysticism and Psychoanalysis', *International Journal of Psychoanalysis*, 83, 2002, 105–118
51 SMSM, p. 259
52 Ibid.
53 Ibid., p. 260
54 Ibid., p. 262
55 Ibid., p. 263
56 Ibid., p. 235f.
57 Ibid., p. 264
58 Ibid., p. 265
59 Ibid., p. 266
60 Ibid., pp. 267, 268
61 Michael Parsons, 'Marion Milner's "Answering Activity" and the Question of Psychoanalytic Creativity', *The International Review of Psycho-Analysis*, 17, 2000, 413–424
62 Mark Epstein, *Thoughts Without a Thinker: Psychotherapy from a Buddhist Perspective,* New York, Basic Books, 1995, pp. 144–145
63 Michael Podro, 'The Landscape Thinks Itself in Me', *The International Review of Psycho-Analysis*, 17, 1990, 401–408

12 BOTHERED BY . . . THE 1990s

1 BBA, p. 1
2 Mathew Hale, personal communications; quotations on the following pages are from conversations and emails between EL and Mathew Hale
3 Mary Reid, interviews, 2011, 2012
4 BBA, pp. 1–2
5 Ibid., p. 5
6 Ibid., p. 9
7 Ibid., pp. 14, 15, 16

8 Ibid., p. 27
9 Ibid., p. 29
10 Ibid., p. 46
11 Ibid., p. 50
12 Ibid., p. 43
13 Ibid.
14 Ibid., p. 51
15 Ibid., p. 53
16 Ibid., p. 54
17 Ibid., p. 66
18 Ibid., pp. 67–68
19 Ibid., p. 69
20 Ibid., pp. 71–110
21 Ibid., p. 123
22 Ibid., p. 124
23 Ibid.
24 Ibid., pp. 125–126
25 Ibid., p. 127
26 Ibid., p. 129
27 Ibid.
28 Ibid., pp. 130–131
29 Ibid., p. 131
30 Ibid., p. 134
31 Ibid., p. 137
32 Ibid., p. 138
33 Ibid., p. 140
34 Ibid.
35 Ibid., p. 142
36 Ibid., p. 145
37 Ibid., pp. 146–147
38 Ibid., p. 148
39 Ibid., p. 148–149
40 Ibid., p. 152
41 Ibid., p. 153
42 Archive papers show that MM and André Green corresponded between 1972 and 1980. MM has annotated a coy of 'The Dead Mother Paper' (1983) indicating links with her husband Dennis's depression and also that of her mother. MMC, PO1/D/D/33
43 Quoted in Alexander Newman, 'A Life of One's Own and An Experiment in Leisure', *The Journal of Analytical Psychology*, 33, 2, 1988
44 BBA, p. 154. William Blake, 'All Religions are One', 1788
45 BBA, p. 154
46 Ibid., pp. 154–155
47 Ibid., p. 157
48 Ibid.
49 Ibid., pp. 157–158
50 Ibid., p. 158
51 Ibid., p. 160f.
52 Ibid., p. 163
53 Ibid., p. 164
54 Ibid., p. 166
55 Ibid., p. 167
56 Ibid., p. 173
57 Ibid., p. 174

58 Ibid., p. 176
59 Ibid., p. 177
60 Ibid., pp. 177–179
61 Ibid., p. 182
62 Ibid.
63 Ibid., p. 183
64 William Blake, 'Auguries of Innocence', 1803(?)
65 BBA, p. 189
66 MM, 'Painting as Playing', typescript, no date, John Milner Papers
67 BBA, p. 192
68 Ibid., pp. 192–193
69 Ibid., p. 195f.
70 Ibid., p. 203
71 Ibid., pp. 206–207
72 Ibid., p. 213f.
73 Letter from Martina Thomson to EL, 20 November 2012
74 BBA, pp. 228, 229
75 Ibid., p. 242
76 Ibid., p. 251
77 Ibid., p. 255
78 Ibid., p. 256
79 Ibid., p. 259
80 Ibid., p. 260
81 Ibid., p. 262
82 Mathew Hale, personal communications; and see BBA, 'Note on Appendix', pp. 269–270
83 Martina Thomson, 'Marion', *Rialto*, 1998

BIBLIOGRAPHY

MARION MILNER WORKS

A Life of One's Own, London, Chatto and Windus, 1934 (as Joanna Field); with a New Introduction by Rachel Bowlby, London, Routledge, 2010

An Experiment in Leisure, London, Chatto & Windus, 1937 (as Joanna Field); with a New Introduction by Maud Ellmann, London, Routledge, 2010

The Human Problem in Schools, London, Methuen, 1938

'A Success and Failure', *The New Era*, February 1940

'Inner Realities', *Home and School*, 5, 6 August 1940

'School Needs of the 12 to 16-year old', *The New Era*, February 1941

'The Child's Capacity for Doubt', 1942, SMSM, pp. 12–15

'The Toleration of Conflict', *Occupational Psychology*, 17, 1, January 1943

'A Suicidal Symptom in a Child of 3', *International Journal of Psychoanalysis*, 25, 1944, 53–61; SMSM, pp. 21–38

'Notes on the Analysis of a 2½ Year Old Boy', 1943, SMSM, pp. 16–20

'Some Aspects of Phantasy in Relation to General Psychology', *International Journal of Psychoanalysis*, 1945, 26, 144–52; SMSM, pp. 39–62

'Some Signposts – Blackness, Joy, Mind', 1947–1948, SMSM, pp. 63–65

'An Adult Patient uses Toys', 1948, SMSM, pp. 66–72

'The Ending of Two Analyses', *International Journal of Psychoanalysis*, 31, 1950, 191–193; SMSM, pp. 73–82

On Not Being Able to Paint, London, Heinemann, 1950 (as Joanna Field); 2nd edition, with Foreword by Anna Freud, London, Heinemann, 1957; with a New Introduction by Janet Sayers, London, Routledge, 2010

'The Framed Gap', 1952, SMSM, pp. 79–82

'Aspects of Symbolism in Comprehension of the Not-Self', *International Journal of Psychoanalysis,* 33, 1952, 181–194; SMSM, pp. 83–111; in version as 'The Role of Illusion in Symbol Formation', SMSM, pp. 83–111; also in S. Gosso, *Psychoanalysis and Art: Kleinian Perspectives*, London, Karnac, 2004

'The Communication of Primary Sensual Experience (The Yell of Joy)', *International Journal of Psychoanalysis*, 1955, 37, 278–281; SMSM, pp. 114–167

'The Sense in Non-Sense: Freud and Blake's Job', *The New Era*, January 1956, 1–13; SMSM, pp. 168–191

'Psychoanalysis and Art', 1956; SMSM, pp. 193–195; also in J. Sutherland (ed.), *Psycho-Analysis and Contemporary Thought*, London, Hogarth and British Institute of Psycho-Analysis, 1958

'The Concentration of the Body', 1960, SMSM, pp. 234–245. Part II, 'Painting and Internal Body Awareness' read at Congress in Athens 1960

'The Hidden Order of Art', 1967, read at ICA London, 21 June 1967; SMSM, pp. 241–244

The Hands of the Living God, London, Hogarth Press, 1969; with a New Introduction by Adam Phillips, London, Routledge, 2010

'Growing Wings in Kashmir', *Review of the Society for Hellenic Travel*, 11, 1, 1971

'Winnicott and the Two-way Journey', 1972, SMSM, pp. 246–252; also in S. Grolnick (ed.), *Between Reality and Fantasy*, Lanham MD, Jason Aronson, 1978

'The Two-way Journey in a Child Analysis', 1972, SMSM, pp. 253–257

'Some Notes on Psychoanalytic Ideas about Mysticism',1973, SMSM, pp. 258–272

'A discussion of Masud Khan's paper "In Search of Dreaming Experience"',1975, SMSM, pp. 275–278

'Winnicott and Overlapping Circles', 1977, SMSM, pp. 279–286; also in *l'arc*, 69

'Clare Winnicott' (Obituary), *Winnicott Studies*, 1, 1, 1985, 4

'Afterthoughts' 1986, SMSM, pp. 287–297

Eternity's Sunrise, London, Virago, 1987; with New Introduction by Hugh Haughton, London, Routledge, 2011

The Suppressed Madness of Sane Men, London, Routledge, 1987

'Autistic Areas in All of Us?', *Winnicott Studies,* 4, 1989, 4–10

[Posthumous] *Bothered by Alligators*, with Introduction by Margaret Walters, London, Routledge, 2012

OTHER WORKS

Abram, J., *The Language of Winnicott*, London, Karnac, 1996

—— *Donald Winnicott Today*, London, Routledge, 2013

AGW, 'Hands of the Living God', *The Psychoanalytic Review*, 59, 1972, 157–158

Balint, M., *The Basic Fault: Therapeutic Aspects of Regression*, London, Tavistock, 1968

Bann, S. (ed.), *The Coral Mind: Adrian Stokes's Engagement with Art History, Criticism and Psychoanalysis*, Philadelphia PA, Pennsylvania University Press, 2007

Baudry, F., 'Revisiting the Freud-Klein Controversies Fifty Years Later', *International Journal of Psychoanalysis*, 75, 1994, 367–374

Berke, J and Barnes, M., *Mary Barnes*, London, Free Association, 1972

Berke, J., Masoliver, C. and Ryan, T (eds), *Sanctuary: The Arbours Experience of Alternative Community Care*, London, Process Press, 1995

Bernstein, J. W., 'Nina Farhi: Leaning on an Annealed Identification: Commentary on paper by Nine Farhi', *Psychoanalytic Dialogues*, 20, 5, 2010, 516–520

Bion, W.R., *Second Thoughts*, London, Heinemann, 1967

Blake, W., *The Complete Poetry and Prose,* ed. D.V. Erdman, newly revised, New York, Anchor Books, 1988

Bollas, C., *Being a Character: Psychoanalysis and Self Experience*, London and New York, Routledge, 1991

—— *Hysteria*, London and New York, Routledge, 2000

Brearley, M., 'Marion Milner; The Suppressed Madness of Sane Men', *Journal of Child Psychotherapy*, 15, 1987, 133–39

Bychowski, G., 'Hands of the Living God', *American Imago*, 28, 1971, 91–9

Caldwell, L. (ed.), *Art, Creativity, Living*, London, Karnac, 2000

—— (ed.) *Winnicott and the Psychoanalytic Tradition*, London, Karnac, 2007

Caldwell, L. and Joyce, A., *Reading Winnicott*, London, Routledge, 2010

Case, C. and Dalley, T., *The Handbook of Art Therapy*, 2nd edition, London and New York, Routledge, 2006

Caudwell, C., *Illusion and Reality*, London, Laurence & Wishart, 1946

Clay, J., *R.D. Laing: A Divided Self*, London, Hodder & Stoughton, 1996

Coltart, N., *Slouching Towards Bethlehem*, London, Free Association, 1992

Davis, M. and Wallbridge, D., *Boundary and Space,* London, Karnac, 1981

Dragstedt, N.R., 'Creative Illusions: The Theoretical and Clinical Work of Marion Milner (1990–1998)', *Journal of Melanie Klein and Object Relations*, 16, 3, 1998

Edwards, D., 'On Re-Reading Marion Milner'. *International Journal of Art Therapy*, 6, 1, 2001

Ehrenzweig, A., 'The Creative Surrender', *The American Imago*, 144, 3, 1957, 193

—— *The Hidden Order of Art*, London, Weidenfeld & Nicolson, 1967

Eigen, M., 'On Not Being Able to Paint', *The Psychoanalytic Review*, 64, 1977, 312–315

—— 'The Area of Faith in Winnicott, Lacan and Bion', *International Journal of Psychoanalysis*, 62, 1981, 413–433

—— 'Dual Union or Undifferentation? A Critique of Marion Milner's View of Psychic Creativeness', *International Review of Psycho-Analysis*, 10, 1983, 415–428

—— *The Psychoanalytic Mystic*, London and New York, Free Association, 1988

Epstein, M., *Thoughts Without a Thinker: Psychotherapy from a Buddhist Perspective*, New York, Basic Books, 1995

Esman, A.H., 'The Hands of the Living God by Marion Milner', *The Psychoanalytic Quarterly*, 40, 1971, 165–166

Farhi, N., 'The Hands of the Living God: "Finding the Familiar in the Unfamiliar"', *Psychoanalytic Dialogues*, 20, 2010, 478–503

Fielding, J., 'Telling the Beads', *Winnicott Studies,* 3, 1988, 64–68

Follett, M.P., *Creative Experience*, New York, Longmans, Green & Co., 1930

Freud, A., 'A Connection between the States of Negativism and Emotional Surrender', *International Journal of Psycho-Analysis*, XXXIII, 1951 (see also 1952)

Freud, S., The Interpretation of Dreams, SE, 5, 1900

—— Three Essays on the Theory of Sexuality, SE, 7, 1905

—— Introductory Lectures on Psychoanalysis, SE, 15–16, 1915–1916

—— The Psychogenesis of a Case of Female Homosexuality, SE, 18, 1920

—— The Ego and the Id, SE, 19, 1923

—— Civilization and its Discontents, SE, 21, 1930

—— Splitting of the Ego in the Process of Defence, SE, 23, 1938

—— Moses and Monotheism, SE, 23, 1939

—— Findings, Problems, Ideas, SE, 23, 1940

Frosh, S., *For and Against Psychoanalysis*, London, Routledge, 1997, 2006

Fuller, P., *Art and Psycho-Analysis*, London, Writers and Readers, 1980

—— Foreword in T. Dalley, *Art as Therapy: An Introduction to the Use of Art as Therapeutic Tool*, London, Routledge, 1984 (see also 2009)

Giannacoulas, A. (1988), 'The Suppressed Madness of Sane Men', no date, MMC, PO1/D/B/04

Gilroy, A., 'On Occasionally being able to Paint', *International Journal of Art Therapy: Inscape*, 9, 2, 2004, 72–78

Glaister, J.N., *The Braziers Approach*, Braziers Park, (?)1952

Glover, N., *Psychoanalytic Aesthetics: An Introduction to the British School*, London, Karnac, 2009

Goldman, D., 'Letting the Sea in: Commentary on Paper by Nina Farhi', *Psychoanalytic Dialogues*, 20, 5, 2010, 504–509

Gordon, J., *A Step Ladder to Painting*, London, Faber & Faber, 1934

Gorer, G., 'The Hands of the Living God by Marion Milner', *The International Journal of Psychoanalysis*, 51, 1970, 531

Gosso, S., *Psychoanalysis and Art: Kleinian Perspectives*, London, Karnac, 2004

Green, A. (1978), 'Potential Space in Psycho-Analysis: the Object and its Setting' in S. Grolnick (ed.), *Between Reality and Phantasy*, Hillsdale NJ, Jason Aronson, 1995

Grolnick, S., 'The Suppressed Madness of Sane Men', *Journal of the American Psychoanalytical Association*, 39, 1991, 292–296

Grosskurth, P., *Melanie Klein: Her World and Her Work*, Cambridge MA, Harvard University Press, 1987

Heimann, P. (1943), 'Some Aspects of the Role of Introjection and Projection in Early Development' in P. King and R. Steiner (eds), *The Freud-Klein Controversies 1941–45*, London, Routledge, 1991, pp. 501–530

—— 'On Counter Transference' *International Journal of Psychoanalysis*, 31, 1950, 81–84

Hogan, S., *Healing Arts: The History of Art Therapy*, London and Philadelphia, Jessica Kingsley, 2001

Hopkins, L., 'Red Shoes, Untapped Madness, and Winnicott on the Cross: An Interview with Marion Milner', *The Annual of Psychoanalysis*, 32, 2004, 233–243

—— *False Self: The Life of Masud Khan*, New York, Other Press, 2006

Isaacs, S. (1943), 'The Nature and Function of Phantasy', in P. King and R. Steiner (eds), *The Freud-Klein Controversies 1941–45*, London, Routledge, 1991, pp. 264–321

Isaacs Elmhirst, S., 'Marion Milner: The Suppressed Madness of Sane Men', *The New Library of Psychoanalysis*, no date, leaflet, John Milner Papers

Jacobus, M., *The Poetics of Psychoanalysis in the Wake of Klein*, Oxford, Oxford University Press, 2005

Jones, E., 'The Theory of Symbolism', *British Journal of Psychology*, 9, 1916, 181–229

Jung, C., *Psychological Types*, London, Kegan Paul, 1933

Kadmon, J., 'Hands of the Living God', *Jerusalem Post Magazine*, no date

Kahr, B., *D.W. Winnicott: A Biographical Portrait*, London, Karnac, 1996

Kanter, J. (ed.) *Face to Face with Children: The Life and Work of Clare Winnicott*, London, Karnac, 2004

Karpf, A., 'Journey to the Centre of the Mind', *The Guardian*, 3 June 1998

Kennedy, R., *The Many Voices of Psychoanalysis*, London, Routledge, 2007

Khan, M., 'Notes on the Dissolution of Object-Representation in Modern Art'; paper presented in either 1950 or 1951; see Hopkins, L., *False Self: The Life of Masud Khan*, New York, Other Press, 2006, p. 409

—— 'Clinical Aspects of the Schizoid Personality', *International Journal of Psychoanalysis*, 41, 1960, 430–437

—— 'The Changing Use of Dreams in Psychoanalytic Practice', *International Journal of Psychoanalysis*, 57, 1975, 324–330

—— 'On Not Being Able to Paint', *International Journal of Psychoanalysis*, 34, 1957(?), 323–336

King, P., *Time Present and Time Past: Selected Papers of Pearl King*, London, Karnac, 2005

King, P. and Steiner, R. (eds), *The Freud-Klein Controversies 1941–45*, London, Routledge, 1991

Klein, M. (1931), 'A Theory of Intellectual Inhibition' in M. Klein (ed.), *Contributions to Psycho-Analysis*, London, Hogarth, 1948

——— *The Psycho-Analysis of Children*, London, Hogarth, 1937

——— 'Infantile Anxiety Situations Reflected in a Work of Art and in the Creative Impulse' in M. Klein (ed.), *Contributions to Psychoanalysis 1921–1945*, London, Hogarth Press, 1948

——— *Developments in Psycho-Analysis*, London, Hogarth, 1952

——— *Envy and Gratitude,* London, Tavistock, 1957

Klein, M., Heimann, P. and Money-Kyrle, R. (eds), *New Directions in Psycho-Analysis,* London, Hogarth, 1948

Kohon, G. (ed.) *The British School of Psychoanalysis: The Independent Tradition*, London, Free Association, 1986

——— (ed.), *The Dead Mother: The Work of André Green*, London, Routledge, 1999

Laing, A., *R.D. Laing: A Life*, London, Harper Collins, 1997

Laplanche, J. and Pontalis, J-B., *The Language of Psychoanalysis*, London, Hogarth, 1988

Little, M., 'On Basic Unity', *International Journal of Psychoanalysis*, 41, 1960, 377–384

——— *Psychotic Anxieties and Containment: A Personal Record of An Analysis with Winnicott*, Hillsdale NJ, Jason Aronson, 1990

Lomas, P., 'Hands of the Living God', *New Statesman*, 30 January 1970

Lucas, R., 'The Relationship between Psychoanalysis and Schizophrenia', *International Journal of Psychoanalysis*, 84, 2003, 3–15

Luepnitz, D.A., 'Thinking in the Space between Winnicott and Lacan', *International Journal of Psychoanalysis*, 90, 2009, 957–981

Meakins, E., 'A Passion for Life', Interview with Marion Milner, *Everywoman*, September 1997

——— *What Will You Do With My Story?* London, Karnac, 2012

Molino, A. (ed.), *Freely Associated: Encounters in Psychoanalysis*, London and New York, Free Association, 1977

Neuburger, R.P., Review Essay 'An Imaginary Trauma?', *Journal of Lacanian Studies*, 4, 2, 2006, 349–353

Newman, A., 'A Life of One's Own and An Experiment in Leisure', *The Journal of Analytical Psychology*, 33, 2, 1988

Nye, M.J., *Blackett: Physics, War and Politics in the Twentieth Century*, Cambridge MA and London, Harvard University Press, 2004

Ogden, T., 'On the Nature of Schizophrenic Conflict', *International Journal of Psychoanalysis*, 61, 1980, 513–533

Parsons, M., 'Marion Milner's "Answering Activity" and the question of psychoanalytic creativity', *International Review of Psycho-Analysis* , 17, 2000, 413–424

——— *The Dove that Returns, the Dove that Vanishes: Paradox and Creativity in Psychoanalysis*, London, Routledge, 2000

Pearson, J. (ed.) *Analyst of the Imagination: The Life and Work of Charles Rycroft*, London, Karnac, 2004

Phillips, A., *The Beast in the Nursery,* London, Faber and Faber, 1999

——— *On Balance*, London, Hamish Hamilton, 2010

Pines, D., *A Woman's Unconscious Use of her Body*, London, Virago, 2010

210

Podro, M., 'The Landscape thinks itself in me', *The International Review of Psycho-Analysis*, 17, 1990, 414–424

Raab, K.A., 'Creativity and Transcendence in the Work of Marion Milner', *American Imago*, 57, 2, 2002, 185–214

Rayner, E. *The Independent Mind in British Psychoanalysis*, London, Free Association, 1990

Rippin, A., 'Refusing the therapeutic: Marion Milner and Me', *Culture & Organisation*, 12, 1, 2006, 25–36

Robinson, H.T., 'Marion Milner; On Not Being Able to Paint and The Hands of the Living God', *British Journal of Psychotherapy*, 27, 3, 2011

Robinson, K., 'A Brief History of the British Psychoanalytical Society', in P. Loewenberg and N. Thompson (eds), *100 Years of the IPA: The Centenary History of the International Psychoanalytical Association 1910–2010, Evolution and Change*, London, IPA and Karnac, 2012, pp. 196–227

Rodman, R.R. (ed.), *The Spontaneous Gesture: Selected Letters of D.W. Winnicott*, London, Karnac, 1999

―――― *Winnicott: Life and Work*, Cambridge MA, Da Capo, 2003

Rose, G.J., 'Suppressed Madness of Sane Men', 1989, typescript, John Milner Papers

Rosenfeld, H., 'Psychotic States: A Psycho-Analytic Approach', in H. Rosenfeld, *Psychotic States: A Psycho-Analytic Approach,* London, Hogarth, 1965

Rudnytsky, P. L., *Psychoanalytic Conversation: Interviews with Clinicians, Commentators and Critics*, Hillsdale NJ, The Analytic Press, 2002

Rycroft, C., 'In conversation with Jeremy Holmes', *The Psychiatrist, Psychiatric Bulletin*, 20, 1996, 726–732

Saketopoulou, A., 'Identification Annealed, Adhesive and Political: Commentary on Paper by Nina Farhi', *Psychoanalytic Dialogues*, 20, 5, 2010, 510–515

Santayana, G., *The Suppressed Madness of Sane Men, Little Essays*, London, Constable, 1920

Saunders, C., Preface to *Marian Bohusz*, Max Wyke-Jones (intro), London, Drian, 1977

Sayers, J., 'Marion Milner: Psychologist to Psychoanalyst', *Psychology of Women Section*, Newsletter 3, 1989.

―――― *Mothering Psychoanalysis*, London, Penguin, 1992

―――― 'Marion Milner, Mysticism and Psychoanalysis', *International Journal of Psychoanalysis*, 83, 1, 2002, 105–120

―――― *Freud's Art: Psychoanalysis Retold*, London, Routledge, 2007

―――― 'Healing Art – Healing Stokes' in S. Bann (ed.), *The Coral Mind: Adrian Stokes's Engagement with Art History, Criticism and Psychoanalysis*, Philadelphia PA, Pennsylvania University Press, 2007

Schacht, L., '"Psycho-Analytic Facilitation in the Subject-Uses-Subject" Phase of Maturation', *International Journal of Child Psychotherapy*, 1, 4, 1972, 71–82

Scott, W.C.M., 'Some embryological, neurological, psychiatric and psycho-analytic implications of the body scheme', *International Journal of Psychoanalysis*, 29, 1948

―――― 'The Body Scheme in Psychotherapy', *British Journal of Medical Psychotherapy*, 22, 1949, 137–143

Searles, H., 'The Effort to Drive the Other Person Crazy – An Element in the Aetiology and Psychotherapy of Schizophrenia', *The Psychoanalytic Quarterly*, 29, 1960, 443–444

Sharpe, E, 'Psycho-physical Problems Revealed in Language: An Examination of Metaphor' in E. Sharpe, *Collected Papers on Psychoanalysis*, London, Hogarth, 1950

Segal, H., 'The Psycho-Analytic Approach to Aesthetics' in M. Klein, P. Heimann and R. Money-Kyrle (eds), *New Directions in Psycho-Analysis,* London, Hogarth, 1948

Siegelman, E., *Metaphor and Meaning in Psychotherapy*, Hove, Guilford Press, 1993

Simon, R., 'Marion Milner and the Psychotherapy of Art', *Winnicott Studies*, 3, 1988

Spitz, E.H., 'The Suppressed Madness of Sane Men', *The Psychoanalytic Quarterly*, 59, 1990, 137–142

Stokes, A., 'Form in Art' in M. Klein (ed.), *New Directions in Psycho-Analysis*, London, Tavistock, 1955

Stonebridge, L., *The Destructive Element: British Psychoanalysis and Modernism*, New York, Routledge, 1998

Strachan. M., 'Hands of the Living God', 1970s, typescript MMC, PO1/A/E/08

Sutherland, J. (ed.), *Psycho-Analysis and Contemporary Thought*, London: Hogarth and British Institute of Psycho-Analysis, 1958

Thomson, M., *On Art and Therapy: An Exploration*, London, Free Association, 1989 (see also 1997)

—— 'Marion Milner Remembered', *International Journal of Art Therapy*, 3, 2, 1988, 83

Tonnesmann, M., 'Michael Balint and Donald Winnicott: Contributions to the Treatment of Severely Disturbed Patients in the Independent Tradition', in L. Caldwell (ed.), *Winnicott and the Psychoanalytic Tradition,* London, Karnac, 2007

Turner, J., 'A Brief History of Illusion: Marion Milner, Winnicott and Rycroft', *International Journal of Psychoanalysis*, 2002, 83, 1063–1082

Tustin, F., *Autistic Barriers in Neurotic Patients*, London, Karnac, 1986

—— 'A Personal Reminiscence', *Winnicott Studies*, 3, 1988, 57, 58

Walker, R., 'Marion Milner at the Drian Gallery', *Art Review*, 1971, XXIII, 2

Walsby, H. *The Domain of Ideologies*, Glasgow, W. MacLellan, 1947

Walters, M., 'On Robinson Crusoe's Island' in L. Caldwell (ed.), *Art, Creativity, Living*, London, Karnac, 2000

Watsky, P., 'Marion Milner's Pre-Freudian Writings 1926–1938', *Journal of Analytical Psychology*, 1992, 37, 4, 455–473

White, J., *Generation: Preoccupations and Conflicts in Contemporary Psychoanalysis*, London, Karnac, 2007

—— 'From Survival to Creative Destiny: The Psychoanalytic Journey of Nina Farhi', *Psychoanalytic Dialogues*, 2010, 20, 5, 533–539

Willoughby, R., *Masud Khan: The Myth and the Reality*, London, Free Association, 2005

Winnicott, D.W. (1945), 'Primitive Emotional Development', in *Collected Papers: Through Paediatrics to Psychoanalysis*, London, Tavistock, 1958

—— *The Child and the Family*, London, Tavistock, 1957

—— *The Child and the Outside World*, London, Tavistock, 1957

—— *Maturational Processes and the Facilitating Environment*, London, Hogarth, 1965

—— 'The Location of Cultural Experience', *International Journal of Psycho-Analysis*, 48, 1967

—— *Playing and Reality*, London, Penguin, 1971

INDEX

213